D1606544

The Catholic
CHARACTER
of Catholic
SCHOOLS

The Catholic
CHARACTER
of Catholic
SCHOOLS

JAMES YOUNISS,
JOHN J. CONVEY,
and
JEFFREY A. MCLELLAN,

Editors

UNIVERSITY OF NOTRE DAME PRESS
Notre Dame, Indiana

Copyright 2000 by
University of Notre Dame Press
Notre Dame, Indiana 46556
All Rights Reserved
http://www.undpress.nd.edu

Manufactured in the United States of America

Library of Congress Cataloging-in-Publication Data
The Catholic character of Catholic schools / James Youniss, John J.
Convey, and Jeffrey A. McLellan, editors.
    p.   cm.
    Includes bibliographical references and index.
    ISBN 0-268-02254-2 (cloth : alk. paper)
    1. Catholic schools—United States.   2. Catholic Church—
Education—United States.   3. Catholics—United States—
Conduct of life.   I. Youniss, James.   II. Convey, John J., 1940–
III. McLellan, Jeffery A.
LC501 .C342   2000
371.071'2'73—dc21   00-025643

Acknowledgments

This book emanates from the project "Legacy at the Cross-roads: The Future of Catholic Schools," which was funded by a grant from the Lilly Endowment. We wish to thank Sister Jeanne Knoerle, Fred Hofheinz, and Craig Dystra of the Endowment for their generous support and helpful counsel.

Several colleagues participated in helping organize and manage parts of the larger project of which the present volume is a major component. We appreciatively acknowledge the work of Carl Pieber, David Baker, and Louis Crishock.

The administration of this project was ably managed by Dorothy Kane and Woinishet Negash, who handled numerous tasks that included budget control, assuaging anxious authors, and advancing public relations. We thank them heartily.

Our work has convinced us that Catholic schooling in the United States is indeed at a crossroads. Our hope is that in publishing the present volume, we can help educators, scholars, and policymakers focus on needs and opportunities. Catholic education has given us a legacy well worth continuing. By clarifying the current status, we want to ensure that its future will be even more worthy of respect.

Contents

Introduction

This volume is the second in a series on contemporary Catholic elementary and secondary schools. The first volume, edited by James Youniss and John Convey, *The Current State and Future Prospects for Catholic Schools* (2000, Teachers College Press), addresses the operational issues of enrollment, staffing, income and costs, academic achievement, and the well-being and travails of inner-city schools. These issues have become important because of recent public debates that have made Catholic schools a lightning rod in national controversies over vouchers, school choice, and tax credits. Our view is that Catholic schools ought to be taken on their own terms, according to the purposes for which they were established (see Youniss and McLellan 1999). In this regard, the present book addresses the chief reason for being of these schools: their religious and Catholic character. This topic is relevant to persons inside the system, such as bishops, pastors, superintendents, principals, teachers, and parents, all of whom have a stake in the schools' religious nature and ability to cultivate a Catholic religious ethos in their students. If this religious perspective cannot be communicated convincingly, then these schools have lost their historic basis. This topic is also relevant for people outside the system because Catholic schools seek to instill religious, moral, and cultural values that serve the wider society and all humanity.

Because of changes over the past forty or so years, it is important to ask the questions of how, and how well, Catholic schools are meeting their religious commitment.

1

Forty years ago, these questions would not have been asked. About 13,000 elementary and secondary schools were educating roughly 5.5 million students in a system that had spread nationwide and seemed inevitably headed for further expansion (Walch 1996). These schools were Catholic through and through, from the common religious curriculum grounded in the Baltimore Catechism to shared rituals such as First Friday Eucharist, the May Queen crowning, and prayers for the Notre Dame football game on Saturday afternoon. Most elementary schools were attached to parishes which served ethnic neighborhoods of believing Catholic families. Hence, schools were embedded in a Catholic context and, in turn, promoted the perpetuation of practices which enhanced that culture.

A high mark in American Catholic history occurred with the election of John F. Kennedy as president. This event stilled any doubt about the validity of the American form of Catholicism. Catholics had come a long way from their immigrant and working-class start in the United States, and the schools were partly responsible for their progress. The future was filled with hope for the next generation which the schools would serve by building on past accomplishments and the new opportunities that had come into view.

Then came the rest of the 1960s. We can see in retrospect the key events which changed Catholicism and the role the schools would have in it. The Second Vatican Council, with its opening of the Church to fresh air, caught Catholics by surprise. It invited lay participation in an expanded definition of the Church as the People of God. For reasons that are still to be explored, the council was followed by a large exodus of individuals who had previously committed themselves to the religious life. Immediate consequences were felt by the schools as their teaching staffs were depleted of sisters, brothers, and priests (Jacobs, chap. 4; Wittberg 1994). This change in staffing, which was dramatic at the time, has continued apace and, coupled with a paucity of new vocations, results today in a ratio of about 12:1 lay: religious/clergy teachers; or about 1.5 religious and clergy available for each school (calculations from data reported by NCEA, 1998).

Simultaneously, there was a new migration of Catholic families out of the large cities where they had lived for two or more previous generations. The original immigrants had settled in the cities, which provided Catholics opportunities for employment and collective sharing of their ethnic heritage. Catholic churches with attached parish schools were at the center of these Irish, Italian, German, Polish, and other ethnic neighborhoods. But having achieved new affluence after World War II, many veterans moved to the suburbs, leaving the old urban settlements as part of a deteriorating urban environment. Young families left their elderly parents behind and were replaced by newcomer minority groups which were mainly African-American and Hispanic (Glazer and Moynihan 1970; McGreevy 1996; McLellan 2000).

A complex dynamic was involved. As young Catholic families moved out and minorities moved in, racial tensions mounted. This posed a difficulty for the concept of social justice which had been recently freshened by Vatican II. Some Catholic leaders called for the peaceful welcoming of the incoming minority groups, whereas parish priests whose congregations were being transformed, empathized with their parishioners who were either elderly or could not afford to migrate to the suburbs. One way out of the tension that satisfied both sides was to open the parish schools to the minority newcomers. The schools provided the opportunity to refocus the social justice mission on minority groups within the parish boundaries. By filling abandoned desks with children of these new neighbors, pastors and principals were fulfilling the traditional mission of offering quality education and religious formation to a population which circumstances had temporarily placed at the lower end of the social-economic structure.

The upward social mobility of the Catholic population did not stop in the 60s, but continued on all fronts. Instead of being defensive and watching the culture being made from the outside, Catholics moved into leadership positions as confident central actors in the construction of society (Morris 1997). Schools had been part of the parallel structures late nineteenth-century and early twentieth-century bishops had created to protect and support the working-class Catholic population. But by the 1960s and more so in the 70s and 80s, Catholics felt less and less the need for separate schools. This viewpoint was articulated in Ryan's (1964) assessment of a new Catholicism that was to be practiced *in* the culture rather than apart from it. Having become incorporated into the American mainstream, Catholics no longer felt threatened by Protestantism or the culture at large. Having moved beyond the "we-versus-they" mentality, Catholics seemed to recognize that the original need for separate schools as a bulwark for an oppressed minority had come to an end.

THE 1980 WATERSHED

The decade of the 80s marked a new era in Catholic education. Sociologists James Coleman and his colleagues, and Andrew Greeley analyzed data that had been collected by the federal government and found, among other things, minority students in Catholic secondary schools out-performing their peers in public schools (Greeley 1982; Coleman and Hoffer 1987). This result caused controversy because it implied an attack on public school education at a time when the political climate was turning conservative and public schools were coming under severe attack. Parents wanted to know how it was possible for Catholic schools with small per-pupil budgets to stimulate higher academic achievement than public schools which were becoming increasingly costly. This concern was turned into political action in several forms, one of which was a national trend of voters rejecting school bond referenda. We now know, of course, that part of this voting pattern may be attributed to a demographic swing in which the proportion of voters who were elderly had increased while the proportion of voters with school-age children was decreasing (Wisensale 1999).

Another political expression was a movement toward a market model of education in which schools were supposed to compete for enrollment. There followed a series of proposals that promoted tax credits and vouchers that parents could use to send their children to schools of their choice, even private religious schools. These proposals took on new seriousness under the Republican presidencies of Ronald Reagan and George Bush, who were not friends to teacher unions or public schools, which they had deemed as failures, especially in our large urban settings. Reagan led the charge when he spoke before the National Catholic Educational Association's national convention in 1982 to promise his support in Congress for state-funded vouchers that could be used at Catholic schools (Walch 1996). This movement has not died down, as several cities, most recently Milwaukee and Cleveland, have issued vouchers to minority families and are willing to serve as test cases in what will surely be judicial challenges. Simultaneously, the private voucher movement is supplying scholarships to poor minority students who would otherwise be unable to attend private schools. In June 1998, the Children's Scholarship Fund was established by philanthropists Ted Forstmann and John Walton, who offered $100 million to cities across the country that could come up with matching funds from local foundations. During the 1998 school year, the local Washington, D.C., Scholarship Fund was supporting 1,300 poor children attending private schools, 70 percent of whom were in Catholic schools (Washington Scholarship Fund 1999).

The number of Catholic schools nationally has not risen, but the decline of the previous decades has leveled off and numbers have increased in certain areas of the country. Despite the fact that only about 5 percent of all school children in the United States attend Catholic schools, interest in Catholic schools remains high. But even this interest is difficult to gauge, most likely because the common focus is driven by diverse motives that are hard to identify.

HETEROGENEITY IN MOTIVES BUT UNIFORMITY IN PURPOSE?

The once relatively homogeneous immigrant working-class background of Catholics accounted for a clear definition of what Catholics were, who attended the schools, and what was taught in them. Today, the portrait is more complex.

1. Inner-city elementary schools. Many of these schools were attached to parishes that historically served particular ethnic groups. As these groups have aged or moved away, the schools have closed, been consolidated, or become affordable private schools for non-Catholic minority children. The latter two categories exemplify the long-term results of the social-justice focus that took shape in the 1960s and which the present bishops still explicitly support. For example, in Cleveland and Washington, D.C., special efforts are being made to keep these schools open, with full recognition that they serve mainly non-Catholic families. Despite this history and continued ideological support, survival of these schools is tenuous. They are at risk for closing because the parishes to which they are attached have only limited funds for them (Harris 2000) and because they are costly (O'Keefe and Murphy 1999). The shift from religious to lay teachers has driven up payrolls, while the

students who attend these schools come from families that are finan-cially stressed.

2. Suburban elementary schools. The movement of Catholics to the suburbs in the 1960s and 70s, coincided with the end of Vatican II and the new sense of social-class arrival that Ryan (1964) had so aptly de-scribed. One consequence was the decision not to build parish schools where the young Catholic families had relocated. The fact that many of these suburbs had excellent public school systems fit neatly with the sense that Catholics did not need cradle-to-grave protection. It is noted further that many of the Catholic families that moved out of northern Rust Belt cities migrated west and south where there was less of a tra-dition of parish schooling. School enrollment in the diocese of Albany declined from 38,000 to 21,000 from 1970 to 1980 and in the diocese of Buffalo from 73,000 to 42,000 during the same period. The numbers of Catholics in the west and south had been small and the new migration was not initially large enough to warrant large expenditures for schools. In 1970, the archdiocese of Atlanta reported enrollments of 5,200 elementary and 1,700 secondary school students. The diocese of St. Petersburg, Florida, had school enrollments of 13,000 elementary and 3,700 secondary students in 1970.

3. Diocesan and parish secondary schools. Of all secondary schools, approximately 59 percent are classified as parish or diocesan high schools. Historically, diocesan high schools were established so that all students, regardless of income, could proceed from parish elementary to Catholic secondary education. These schools traditionally charged low tuition so that any student might have access to them. These schools were hard hit in the post-1965 decline, although large dioceses have been able to maintain them. Even harder hit were parish high schools, which were mainly in urban centers from which Catholic families moved during the past three decades.

4. Private secondary schools. Some high schools were always run by religious congregations such as the Jesuits, the Benedictines, or the Madames of the Sacred Heart. These schools have tended to survive during the period of decline, although many have loosened ties with their founding religious congregations (see Mueller, chap. 2). The teacher-members of their founding congregations have been replaced by lay teachers who command market-rate salaries and benefits. This may be less true of elementary school teachers (Schaub 2000), if only

because secondary schools are under more pressure to provide specialized education expressed in high academic achievement. Consequently,
tuition is relatively high and it is no wonder that an estimated 45 to 50
percent of Catholic secondary school students come from families in
the upper one-fourth of the income scale (Riordan 2000).

5. Non-Catholic students. In 1965, a minuscule proportion of all
students in Catholic schools were not Catholic. It is estimated that
today 13 percent of students in these schools are not Catholic (NCEA
1998). Some proportion of them are in inner-city elementary schools
and another proportion attend private secondary schools. These are
two vastly different populations in terms of income, but the majority of
such schools are probably Christian in both instances.

6. Minorities. Many of the non-Catholic students are also minorities, primarily African-American. Some schools, especially in the South
and East, were founded to serve this population and some have come to
serve it through urban migration (Polite 2000). Recent immigration
has made the schools even more ethnically diverse. Students from various Spanish-speaking countries and from several Asian countries have
now entered the system, although not in numbers similar to those that
were associated with previous immigrations to the United States. Nev-
ertheless, dioceses in certain states such as California serve diverse ethnic language groups and cultures, as do the public schools (Lawrence
2000).

These categories do not exhaust the variation that complicates the
term "Catholic schools." Perhaps in times past, diversity was hidden by
a homogeneous definition of Catholicism which was reinforced by a
well-trained cadre of teachers with a commonly avowed religious life.
Today, the diversity of the students' backgrounds is complicated by diversity in the meaning of "Catholic." One can see then why observers
might ask just how Catholic the schools are and how high a priority
being Catholic ranks, say, in comparison with academic achievement
(Baker and Riordan 1998; Greeley 1998; Youniss and McLellan 1999).

THE PRESENT BOOK

One would think that with all the publicity given to Catholic schools
since the 1980s, we would know much about them, how they operate,
and what precisely distinguishes them from public and other private

schools. Yet, when one looks carefully at published studies, few details are available. The best of the studies are by Cibulka, O'Brien, and Zewe (1982) in a nearly two-decades-old survey of principals from fifty-four elementary schools and by Bryk, Lee, and Holland (1993) on a mid-1980s ethnographic report on seven secondary schools. These studies are valuable for hypotheses about the features which make Catholic education successful and distinctive. These schools are locally managed, offer a single stringent curriculum for all students, and promote an ethos of respect for individuals and the community. Such features are self-explanatory and sufficiently important to warrant further probing. If they constitute the structure of Catholic schools, then the religious component is clear, palpable, and worthy of the tradition from which the schools have sprung.

Still, the cultural context in which Catholic schools operate today is complex and different from what it was at the start of the twentieth century. Discussions of Catholicism are too often blinded by debates over Vatican II that tend to dwell on whether the Church has drifted too far from some unspecified pre-1960 norm or whether it has lived up to the options the council glimpsed for the future. This form of debate distracts us from a fundamental point: history does not move backward in time and any viable religion must be practiced and understood in the context of real lives and living cultures. In the case of schools, the question is not whether schools today are the same as they were forty years ago or whether they are Catholic as that term was understood prior to 1960. The more productive questions and those on which we based this book are: How are Catholic schools maintaining their religious character today and what are the issues they must face in order to fulfill their Catholic heritage?

Church Leadership

In chapter 1 John Convey reports results from a 1996 survey of bishops and pastors who were asked to describe their orientations to Catholic schools. In a Church that depends to a large extent on its clergy for leadership, these views are central to understanding how resources will be expended on the schools and what choices need to be made to sustain the schools as quality educational institutions. The survey was based on an earlier one conducted in 1986 so the results permit some examination of trends. Over the ten-year period, the bishops maintained an extremely high level of agreement (over 90 percent) with statements that Catholic schools are needed and that they reflect an effective use of diocesan resources. More than two-thirds of priests also agreed with such statements at both time-periods. One significant trend over time was for priests to be more likely to endorse the statement "The need for Catholic schools is at least as great today as in the past," in 1996 than in 1986. Although both bishops and priests responded in a way indicating strong support for Catholic schools, it is clear that priests are not as overwhelming in that support as bishops. One possible reason for this difference is that priests in many parishes are confronted daily with the heavy burden of managing and financing their schools. Thus their enthusiasm for Catholic schooling in principle might be tempered by the difficult reality of their operation. However, Convey's analyses show that pastors of parishes with schools are at least as positive in their responses as pastors of parishes without schools and sometimes more so.

In his introduction to chapter 2, Brother Frederick Mueller points out the burgeoning popularity, according to his own new data, of the sponsorship of schools by religious congregations. When most of these schools were first established, they typically were under the sole ownership and control of their founding congregations. Sponsorship represents a change in the original relationship of the congregations to the schools. In some cases, sponsorship might mean that the school is sold and members of the congregation continue only in a consultative or advisory role. In others, the congregation maintains ownership of the physical plant and has reserved powers in certain areas of school operation. Mueller's thorough review of the literature on sponsorship as a strategy covers practical points of personnel and governance. His main point, however, is that sponsorship offers a means by which the traditions and spirituality of the congregations can be passed on to succeeding generations of students who do not have the benefit of extended direct contact with the religious as teachers.

Staffing and Internal Workings

In chapter 3 Sister Kathleen Carr reports results of a 1995 survey of 887 elementary school principals, 56 percent of whom were lay persons, in 156 dioceses. Questions were focused on the principals' self-perceptions as leaders to cultivate the students' religious-spiritual development. Lay and religious principals equally valued this function and viewed it to be as important as academic achievement. Her data also indicate that the longer principals are in the system, the more satisfaction, feelings of self-efficacy, and motivation they experience.

Rev. Richard Jacobs structures chapter 4 around the historical shift from religious to lay teachers. He then raises the question of whether lay leadership will accept the mission that religious teachers once put into practice. Religious teachers laid out a model of how the religious function could be activated. The challenge is for lay teachers to adapt that model or discover new ones that will allow the religious mission to remain central to the schools.

In chapter 5 Merylann Schuttloffel reviews documents from various dioceses in order to identify common philosophical threads among the nation's Catholic schools. She identifies two qualitative dimensions of diocesan curricula: centralization and Catholicity. Her discussion focuses on the key role of the teacher in implementing these curricula.

Rev. Paul Galetto, in chapter 6, reports on a national sample of over 2,000 Catholic elementary school teachers of religion surveyed in 1994. The focus of this study was on their knowledge of core beliefs central to the Catholic faith and their personal belief therein. Galetto shows that older teachers who have had more formal instruction in Catholicism score higher on religious knowledge and have more orthodox personal beliefs. He discusses implications for the preparation of religion teachers.

In chapter 7, George Elford discusses the potential use in Catholic schools of ways of creating and using information developed in business. As an example, he presents results from an assessment of faith-knowledge and Catholic values conducted with students from twenty dioceses. An important finding here is that students in Catholic schools consistently score higher on knowledge of the Catholic faith than do students in parish religious education programs.

CATHOLIC IDENTITY

Sister Catherine Dooley in chapter 8 provides a historical overview of theories and controversies in the field of religious education through an examination of religious curricula. She shows how curricula (i.e., nationally distributed textbook series) reflected shifts in catechetical emphases in the Church. She concludes with a commentary on the implications of these developments for the Catholic identity of Catholic schools.

In chapter 9, Timothy Walch describes three eras in the history of Catholic schooling in the United States. His thesis is that Catholic schools have undergone a series of changes as the Catholic population has faced and met cultural challenges. His positive perspective replaces the more typical pessimistic stance that the golden age of Catholic schools can never be achieved again. In Walch's view, each age brings new challenges and opportunities. Schools must be open to change as each generation constructs solutions for its moment while it retains a basic Catholic character.

Timothy Meagher offers a historical essay in chapter 10 that tracks the role of Catholic schools in helping to form and sustain ethnic-religious identity. He proposes that as the link with ethnicity has been weakened, the schools need to alter the way they foster identity. Because much debate about the schools assumes a constant function, this essay opens educators to a fresh perspective on why schools must change in light of changes within the Catholic population and its relationship to American culture.

Jerome Porath, in chapter 11, presents a thorough analysis of the religious mission of Catholic schools, how this mission relates to official Church doctrine, and how administrators can blend the two in the everyday world of educational practice. Porath embeds his analysis in a firm theological position which gives schooling a legitimate basis and motivation. But he too is historically sensitive and notes that Catholic schools of the past cannot be the sole model for Catholic schools of tomorrow. He shows how the Catholic character is the reason for having the schools, and he demonstrates how this principle can be put into practice as we reach the twenty-first century.

<h3 style="text-align:center">REFERENCES</h3>

Baker, D. P., and C. Riordan. 1998. "The 'Eliting' of the Common American Catholic School and the National Education Crisis." *Phi Delta Kappan*, September, pp. 15–23.

Bryk, A., V. Lee, and P. Holland. 1993. *Catholic Schools and the Common Good.* Cambridge: Harvard University Press.

Cibulka, J., T. O'Brien, and D. Zewe. 1982. *Inner-City Private Elementary Schools: A Study.* Milwaukee: Marquette University Press.

Coleman, James S., and Thomas Hoffer. 1987. Public and Private High Schools: The Impact of Communities. New York: Basic Books.

Glazer, N., and D. P. Moynihan. 1970. *Beyond the Melting Pot: The Negroes, Puerto Ricans, Jews, Italians, and Irish of New York City,* 2d ed. Cambridge: M.I.T. Press.

Greeley, A. M. 1998. "The So-Called Failure of Catholic Schools." *Phi Delta Kappan,* September, pp. 24–25.

Greeley, A. M. 1982. *Catholic High Schools and Minority Students.* New Brunswick, N.J.: Transaction Books.

Harris, J.C. 2000. "The Funding Dilemma Facing Catholic Elementary and Secondary Schools." In J. Youniss and J. Convey, eds., *Catholic Schools at the Crossroads: Survival and Transformation.* New York: Teachers College Press.

Lawrence, S. 2000. "'New' Immigrants in the Catholic Schools: A Preliminary Assessment." In J. Youniss and J. Convey, eds., *Catholic Schools at the Crossroads: Survival and Transformation.* New York: Teachers College Press.

McGreevy, J. 1996. *Parish Boundaries.* Chicago: University of Chicago Press.

McLellan, J. A. 2000. "Rise, Fall, and Reasons Why: U.S. Catholic Elementary Education, 1940–1995." In J. Youniss and J. Convey, eds., *Catholic Schools at the Crossroads: Survival and Transformation.* New York: Teachers College Press.

Morris, C. 1997. *American Catholic: The Saints and Sinners Who Built America's Most Powerful Church.* New York: Holt, Rinehart, and Winston.

National Catholic Educational Association (NCEA). 1998. *United States Catholic Elementary and Secondary Schools 1997–1998: The Annual Statistical Report on Schools, Enrollment and Staffing.* Washington, D.C.

O'Keefe, J., and J. Murphy. 2000. "Ethnically Diverse Catholic Schools: School Structure, Students, Staffing, and Finance." In J. Youniss and J. Convey, eds., *Catholic Schools at the Crossroads: Survival and Transformation.* New York: Teachers College Press.

Polite, V. C. 2000. "Cornerstones: Catholic High Schools That Serve Predominantly African American Student Populations." In J. Youniss and J. Convey, eds., *Catholic Schools at the Crossroads: Survival and Transformation.* New York: Teachers College Press.

Riordan, C. 2000. "Trends in Student Demography in Catholic Secondary Schools, 1972–1992." In J. Youniss and J. Convey, eds., *Catholic Schools at the Crossroads: Survival and Transformation.* New York: Teachers College Press.

Ryan, M. P. 1964. *Are Parochial Schools the Answer?* New York: Holt, Rinehart, and Winston.

Schaub, M. 2000. "A Faculty at a Crossroads: A Profile of American Catholic School Teachers." In J. Youniss and J. Convey, eds., *Catholic Schools at the Crossroads: Survival and Transformation.* New York: Teachers College Press.

Walch, T. 1996. *Parish School: American Catholic Parochial Education from Colonial Times to the Present.* New York: Crossroads.

Washington Scholarship Fund. 1999. *Facts and Figures.* [On-line]. Available: http://www.wsf-dc.org.

Wisensale, S. K. 1999. "Grappling with the Generational Equity Debate." *Public Integrity,* 1, pp. 1–19.

Wittberg, P. 1997. *The Rise and Fall of Catholic Religious Orders.* Albany: State University of New York Press.

Youniss, J., and J. A. McLellan. 1999. "Catholic Schools in Perspective: Religious Identity, Achievement, and Citizenship." *Phi Delta Kappan,* October, pp. 105–13.

1 Views of Bishops and Priests Concerning Catholic Schools

A TEN-YEAR PERSPECTIVE

John J. Convey

During the 1985–86 school year 2.821 million students enrolled in 9,340 Catholic schools nationwide. What might seem to be respectable numbers for a nonpublic "system" of parish and diocesan schools were almost 50 percent less than the peak numbers twenty years earlier, when 5.574 million students enrolled in 13,292 Catholic schools. The reality was that in 1985 Catholic school enrollment was in a free fall, schools were closing at the rate of 50 to 100 per year, and costs were escalating rapidly. Elementary school costs had reached $1,000 per student and high school tuition averaged over $1,600, remarkable numbers for schools whose costs were kept in check for decades by large parish and diocesan subsidies and low wages paid to religious teachers. Instead of automatically enrolling their children at the nearest Catholic school, many Catholic parents carefully studied their options and often selected public education, simply because of the cost of sending their children to a Catholic school.

Bishops around the country were scrambling to shore up the schools, attempting to stop the hemorrhaging and to find ways to support financially the schools that remained, particularly those in the center cities of large urban areas. Many dioceses commissioned strategic plan-

The research for this study was supported by a grant from the Lilly Foundation, Inc.

ning studies to secure the future of their schools. In addition to questions dealing with finances, curriculum, Catholic identity, and governance themes, these studies usually took a hard look at whether the diocese could continue to operate as many schools as it did.

It was in this context that J. Stephen O'Brien, the executive director of the Chief Administrators of Catholic Education (CACE), a division of the National Catholic Educational Association (NCEA), set out to survey bishops and priests nationwide concerning their perceptions of the value, effectiveness, funding practices, and future structure of Catholic schools. O'Brien (1987) wanted to know what value bishops and priests placed on Catholic schools as a work of the Church; how they viewed the effectiveness of the schools and the methods of financing them; their acceptance of a relatively new phenomenon, regionalization of schools; and their views on parental involvement in decision-making about the schools.

To accomplish his objectives, O'Brien adapted a questionnaire that Sullivan (1982) used to study the sentiments of priests in the archdiocese of Boston. Overall, Sullivan had found that the majority of priests were supportive of Catholic schools, with length of time ordained and years of service in a parish with a school having a positive influence on a priest's perception of the value and effectiveness of Catholic schools. Schipper (1982) in the archdiocese of San Francisco had replicated Sullivan's study with similar results. Later, Tacheny (1988) would do the same in the dioceses of Winona and New Ulm, Minnesota. All three studies had surveyed priests only; O'Brien's study added the perspective of bishops to that of the priests.

O'Brien sent his questionnaire to the 273 active bishops in the United States and to a sample of 660 priests selected systematically from a mailing list generated randomly by the publishers of *The Official Catholic Directory*. Just over 80 percent of the bishops (219) and slightly more than half of the priests (346) returned a completed questionnaire. What O'Brien found was a "mixed message." Bishops and priests were very strong in their affirmation of the value of Catholic schools. Virtually all bishops (93 percent) and a large majority of priests (72 percent) agreed that the need for Catholic schools was at least as great today as in the past. However, in all issues concerning the value of Catholic schools—their need, their role in the mission of the Church, their preparation of students for roles in the Church and society—priests were less in agreement than were the bishops.

By 1996 the general feeling about the future of Catholic schools within the Catholic school community had changed to a more positive perception about the viability and future of the schools than in 1986. National enrollments in Catholic schools started to increase in 1992 after decades of decline and continued to rise since then. The demand for a Catholic school education had increased in many areas, new schools were built, and existing schools were expanded. Between 1985 and 1995, 120 new Catholic elementary schools and 14 new secondary schools had been established, mostly in the southeast, southwest, and western parts of the country (Meitler Consultants 1997). But demand was also building in the suburbs of large eastern dioceses, where, in some cases, new schools had not been established in thirty years. In addition, a series of well-publicized research studies (Convey 1992; Bryk, Lee, and Holland 1993) with favorable results concerning Catholic schools and the accompanying good publicity in the popular media certainly contributed to an increased optimism about the schools.

The situation was not entirely rosy, however, as many Catholic schools continued to struggle, particularly in rural areas and in the inner cities of large urban areas. Costs also continued to escalate rapidly in all schools, with the average cost per student in elementary schools exceeding $2,000 and average high school tuition approaching $4,000. On the whole, though, more optimism involving Catholic schools was present in 1996 than in 1986.

The purpose of this study is to ascertain whether any changes have occurred in the sentiments of bishops and priests concerning Catholic schools in the ten years since O'Brien's study. The issues examined in the study are limited to the need for Catholic schools and their value, their quality and effectiveness, financial issues concerning the schools, and parental involvement in governance. In addition, the study attempts to determine whether perceived demand for Catholic schools is related to the sentiments of bishops and priests towards these issues.

METHOD

Sample

The data come from a questionnaire, adapted from O'Brien's and expanded, sent in May 1996 to all diocesan, auxiliary, and retired bishops in the United States and, using a list provided by the publishers of *The Official Catholic Directory*, to a 10 percent random sample of priests within each of the thirteen episcopal regions, as defined by the National Conference of Catholic Bishops. The sample of priests was stratified into three categories: pastors of parishes with schools (696 sampled), pastors of parishes without schools (1,053 sampled), and other clergy (1,263 sampled). In all, questionnaires were mailed to approximately 400 bishops and to 3,012 priests.

Completed questionnaires were received from 184 bishops (46 percent response), including 119 diocesan bishops (66 percent response), 36 auxiliary bishops, 27 retired bishops, and two bishops who did not provide sufficient information to permit classification.

Two-thirds of the 1,026 priests (33 percent response) that returned a questionnaire are pastors, 328 of parishes with schools (47 percent response) and 354 others (34 percent response), including 212 of parishes that cooperate in the support of schools, and 142 without a school affiliation. The 344 other clergy (28 percent response) are distributed as follows: 200 associate pastors/parochial vicars, 88 in other ministries, and 56 retired priests.

Table 1 (see Appendix at the end of this chapter) shows the distribution of respondents according to the thirteen episcopal regions. The highest rates of return (approximately 40 percent) were from priests in the midwest (regions 6,7,8). Priests from the mid-southwest (region 10) and far west (regions 11 and 12) had returns of less than 30 percent. Overall, priests from 165 dioceses returned completed questionnaires. The ten dioceses yielding the largest number of priests responding to the questionnaire were New York (46), Chicago (35), Boston (23), Los Angeles (22), Newark (22), Detroit (20), Brooklyn (19), Philadelphia (19), Cincinnati (19) and Minneapolis/St. Paul (16).

Overall, slightly more than half (53 percent) of the priests were current or former pastors of parishes with schools, while a third (33 percent) had never been assigned to a parish with a school. In addition, 83 percent of the priests had attended a Catholic elementary school and 70 percent a Catholic high school.

The associate pastors were a heterogeneous group since some had not yet been eligible to be pastors due to their age, while others were old enough but had not yet been given the responsibility as pastor. Still others (22 percent) had once been pastors, 59 percent of them (13 percent of all the associate pastors) in parishes with schools. In addition, a third of priests in other ministries (20 percent of them in parishes with schools) and 86 percent of retired priests (80 percent of them in parishes with schools) had been pastors.

Instrumentation

The questionnaires for bishops and for priests contain demographic items appropriate to each group and a common set of 64 sentiment items, including a number of items from O'Brien's questionnaire. Respondents used a 5-point Likert scale from Strongly Agree to Strongly Disagree, including an Uncertain option, to address 62 of the sentiment items. The scale used by O'Brien did not contain the Uncertain option. The other two items employed a multiple choice format to determine perceptions of the most important purpose of a Catholic school and how demand has changed in the past five years.

Analysis

This study uses the data from 19 items, including 15 that were also on O'Brien's questionnaire. For purposes of analysis, the items are divided into four clusters representing the need for Catholic schools and their value, their quality and effectiveness, financial issues concerning the schools, and parental involvement in governance. For each item, an agreement index was computed by combining the Strongly Agree and Agree options on the scale. Two analyses are displayed for the items in each cluster: (1) the change in percent agreement of bishops and priests between 1986 and 1996 and (2) the percent agreement in 1996 by six subgroups of priests: pastors of parishes with schools, pastors of parishes that assist in the sponsorship of schools, pastors of parishes without schools, associate pastors, priests in other ministries, and retired priests. This latter analysis provides a level of precision not available in O'Brien's study.

Results

Need for Catholic Schools and Their Value

Table 2 shows the percent agreement of the bishops and priests to six items that address the need for Catholic schools and their value to the Church. The bishops on the whole were very supportive of the need for the schools and their value. Virtually all of the bishops (over 95 percent) agreed that schools are needed as much today as in the past, they are an essential part of the Church's educational ministry, and maintaining them is an effective use of resources. Ninety percent of the bishops also agreed that the schools are one of the best means of evangelization. In addition the vast majority of bishops continued their overall assessment of the schools' value by disagreeing with the view that the schools were not different enough from public schools to justify their continuation and that improved parish programs should replace Catholic schools in most parishes. Overall, the bishops were more supportive than priests regarding the need and value of the schools both in 1986 and in 1996.

Although less supportive than the bishops, the priests showed substantial agreement to the four items for which agreement was a supportive response and substantial disagreement to the two items for which agreement was a nonsupportive response. The largest disparity in agreement between bishops and priests concerned whether maintaining Catholic schools was an effective use of diocesan resources, whether the Catholic school is one of the best means of evangelization in the Church today, and whether improved parish religious education programs should replace Catholic schools in most parishes. Still, approximately two-thirds of the priests agreed with the first two of these sentiments and disagreed with the last one.

The agreement of both bishops and priests to four items did not change substantially between 1986 and 1996. Both groups had views similar to those of their counterparts ten years ago regarding the essential role that Catholic schools play in the Church's educational ministry and whether Catholic and public schools' differences are great enough to warrant the continuation of Catholic schools. In addition, no change in agreement occurred on whether Catholic schools are an effective use of the Church's resources and the best means for evangelization. These last two items, however, received a large number of "Uncertain" responses from priests, a response not available in the 1986 survey, so the percent of priests who disagreed with these items was substantially less in 1996 than in 1986.

The ten years from 1986 to 1996 saw a significant change in the responses of priests to two issues. The sentiments of priests regarding the need for Catholic schools being at least as great today as in the past increased by over 12 percentage points. In addition, priests were less likely to agree that improved parish religious education programs should eventually replace Catholic schools. The agreement of the bishops was slightly higher in 1996 than in 1986 to the first of these items and slightly lower towards the second, but neither difference was statistically significant.

As is evident in table 3, however, the sentiments of priests to all items within this subset varied by the priest's current ministry. Among pastors, for example, those whose parishes had schools showed the strongest support for issues pertaining to the need for Catholic schools and their value. Pastors of parishes that assisted in the sponsorship of schools had substantially lower levels of support than did pastors of parishes with schools, and, in most cases, pastors of parishes without schools had even lower support. Similar levels of agreement occurred among associate pastors, priests in other ministries, and retired priests, who generally were somewhat less supportive than pastors of parishes with schools, but somewhat more supportive than other pastors.

Quality and Effectiveness of Catholic Schools

Table 4 shows the agreement of bishops and priests to four items regarding the quality and effectiveness of Catholic schools. Bishops and priests showed very high levels of agreement regarding the quality of the Catholic schools in the diocese both in 1986 and 1996. Virtually all bishops and over 90 percent of the priests agreed that the schools have high quality. This assessment was uniformly shared among the priests, including pastors of parishes without schools and those whose parish sponsored a school (see table 5), albeit with slightly lower levels of agreement (86 percent as opposed to over 90 percent), but with a higher number (10 percent) of "Uncertain" responses than the other subgroups of priests.

On the remaining items, however, bishops and priests demonstrated more discrepant views. Bishops were more likely than priests to believe that Catholic schools strengthen parish unity, although both groups were somewhat less likely to believe this in 1996 than ten years earlier. The lower level of agreement to this item, even on the part of school pastors, may have resulted from some bishops and priests experiencing at least mild levels of dissent from certain parishioners whenever the issue arises of the parish supporting its own school or helping to support other schools.

Bishops were also more likely than priests to believe that Catholic schools have a positive impact on the adult religious behavior of their graduates. Although both bishops and priests had lower levels of agreement in 1996 than in 1986, only priests showed a statistically significant decline for this item. On both items, the differences between the subgroups of priests were smaller than occurred on the items measuring need and value. A significant amount of uncertainty existed among priests, however, regarding these items, with approximately 20 percent choosing the "Uncertain" response, which makes the comparison to 1986 uneven since priests did not have the option to choose this response then.

Finally, bishops were much less likely than priests to agree that Catholics who go to public schools generally turn out to be as good Catholics as those who attend Catholic schools. The agreement of both groups, however, declined significantly from 1986 to 1996. The amount of uncertainly about this sentiment is extremely high on the part of both bishops and priests, about 40 percent, probably due the lack of information to make a proper judgment about this issue, which makes the comparison with 1986 even more tenuous. Even so, priests, who are more likely to have some personal experience with this issue in their parishes, were three times more likely than bishops to agree with this statement. The strongest agreement to this issue comes from pastors of parishes without schools and those whose parishes assist in the sponsorship of schools, who may have more Catholics in their parishes who have attended public schools than pastors of parishes that have a school.

Financial Issues

Table 6 displays a variety of items dealing with financial issues concerning Catholic schools. Three items deal with financial support, one with sponsorship that has financial implications, and another with tuition as a deterrent for enrolling in Catholic schools. Bishops were somewhat more supportive than priests regarding the responsibility of parishes and all Catholics to support Catholic schools, but even the agreement of priests was rather substantial, with approximately three-quarters indicating their support. Having several parishes financially support a single Catholic school received less agreement from priests in

1996 than in 1986; still, 83 percent of priests agreed. Pastors of parishes with schools and whose parishes assist in the support of schools were much more likely to agree with this shared support by parishes. In general, however, pastors of parishes without schools were much less likely than the other priests to support any effort for shared financial responsibility (see table 7).

Bishops and priests differed markedly over whether every parish should have its own Catholic school, when that is possible and practical. Three-quarters of the bishops supported this, but less than half of the priests did, with pastors of parishes without schools and whose parishes assist in sponsoring a school showing the least agreement. Some priests in their response to this item may have been considering difficulties faced by parishes with schools. In some priests' minds, having a school is a burden and results in extra work for the pastor. Some priests would rather not take on this responsibility. However, there was considerable uncertainty about this issue, with 14 percent of the bishops and 22 percent of the priests choosing the Uncertain option on the questionnaire.

Bishops and priests held similar views regarding parents' inability to afford the tuition being the main reason for not selecting Catholic schools. In addition, both groups showed a similar increase in agreement between 1986 and 1996, but only the increase of the priests was statistically significant, due mainly to their larger numbers. The questionnaire did not include questions as to what may be the principal reason for not selecting Catholic schools, if inability to pay the tuition is not. Other studies have indicated that some parents choose an academic reason, the need for special programs not offered in the Catholic school, or simply support for public education as being reasons for not selecting Catholic schools (Convey 1992).

Parental Involvement in Governance

Although bishops are much more supportive than priests about giving parents more say in the development of policy for the schools, both bishops and priests were more willing to do this in 1996 than they were in 1986 (see table 8). The increase between 1986 and 1996 in the agreement to this item was the largest in the entire questionnaire. In 1996 about 85 percent of bishops and over two-thirds of the priests agreed that parents must be given a substantial role in the development of policy for Catholic schools. In addition, another 20 percent of the priests were uncertain about this.

On three additional items not included during the 1986 survey, bishops were somewhat more supportive than priests of parents' voice in governance, the need for boards for all schools and representative boards for schools serving several parishes. On each of these items, however, the support of priests was higher than on the item concerning parental role in policy development. Bishops and priests seemed to acknowledge the growing role of parents on school boards and other policy groups. Surveys of diocesan boards and local school boards have confirmed the increased participation of parents, which bishops and priests have facilitated and encouraged (Convey and Haney 1997).

In contrast to patterns on other issues, pastors of parishes with schools were not quite as supportive as other pastors (see table 9). Apparently, some pastors would prefer not to deal with parental participation in governance, which they may perceive as "a hassle."

Relationship with Growth

Diocesan bishops ordained after 1985 (71 percent) were more likely than those ordained before 1985 (61 percent) to indicate that the demand for Catholic schools had increased in their diocese during the previous five years. About 3 percent of all diocesan bishops indicated that the demand had decreased during that period. Bishops who reported that the demand for Catholic schools had increased were slightly more likely than other bishops to have higher levels of agreement with each subset of items.

Approximately 45 percent of priests reported increased demand for Catholic schools during the previous five years, 36 percent indicated demand had remained stable, and 19 percent that it had diminished. Pastors of parishes with schools, those whose parishes cooperated in the sponsorship of schools, and associate pastors were more likely than the other priests to report an increase in demand for Catholic schools in their areas. Priests who lived in parishes located in rural areas, urban areas, or the inner city were more likely than priests in parishes in suburban areas to report a decrease in demand over the previous five years.

The relationships between perceived increases in demand for Catholic schools and their value, quality, effectiveness, and financial support were much stronger for priests than for bishops. Priests who reported increases in enrollment were more likely to have higher agreement than priests who reported stable or decreasing demand for each of the issues, except those concerning parental involvement and governance of the schools, where the agreement was independent of perceived increases.

Discussion

The good news in these findings is the very strong support that bishops have for Catholic schools—their need and value to the Church, their quality and effectiveness, the necessity of widespread financial support for them, and the importance of parental involvement in their governance. Bishops were united in their assessment, and their support is at least as strong as it was ten years earlier. Compared to the responses on O'Brien's questionnaire, bishops today are as favorable as or more favorable than bishops ten years ago on all issues, except that Catholic schools strengthen parish unity. Particularly evident is the increase in the bishops' support for parental involvement in the development of school policy. These results are good news indeed for Catholic schools, for the support of the bishop is critical to the success of schools. Many of the bishops surveyed were instrumental in keeping Catholic schools financially viable during difficult periods of declining enrollments and rising costs. The continued support of bishops is critical for the future success of the schools. According to the findings in this study, the support from the bishops is present, and if the general stability in their sentiments can be used as a benchmark, can likely be counted on in the future.

The support of priests is also very positive and very encouraging. Priests show more mixed results than do bishops, being more agreeable than ten years ago regarding the need for Catholic schools, giving parents more say in school affairs, and the importance of tuition as a deterrent for some parents in choosing Catholic schools. On the other hand, priests are less agreeable than ten years ago regarding Catholic schools as strengthening parish unity, having an impact on adult religious behavior, parish schools being the best model, and graduates of public schools being as good Catholics as graduates of Catholic schools. Overall, however, priests, on average, remain quite supportive of Catholic schools, but less so than the bishops.

However, these findings still very much contain a "mixed message," but in a different sense than occurred in O'Brien's study. Assessment of value, effectiveness, financial support, and parental involvement clearly differ among the priests according to the type of their ministry. A key variable here is the different parish circumstances in which pastors find themselves, a factor that O'Brien was not able to explore because he did not ask for these distinctions in his questionnaire. Pastors of parishes with schools and retired priests generally have the highest assessments, followed, in order, by associate pastors, priests in other ministries, pastors of parishes that cooperate in the sponsorship of a school, and, finally, pastors of parishes without schools. The exception to this pattern occurs on sentiments toward parental involvement in governance, where pastors of parishes with schools are the most reluctant to give parents a voice in school affairs.

Associate pastors generally have the same levels of agreement as pastors with schools and they show higher agreement than pastors without schools do. The interpretation of the data from associate pastors, however, is complicated since some have been pastors in the past. In general young associate pastors ordained less than twenty years who had not yet been pastors are very supportive of Catholic schools, as are older associate pastors who are former pastors. The support of the younger associate pastors is particularly encouraging for the future of Catholic schools since these men will someday be pastors, in all likelihood associated with a parish that has a school or assists in the sponsorship of a school.

What is critical to note here is that priests directly involved with schools are among the most supportive of schools, as are many of the younger priests who are likely, in due time, to become pastors of parishes with schools. Priests who are pastors of parishes that do not have schools often self-select themselves away from a parish with a school or they are not assigned to parishes with schools by bishops because they are less supportive of Catholic schools.

Another particularly significant finding of this study is the relationship, for both bishops and priests, but particularly for the priests, between perceived increases in demand for Catholic schools during the previous five years and support for the issues addressed in the study. A strong, positive relationship exists between a priest's perception of growth in his area and his assessment of worth, quality, and access. The relationships, while still significant, are lower for bishops, which may be due to their more homogeneous, and more favorable, views on Catholic schools compared with the views of the priests.

One might ask which is the antecedent, the demand or the affirmation? Does the demand result in the affirmation of bishops and priests? Or does the support of bishops and priests bring about an increased demand? In fact, both cases likely occur.

Strong leadership is necessary for the effective running of any organization, and Catholic schools are not different in this respect. A successful Catholic school requires both a supportive bishop and one or more supportive pastors. These leaders put into place the structures—physical and financial—that make it possible for schools to prosper. Supportive leaders find ways to make schools work. Visionary bishops and energetic pastors are ultimately responsible when new schools are built in dioceses and existing schools are expanded. "Build it and they will come" is a dictum that has experiential validity in many dioceses.

In times of decreasing enrollment and increasing costs, bishops and priests have many difficult choices to make. Will it be possible to keep all the schools open? Is it desirable to do this? How will the schools be financed, particularly those that experience declining enrollment? Should schools remain open if it means that the majority of the students will not be Catholic? How should the school's Catholic identity be preserved when Catholic students no longer constitute the majority in a school? Wrestling with these issues can engender on the part of some a pessimism that could result in a decreased level of support for Catholic schools. Every diocese has limited resources, and judicious stewardship is required to make the best use of these resources. Declining enrollment, increasing costs, and more non-Catholics in the schools can often lead to a lack of support for Catholic schools by some.

On the other hand, increases in enrollment and increased demand on the part of parents for Catholic schools leads to an optimism about the future of the schools and can result in more supportive sentiments concerning the schools. Has that happened in this study? Perhaps. But whatever the reason, the sentiments of bishops and priests remain supportive of Catholic schools with regard to their value, quality, effectiveness, sources of support, and parental involvement.

APPENDIX

Table 1.   Distribution of Respondents by Episcopal Regions

Region	Bishops			Priests		
	N	Percent Total	Percent Return[a]	N	Percent Total	Percent Return
1 NEW ENGLAND	13	7.1%	63.6%	93	9.1%	32.2%
2 NY	14	7.6%	75.0%	123	12.0%	33.7%
3 PA & NJ	17	9.2%	84.6%	131	12.8%	32.0%
4 SOUTHEAST	16	8.7%	61.1%	88	8.6%	31.5%
5 KY,TN,AL,MS,LA	13	7.1%	61.1%	61	6.0%	35.1%
6 OH & MI	20	10.9%	69.2%	99	9.7%	40.9%
7 WI,IL,IN	22	12.0%	75.0%	134	13.1%	40.0%
8 ND,SD,MN	9	4.9%	70.0%	43	4.2%	39.8%
9 NE,IA,KS,MO	14	7.6%	60.0%	72	7.0%	37.9%
10 AR,OK,TX	11	6.0%	58.8%	48	4.7%	27.7%
11 CA,NV,HI	18	9.8%	85.7%	73	7.1%	26.6%
12 WA,OR,ID,AK,MT	9	4.9%	63.6%	18	1.8%	22.8%
13 WY,UT,CO,AZ,NM	7	3.8%	63.6%	35	3.4%	37.2%
(Missing)	1	0.5%		8	0.7%	
Total	184			1,026		

[a]Percentage of diocesan bishops returning a questionnaire.

Table 2. Percent Agreement of Bishops and Priests to Need and Value of Catholic Schools

Item	Bishops			Priests		
	1986	1996	Change	1986	1996	Change
The need for Catholic schools is at least as great today as in the past.	92.7%	96.7%	4.0	71.6%	84.0%	12.4*
Catholic schools are an essential part of the Church's educational ministry.	96.8%	95.1%	−1.7	83.4%	86.5%	3.1
Maintaining Catholic schools is an effective use of diocesan resources.	91.7%	95.6%	3.9	66.2%	68.6%	2.4
The Catholic school is one of the best means of evangelization in the church today.	87.0%	89.7%	2.7	69.2%	65.7%	−3.5
Percent Disagreement:						
Catholic and public schools are not different enough to justify the continuation of most Catholic schools.	96.8%	96.7%	−0.1	80.0%	79.3%	−0.7
Improved parish religious education programs should eventually replace Catholic schools in most parishes.	92.2%	90.2%	−2.0	71.2%	62.9%	−8.3*

Note: * denotes a significant change at .05 level.

Table 3. Percent Agreement by Subgroups of Priests in 1996 to Need and Value of Catholic Schools

Item	Pastor School	Pastor Sponsoring	Pastor No School	Associate	Other Ministry	Retired
The need for Catholic schools is at least as great today as in the past.	90.2%	79.2%	73.9%	84.3%	83.0%	91.1%
Catholic schools are an essential part of the Church's educational ministry.	91.1%	84.8%	76.8%	88.3%	85.2%	85.7%
Maintaining Catholic schools is an effective use of diocesan resources.	78.0%	59.2%	51.1%	71.1%	72.4%	78.6%
The Catholic school is one of the best means of evangelization in the church today.	71.0%	56.9%	56.3%	70.4%	67.8%	71.4%
Percent Disagreement:						
Catholic and public schools are not different enough to justify the continuation of most Catholic schools.	83.2%	76.6%	71.6%	80.1%	84.1%	75.0%
Improved parish religious education programs should eventually replace Catholic schools in most parishes.	73.9%	51.7%	49.6%	66.2%	62.5%	62.5%

Table 4.   Percent Agreement of Bishops and Priests to Quality and Effectiveness of Catholic Schools

Item	Bishops			Priests		
	1986	1996	Change	1986	1996	Change
Generally, I believe that the Catholic schools in the diocese have high quality.	95.9%	98.9%	3.0	88.7%	90.4%	1.7
Where they exist, Catholic schools strengthen the bonds of unity within a parish.	92.5%	84.8%	−7.7*	78.4%	68.6%	−9.8*
Catholic schools have a positive impact on the adult religious behavior of their graduates.	97.2%	92.9%	−4.3	84.4%	72.2%	−12.2*
Catholics who go to public schools generally turn out to be just as good Catholics as those who attend Catholic schools.	20.7%	11.5%	−9.2*	46.7%	35.1%	−11.6*

Note: * denotes a significant change at .05 level.

Table 5. Percent Agreement by Subgroups of Priests in 1996 to Quality and Effectiveness of Catholic Schools

Item	Pastor School	Pastor Sponsoring	Pastor No School	Associate	Other Ministry	Retired
Generally, I believe that the Catholic schools in the diocese have high quality.	93.6%	85.8%	85.9%	90.9%	92.0%	90.9%
Where they exist, Catholic schools strengthen the bonds of unity within a parish.	70.7%	62.1%	62.7%	72.6%	65.9%	85.7%
Catholic schools have a positive impact on the adult religious behavior of their graduates.	76.1%	68.4%	68.1%	73.1%	72.4%	69.6%
Catholics who go to public schools generally turn out to be just as good Catholics as those who attend Catholic schools.	27.7%	45.0%	43.7%	21.1%	18.2%	28.6%

Table 6.   Percent Agreement of Bishops and Priests to Financial Issues Concerning Catholic Schools

Item	Bishops			Priests		
	1986	1996	Change	1986	1996	Change
The financial support of Catholic schools is the duty of all Catholics whether or not they have children in the schools.	95.9%	91.3%	-4.6	79.2%	74.4%	-4.8
In areas where there are only one Catholic elementary school and several parishes, each of the parishes should financially support the school.	94.9%	95.1%	0.2	93.2%	82.8%	-10.4*
Where possible and practical, it is best if each parish has its own Catholic school.	74.2%	75.0%	0.8	56.4%	47.4%	-9.0*
Every parish should provide some financial support for Catholic schools.	n/a	82.0%	n/a	n/a	71.6%	n/a
I believe that the main reason parents do not select Catholic schools for their children, when such choices are available, is their inability to afford the tuition.	59.0%	66.3%	7.3	58.3%	66.1%	7.8*

Note: * denotes a significant change at .05 level.

Table 7. Percent Agreement by Subgroups of Priests in 1996 to Financial Issues Concerning Catholic Schools

Item	Pastor School	Pastor Sponsoring	Pastor No School	Associate	Other Ministry	Retired
The financial support of Catholic schools is the duty of all Catholics whether or not they have children in the schools.	83.7%	70.7%	54.9%	73.6%	78.4%	80.4%
In areas where there are only one Catholic elementary school and several parishes, each of the parishes should financially support the school.	88.3%	81.7%	63.1%	86.3%	86.4%	85.7%
Where possible and practical, it is best if each parish has its own Catholic school.	57.1%	34.4%	34.5%	49.7%	47.7%	69.6%
Every parish should provide some financial support for Catholic schools.	80.7%	71.2%	45.1%	73.8%	73.9%	75.0%
I believe that the main reason parents do not select Catholic schools for their children, when such choices are available, is their inability to afford the tuition.	59.8%	66.8%	63.1%	74.6%	70.1%	71.4%

Table 8.   Percent Agreement of Bishops and Priests to Parental Involvement in Governance of Catholic Schools

Item	Bishops			Priests		
	1986	1996	Change	1986	1996	Change
Parents must be given a substantial role in the development of policy for Catholic schools.	63.4%	84.8%	21.4*	40.1%	68.1%	28.0*
Parents should have a substantial voice in the governance of Catholic schools.	n/a	83.7%	n/a	n/a	71.8%	n/a
All Catholic schools should have school boards/councils.	n/a	92.9%	n/a	n/a	87.1%	n/a
When a school serves several parishes, a representative board/council should be responsible for the school's governance.	n/a	84.2%	n/a	n/a	78.1%	n/a

Note: * denotes a significant change at .05 level.

Table 9.   Percent Agreement by Subgroups of Priests in 1996 to Parental Involvement in Governance of Catholic Schools

Item	Pastor School	Pastor Sponsoring	Pastor No School	Associate	Other Ministry	Retired
Parents must be given a substantial role in the development of policy for Catholic schools.	68.0%	69.0%	72.5%	61.4%	71.6%	71.4%
Parents should have a substantial voice in the governance of Catholic schools.	69.3%	73.8%	76.8%	66.7%	73.6%	81.4%
All Catholic schools should have school boards/councils.	86.0%	89.0%	93.0%	86.2%	82.8%	82.1%
When a school serves several parishes, a representative board/council should be responsible for the school's governance.	71.8%	84.7%	83.1%	77.6%	77.0%	82.1%

Table 10.   Average Percent Agreement in 1996 According to Perceived Demand for Catholic Schools During Past Five Years.

Issue	Bishops			Priests		
	Increase	Stable	Decrease	Increase	Stable	Decrease
Need and value of schools	94.9%	93.6%	86.1%	84.4%	72.9%	53.9%
Quality and effectiveness	92.4%	90.0%	89.9%	79.4%	73.4%	61.6%
Financial issues	84.5%	78.2%	76.7%	74.4%	66.0%	59.1%
Parental involvement and governance	89.1%	82.2%	81.3%	76.9%	75.2%	76.3%

References

Bryk, Anthony, Valerie Lee, and Peter Holland. 1993. *Catholic Schools and the Common Good.* Cambridge: Harvard University Press.

Convey, John J. 1992. *Catholic Schools Make a Difference: Twenty-Five Years of Research.* Washington, D.C.: National Catholic Educational Association.

Convey, John J., and Regina M. Haney. 1997. *Benchmarks of Excellence: Effective Boards of Catholic Education.* Washington, D.C.: National Catholic Educational Association.

Meitler Consultants. 1997. *New Catholic Schools 1985 to 1995.* Washington, D.C.: National Catholic Educational Association.

O'Brien, J. Stephen. 1987. *Mixed Messages: What Bishops and Priests Say About Catholic Schools.* Washington, D.C.: National Catholic Educational Association.

Schipper, C. A. 1982. "A Study of the Perceptions of Catholic Schools by Diocesan Priests of the Archdiocese of San Francisco." Doctoral Dissertation, University of San Francisco.

Sullivan, Eugene P. 1982. "A Study of the Perceptions of Catholic Schools by Diocesan Priests of the Archdiocese of Boston." Doctoral Dissertation, Boston College. Dissertation Abstracts International 42: 3834A.

Tacheny, T. S. 1988. "A Study of the Perceptions of Catholic Schools by Diocesan Priests of the Winona and New Ulm Dioceses of Minnesota." Doctoral Dissertation, Saint Louis University. Dissertation Abstracts International 48: 802A.

2 Sponsorship of Catholic Schools

PRESERVING THE TRADITION

Frederick C. Mueller, F.S.C.

AMERICAN LEGACY AT A CROSSROADS:
RESEARCH SYNTHESIS AND POLICY
ANALYSIS OF CATHOLIC SCHOOLS

Over the past thirty years the role of religious congregations in the management of Catholic schools and in
providing a teaching force for those schools has changed
radically. Parish and diocesan schools which had been conducted by religious congregations for years witnessed the
withdrawal of members of those congregations. Some con-
gregation-owned schools closed; others were given over
to dioceses and to lay boards. In many cases all that remained of the religious congregation was a rich oral history, a school name, or physical artifacts like windows, wall
plaques, and statues. In some cases, however, far-seeing religious leadership developed new governance models, established new models of staff development and training,
and provided on-going education for the school's constituencies regarding institutional identity and its relationship to the charism of the religious congregation. These
initiatives, which could be conceived of broadly as elements of religious congregation sponsorship of schools,
have grown and continue to grow, albeit in an uneven fashion, among religious congregations.

Although lay trusteeship was a common form of governance for some parochial elementary schools in the first
half of the nineteenth century in the United States (Guerra

1996), the history of Catholic elementary and secondary schools in the United States has been perceived, justifiably so, as a history that paralleled the development and growth of religious congregations of women and men. These groups built and staffed schools across the country, provided the work force for countless parish, and later diocesan, schools, and gave a distinctive identity to many of those schools (Fichter 1964; McCluskey 1964). However, by the mid-1960s new forces pressured religious congregations and Catholic schools. The numbers of members of religious congregations available for teaching declined. Initially this was due both to a drop in the number of vocations to those religious congregations and to the losses suffered when members left those religious congregations in the post–Vatican II period. A second factor was the newfound freedom of men and women in religious congregations to choose other than the traditional ministries of their particular congregations. Cultural factors in the United States and in the American Catholic Church, bolstered by new theological and pastoral directions from Vatican II, directions which urged religious congregations to rediscover their original founding charism, which affirmed the role of the laity in ministry, and which invited a reading of the signs of the times, caused religious congregations to reassess their traditional ministries, including Catholic schools.

Munley (1992), in a study conducted by the Leadership Conference of Women Religious, has shown some of the recent effects of those years of changes. The study noted that 31.0 percent of the membership of the religious congregations of women which responded could be classified as retired non-wage earners, 45.3 percent as active, full-time wage earners, 8.2 percent as active, part-time wage earners, 13.6 percent as active, non-wage earners, and 1.8 percent as unemployed. In addition, the projected median age for members of the congregations responding to the study would be 68 years of age in 1995. That study also noted that in the five years prior to 1992 those religious congregations who had responded to the survey had sold, closed, or merged 18 elementary schools and 50 secondary schools. The two major reasons given for that eventuality were rising costs (87.0 percent of the respondents) and lack of religious personnel (58.0 percent).

Cada (1979, 60) viewed this ongoing transition to a new paradigm of mission and ministry as involving "a transforming response to the signs of the times; a reappropriation of the founding charism; and a profound

renewal of the life of prayer, faith and centeredness in Christ." In light
of their emerging image of self and their new vision of mission and ministry, religious congregations have gone through a thirty-year period of
redefinition and renewal. Munley (1992, 2) noted:

> Religious organizations, like all other social organizations, must
> deal with a tendency toward over-institutionalization and entrench-
> ment. It is healthy that periodic assemblies and chapters provide re-
> ligious institutes with built-in opportunities to keep structures from
> becoming static. When structures become static, there is a loss in
> liminality and an inevitable decline in the prophetic impact of the
> group.

Religious congregations responding to the signs of the times and to
their own internal renewal needs, often found themselves "situated at
the threshold, the place or point of entering or beginning. . . . [a place
of liminality which demanded] focus and flexibility, willingness to pur-
sue the vision without total clarity, and ongoing personal conversion
and organizational transformation" (Munley 1992, 1–2).

It was within this context that the concept of sponsorship arose.
Rather than close schools and hospitals or give them over to other
groups, religious congregations viewed sponsorship as a way to maintain some influence over their ministries in the face of declining personnel. First with institutions of higher education and with health service institutions, and later with secondary and elementary schools,
new personnel deployment strategies, new governance structures,
and new administrative arrangements were introduced. Sometimes
these changes were measured and planned; often these changes were
reactive and completed without a long-sighted view of the implications of such changes. Salvaterra (1991) has pointed out that changes
have a continuous effect; and, that, although institutions do not usually experience immediate transformation at the time of adaptation,
gradual changes in goals, governance, and mission over a significant
period of time may cause such institutions to evolve into different
entities.

Over the past thirty years sponsored institutions and sponsorship itself have evolved in a variety of ways. The need to gather information
on sponsorship was recognized in 1987 at a symposium on the Catholic

high school teacher which was cosponsored by the Secondary School Department of the National Catholic Educational Association and Fordham University. Among the recommendations of that symposium (NCEA 1987) was a call for the identification and dissemination of useful models of successful programs developed by religious congregations regarding the faith formation of teachers and the initiation of dialogue and further collaboration with the Conference of Major Superiors of Men and the Leadership Conference of Women Religious in this regard. At the 1995 convention of the National Catholic Educational Association in Cincinnati, another symposium was sponsored by the Secondary School Department of that organization. This symposium was entitled "Sponsorship, Colleagueship, and Service" and its purpose was described by Guerra (1996, v):

> While there are many thoughtful initiatives at work within religious communities and particular dioceses, there has been little or no effort to open the conversation to representatives from a variety of different religious communities and regions. Bridges of various kinds are being built, but there has been little communication among the builders.

In light of these prior initiatives to raise, discuss, and investigate the issue of religious congregation sponsorship practices and in light of the ministry study *Threads for the Loom* (Munley 1992), a section of which reviews sponsorship as seen through the eyes of United States women religious and members of the Leadership Conference of Women Religious, the research reported here was designed to investigate as systematically as possible the current conception and practice of sponsorship of Catholic elementary and secondary schools by religious congregations of women and men in the United States. A brief review of the literature on sponsorship was done, most of which pertained to higher education and health services; survey research was completed in which religious congregational leadership was asked to reflect on specific issues connected with sponsorship of Catholic elementary and secondary schools; and follow-up interviews were conducted with representatives of six religious congregations of women and men to gather more detailed information on how sponsorship theory and practices have developed over time.

KEY ISSUES IN SPONSORSHIP

The Ambiguity of the Concept

Welch (1994, 1) has noted that there is little consistency for the meaning of sponsorship either in civil or church law, so that "each use is based on a particular set of circumstances and its meaning is limited by the interests and by the foresight of those who give it its definition." Responsibilities of sponsorship could range from influence to financial backing to endorsement; they could be as broad or narrow as are the interests and concerns of the religious congregation; they could exist with or without provision for congregational representation in the governance structure. Among the most common meanings of sponsor, according to Welch, are: (1) the assumption of responsibilities for mission and identity; (2) the maintaining of communion with the spiritual source; and (3) a relationship of benevolence, i.e., a quid pro quo in terms of lending support and receiving some benefit in terms of good will.

In the 1970s and 1980s sponsorship descriptions, particularly those connected to health care institutions, concentrated on the controls the religious congregation should have in place in its corporate ministries and emphasized such things as the roles of the "members" of the corporation, who usually were the religious congregational leadership, the division of authority within and among sponsored corporations (the reserved powers), and expectations of how mission could be accomplished (Campbell 1995). The 1990s brought new questions to religious congregations in terms of sponsorship of health care institutions: "Does sponsorship mean control of assets and ownership? Can sponsorship mean having presence and/or influence without ownership or control of institutions? Can the congregation continue its mission without ownership?" (Cassidy 1994, 20).

Sponsorship, therefore, has yielded itself to a certain ambiguity both in theory and in practice. H. Amos (1996, 21–22), in investigating sponsorship itself as an institution, raised a series of questions about "sponsorship capability": (1) Whether and how sponsorship could be a force in works that holds the sponsor to its original purpose; (2) Whether and how sponsorship could provide stability but not rigidity for works; (3) Whether and how sponsorship could be an enabler of life and progress; (4) Whether and how the sponsoring of works could be a source of organizational coherence as well as flexibility and adaptability; (5) Whether and how the sponsoring of works (and not just the works themselves) could give a sense and purpose to the life of the members and the group; and (6) Whether the loss of corporate influence was something which religious congregations would change if they could or which they had freely chosen in light of another value such as ministerial diversity.

As religious congregations have struggled with their appropriate role in specific works and ministries, they have been faced by additional questions: How do they deal with specific works which historically were a part and parcel of the very identity of the religious congregation, a part of its nature, purpose, spirit, and character (Welch 1994)? Are the members of the religious congregation willing to share responsibility with laity or do they insist on employer-employee relations? Are lay teachers and administrators willing to accept apostolic coresponsibility for the integral formation of students or do they wish to remain academic professionals? Is the Catholic population at large willing to prize religious-lay collaboration or do they continue to judge Catholicity by the number of religious (Duminuco 1996)?

Thus, sponsorship has been both a concept and a resultant practice open to many different definitions and interpretations. Savage (1991) claimed that there is no single model of sponsorship to fit all circumstances; rather, the model would be determined by local history, the influence of particular traditions and needs, flexibility, inaction, or the inability to respond to changing circumstances. Warner (1991, 15) further specified that:

> It is highly doubtful that larger institutions will preserve and develop their Catholic character without an important, appropriate, and determinative role for and by the founding religious congregation. Such a role must be derived from the current circumstances and best future hopes of both the institution and the sponsoring religious community. And it must be carried out in close collaboration with lay persons, many of whom are partners in the ministry.

To speak, therefore, in generalities about sponsorship has been difficult, if not impossible, since the same words can in fact mean very different things to different people. Larkin, in Salvaterra (1991, 8), defined sponsorship as "an ongoing relationship whereby the sponsored institution and the religious congregation identify with each other to the public, giving to the institution the benefit of the name and reputation of the religious group." Munley (1992, 167) referred to sponsored works as those "institutions, agencies, or entities founded or acquired by a religious institute to carry out its mission. The institute exercises some significant level of governance. The work may or may not be separately incorporated and the property may or may not be owned by the institute." In this definition, parish elementary and diocesan high schools could not be considered sponsored. However, Gray's (1996, 23) definition would allow such schools to be considered sponsored since "sponsorship involves the religious community's overall support of the school as part of its apostolic network. That support can range from simply allowing its name to be used to a commitment of personnel, money, and oversight. It manifests a willingness to take some responsibility for a school as part of the community's work." Welch (1994, 3), on the other hand, offered a more formal definition that: "a congregation exercises sponsorship of an institution through a civil structure or by reserving powers in the civil structure of the institution to a class of members who are the persons charged with administration of the congregation."

For the sake of this research, sponsorship was used to include the planned efforts by religious congregations to do any or all of the following: (1) preserve the identifying character or charism of the religious congregation within a school that had been or presently is identified with that particular religious congregation; (2) insure religious congregation influence on a school; (3) share responsibility for the administration and/or governance of the school with lay colleagues; and (4) deal with ownership issues. The school(s) in question might be those schools, past and present, owned, operated, and administered by the religious congregation or those parochial and diocesan schools closely identified with a religious congregation through history, tradition, and past practice. This working definition was examined in the survey research to see if a common definition could be arrived at which would be general enough to encompass the variety of expressions of sponsorship and which would be specific enough to have some meaning.

Religious Underpinnings

Campbell (1995) referred to sponsorship as fundamentally a religious activity of the sponsor rather than a governance question. The religious question represented the reason for sponsoring the ministry. According to Welch (1994), the decline in the membership of religious congregations forced a need to refocus resources so that the gift of the corporate existence of religious congregations was not lost to the Church. This refocusing of resources led to sponsorship through which communion with the source of tradition, the spirit of the congregation, the charism of the congregation, could be maintained and nourished. Sponsorship, therefore, was to be seen as an institution's relationship with a religious body and not just with individual members of the congregation. As such, the institution had to be rooted in a faith tradition and "needs to draw from something deeper than itself to be able to sustain that aspect of its identity through various periods of transition and change" (Welch 1994, 4). This communion or spiritual/religious aspect had to be worked out through mission effectiveness strategies; board, staff, and faculty workshops; handbooks reflecting and summarizing the spirit of the institution in the tradition of the congregation; service programs and liturgies; and a connection to and collaboration with other institutions in the religious congregation's tradition.

One way that religious congregations have viewed sponsorship has been as a means of evangelization, marked by the witness of personal contact, the catechesis of oral instruction, and the sacraments of ritual and symbol (Hauke 1993). Another viewpoint has been that sponsorship required from the religious congregation an act of faith. According to Munley (1992, 13), the religious congregation had to become vulnerable, i.e., moving from the familiar and secure; open to change and being changed, i.e., "letting go of images of what constituted effective ministry in the past and being willing to learn from the perspective of those with whom and among whom one may wish to minister"; and interdependent, i.e., breaking free of relationships based on dominance and subordination to a structure of webs of relationships, value-based networks, teams, rather than hierarchical pyramids.

Thus, sponsorship was not simply a question of governance but was inextricably tied into religious motivation and values as well.

Evolving Personnel Patterns

Another key issue in considering sponsorship was the role of the laity in relationship to the religious congregation. Although the spirit of the Second Vatican Council was one of collaboration between religious and lay, there was no injunction for religious congregations to turn over works to the laity or to share governance with them; rather, religious were to remain as the guardians and promoters of the charism, custodians of the works, and trustees for the future (Welch 1994). The laity had no particular responsibility for the charism or mission of a religious congregation.

However, at the same time, laity were being called upon to serve in leadership positions within the sponsored institutions, whether in board or administrative positions. This required the development of programs of in-service and formation both to inform lay colleagues of the charism and mission of the religious congregation and its application in a specific institution and to share with them the deeper spiritual realities of such a charism and mission. It was this latter function which prompted Magnetti (1996) to urge that the leadership come from within an institution, a school in this case, since from within the institution, it could be hoped, the spirituality was already present.

As regards board members, Warner (1991) noted that, as the number of religious dropped, this not only would reduce the possibility of turnover among representatives of religious congregations, but also would in time reduce the number of laypersons who had been significantly influenced by members of the religious congregation, thus having an impact on future boards and on those who would represent the common religious heritage in future board dialogues regarding mission, identity, and charism.

Although the programmatic consequences of such attempts to both inform and form could be considered major, even more significant would be the resolution of a question such as: to what extent can it be expected that lay colleagues will make their own the charism and mission of a religious congregation? Warner (1991, 15) has written:

How does a religious congregation exercise influence within a complex educational setting with a dwindling number of academics, administrators, and personnel available for service in crucial areas of student life? . . . The question here is not whether lay persons appreciate or understand an institution's or a congregation's charism, or whether they are as generous as individual religious in service of the institution within this framework. Rather, the problem arises from the simple reality that charism by its very nature is most effective when people see and appreciate its value personified in men and women who dedicate their lives in public witness and service to the values derived from it.

Thus, the issue of personnel would have to go far beyond leadership training, talking about history and tradition, or even formational elements. The real challenge, therefore, of sponsorship was how to include others, rather than absorb them, into the experience of the charism of the religious congregation (Gray 1996).

Governance

Issues of governance have been equally complex. Ownership, the role of boards, trusteeship, financial responsibility, and alienation of property have grown into overlapping realities. Gray (1996) has written that it is impossible to prescribe or endorse a specific legal arrangement which would universally insure the canonical oversight of the school as an apostolic instrument, its specific characteristics, and the invitation to lay colleagues to full partnership.

Welch (1994) has warned that religious congregations ought not confuse issues of religious life with issues of civil law. To incorporate a work or ministry and to operate it as an independent civil entity did not, in and of itself, mean that the religious congregation sought to distance the institution from the mission of the congregation. Rather, such a move was to limit liability so that there would be a line of demarcation between the religious congregation and the operation of the institution. There have been numerous ways that independent corporations (sponsored institutions) could accept control and limitation from an outside agency such as the religious congregation without the outside agency becoming responsible for the corporation or its liabilities. One model, suggested by Campbell (1995), was for the religious congregation to have one corporation that held congregation property and one or more corporations that provided legal structures for the ministry entities, with the religious congregation corporation not as the sponsor of the ministry corporations. According to Welch (1994), such an arrangement kept the religious congregation's identity distinct from that of the institution or ministry, on one level, but also allowed, on another level, that of participation in the governance structure of individual ministries, the religious congregation to safeguard the dedication of the property or of the endowments to a certain use and to safeguard the identity and to promote the mission of the institution.

Guerra (1996) has noted that ownership and trusteeship were not the same thing. In the nonprofit world, owners held title to the assets while trustees held the mission in trust and employed administrators who were to carry out that mission. Gray (1996, 23) has described ownership as "those who can close the school—not merely withdraw personnel or sponsorship but transfer or sell the buildings, equipment, grounds . . . the notion of ultimate financial title is involved." On the other hand, trusteeship "involves the direct oversight of the school regarding policy, hiring of the chief executive officer of the school, control of finances, and the implementation of the mission of the school" (Gray 1996, 23).

Reserved powers have been one way for a religious congregation to insure that they would be able to fulfill their stewardship responsibilities. Persons in congregational leadership served or acted as corporate members and reserved to themselves powers not given to the trustees, items such as control of the basic documents (articles of incorporation and bylaws); selection of the trustees, key corporate officers, and members of subsidiary boards; property alienation and asset distribution; approval of indebtedness; and the right to the appointment of an independent auditor with the receipt of its report (Welch 1994; Campbell 1995). Although this separation of powers has allowed for both protection from liability and accountability for mission, it has had some limitations. These have been noted by Welch (1994) as instability when embarking on joint ventures and either the pro forma role of the corporate members or their micromanagement.

Another model for sponsorship has been the transfer of property in which the religious congregation has set down the purposes of the institution as well as events that would either return the property or its value to another work of the congregation or trigger the dissolution of the corporation (Welch 1994). This transfer has sometimes been made to a lay model of sponsorship, a public juridic person of pontifical right (Mulvihill 1996), described as "aggregates of persons or things constituted by the competent ecclesiastical authority to fulfill a proper function given them in view of the common good" (J. Amos 1996, 31), e.g., a lay school board.

Gray (1996) has outlined seven possibilities for school sponsorship, some of which incorporate the models and principles noted previously: (1) a consultative, advisory board; (2) the religious leader or provincial as the "trustee" who works with a board which has genuine responsibility for the policy and functioning of the school; (3) a two-tier board, one of which is a small board of members (generally all religious) with reserved powers and the other of which is a larger board of trustees; (4) a one-tier board with 50 percent plus one members from the religious congregation and in which a majority vote is required to change the mission of the school, etc.; (5) tripartite agreements with specific contractual arrangements among the board of directors or trustees of the school, the religious congregation, and the local religious community; (6) a franchise model in which authorization is granted by the religious congregation to local schools to market the religious congregation name and products under strict conditions and with ongoing supervision; and (7) an association model in which the religious congregation has no special rights but only moral persuasion.

Regardless of the model, Gallin (1984) has advised that the overall theoretical concept in sponsorship which has to find expression in the governance model is partnership. Whatever the model, it must make provision for: a distribution of power, a distribution of responsibility, the implications of those distributions in terms of legal accountability and liability, justice in financial arrangements, the ministry goals of individuals and communities and the various modes of exercise of those goals, and the mission of the institution as acknowledged by the various constituencies.

These many models and overlapping realities, evidenced in the research done, have corroborated the position that no one governance model was an ideal model.

Project Design

The research was done in two phases. The first phase was survey research of the leadership of religious congregations of women and men. The second phase was structured, follow-up interviews with the leadership or representatives of six religious congregations whose sponsorship policy and practices were rather well-developed and were representative of somewhat diverse approaches to the question. These particular congregations were chosen as a result of the written responses to the survey.

The Survey

The researcher developed a survey instrument in order to elicit information in a number of different areas: general information, including basic demographic data and background information on sponsorship (whether or not there was a written policy for sponsorship, the number of years a sponsorship model had been in place, the number of schools in which a sponsorship model was in place, and the percentage of total number of schools which operated under a sponsorship model); a proposed definition of sponsorship; whether or not sponsorship extended to schools not owned by the religious congregation; formation and training procedures and practices; financial commitment; governance models; sponsorship staffing; level of support by the members of the religious congregation; perceived strengths and weaknesses; and other miscellaneous information, such as whether or not the chief administrator of a school had to be a member of the religious congregation, new initiatives, and the level of participation of congregational leadership in Catholic educational activities.

In the late spring of 1996 the survey was mailed out to the men and women leadership of 288 congregations or provinces which owned private elementary and secondary schools. In all, 146 surveys were returned (50.7 percent response rate) over a two-month time period. Of the total number of returns, 143 were entered for data analysis.

Having compiled the data from the surveys, the researcher chose six religious congregations for follow-up interviews. These congregations were a religious congregation of men (clerical), the Society of Jesus (S.J.); two religious orders of men (nonclerical), the Congregation of Xaverian Brothers (C.F.X.) and the Brothers of the Christian Schools or De La Salle Christian Brothers (F.S.C.); and three religious congregations of women, the Society of the Holy Child Jesus (S.H.C.J.), the Religious of the Sacred Heart (R.S.C.J.), and the Sisters, Servants of the Immaculate Heart of Mary (I.H.M.). All six congregations have had a clear and strong commitment to education. In addition, each congregation has had sponsorship practices in place which encompassed a wide variety of schools and gave evidence of a diversity of approaches.

The research on religious congregation sponsorship of Catholic schools yielded conclusions in three areas: general conclusions; a working definition of sponsorship in this context; and implications for the future of sponsorship.

Religious congregations whose ministry or a part thereof is Catholic schools are well aware of sponsorship. Some 63.4 percent of the respondents indicated that some sponsorship model was already in place. Of those, 78.3 percent have had a model in place for five years or more. Even though, for 68.9 percent of the religious congregations or provinces with a sponsorship model in place, this represented three schools or less, about two-thirds of those with an operative model reported that sponsorship extended to all of their schools. Thus, in many elementary and secondary Catholic schools with ties to religious congregations, sponsorship is already a reality.

In addition, some 56.6 percent of religious congregation or province respondents indicated that a written sponsorship policy was in place. A number of the remaining respondents noted that a policy was being worked on or that a written policy was being planned. Some responded that they were seeking assistance and guidance in formulating such a written policy.

Thus, sponsorship of Catholic elementary and secondary schools is a concept and practice which is not new to many religious congregations or provinces. For many it is a reality. What is not always clear is whether the term "sponsorship" is being used to describe the same reality, and how the future of sponsorship will be shaped.

A Working Definition of Sponsorship

Using the tentative definition offered for sponsorship in the survey document as a starting point, the following would appear to be a working definition of sponsorship which would reflect the theoretical and organizational priorities of religious congregations and provinces for whom Catholic schools are a ministry:

Sponsorship is the planned effort by a religious congregation primarily to preserve the identifying character or charism of that congregation and to insure its continuing influence within a school that had been or presently is associated with that particular congregation; this is accomplished through sharing responsibility for the administration and/or governance of that school with lay colleagues.

In addition, the religious congregation seeks, through sponsorship, to deal with ownership issues should they arise. Although, in many cases, sponsorship is applicable only to a school owned, operated, and administered by the religious congregation, at present or in the past, sponsorship can also be used in reference to a school not owned by the religious congregation (a parish or diocesan school) which is closely identified with that religious congregation through history, tradition, and past practice.

This working definition reflects the importance placed on preservation of charism and influence by the religious congregation, as well as the willingness to share responsibility with lay colleagues to accomplish the mission (more than 90 percent of the total respondents indicating that these three areas were of high or very high importance to them as regards sponsorship). Ownership, though of less importance, gains in degree of importance the longer the sponsorship model has been in place, whether or not a written policy has been developed. The structured interviews with religious congregations or provinces revealed that the longer the model was in place the more the ownership issue emerged. From a positive point of view, it was seen that sponsorship could in fact work even with a different governance structure and a different set of relationships between the religious congregation or province and the individual school; thus, new models could be thought about and implemented (cf. Cassidy 1994, 20). However, from a less positive point of view, the ownership issue would emerge after time because early attempts at sponsorship, though appearing to meet the needs of the religious congregation, had not always been successful in achieving the hoped for goals or might need to be rethought in the light of new needs of the religious congregation, be they financial or personnel-related.

This working definition also extends to schools not owned or administered by a religious congregation or province since, in fact, some religious congregations are choosing to continue their unique relationships with parish and diocesan schools where there is no question of ownership. Among the elements of those relationships are the preservation of congregational character within the school, the continuation of influence often through on-site personnel or outside support personnel and services (formational opportunities, for example), and the willingness to share responsibility for administration and leadership with lay colleagues, as well as with parish and diocesan leadership. This reality exists at present and was also mentioned in the structured interviews as a possibility for the future in terms of a new model of religious congregation influence on and support for Catholic elementary and secondary schools. In fact, this is in the process of occurring with one of the interviewed groups, i.e., a newly created school seeking sponsorship even though no members of the religious congregation or province would staff the school.

Some Implications for the Future of Sponsorship

The time for religious congregational sponsorship of Catholic schools would appear to be now. Munley's (1992) study of ministries pointed out that the respondents (leadership from the Leadership Conference of Women Religious) projected dramatic personnel shifts from 1991 to 1996; 62.0 percent projected a decrease in the full-time professional staffing of secondary schools by their membership and 74.0 percent projected a decrease for elementary schools. Likewise they anticipated the sale, closing, or merger over the same time period of 12 elementary schools and 29 high schools. The three most-supported reasons offered for this projection were: rising cost (77.8 percent), lack of religious personnel (68.9 percent), and declining need (51.1 percent). Only 15.67 percent gave "desire for collaboration" as a reason. Only 59.7 percent of the respondents assessed as good or excellent their ability to continue sponsorship of elementary schools and only 48.0 percent assessed that as regards secondary schools. Munley (1992) further explored this possibility of school closings, sales, or merger by examining the factors which would influence decisions to collaborate or cosponsor. Those factors with a positive impact were: commitment to common values, commitment to a common work, economic factors, and commitment to a common charism. Those factors which militated against collaboration were: lack of diocesan interest, fear of loss of control, inadequate sponsorship models, fear of loss of identity, and inter-congregational competition (to a lesser degree). If Munley's findings were to be extended to other congregations of women religious and to congregations of men religious, then the question of sponsorship is indeed one whose time has come, and perhaps is near to passing as new models of collaboration and cosponsorship emerge by necessity.

One urgent implication for sponsorship from the present research is the need for the development of a written sponsorship policy by religious congregations or provinces. The lack of a written policy was a weakness noted by a number of respondents. The data gathered revealed that those religious congregations or provinces with a written policy were more attentive to formational efforts for the various constituencies of the school, more likely to provide sponsorship support staff from the congregation or province, more open to the chief administrator of the school being a nonmember of the congregation, and more likely to report that the general membership of the religious congregation or province supported sponsorship.

A written sponsorship policy or agreement forces a religious congregation or province to reexamine itself repeatedly and to be clear about what is said and done (Hauke 1993), to look at the unstated beliefs and disparity of beliefs and assumptions among the parties to the sponsorship agreement (DiPietro 1991), to clarify any ambiguity that exists in the minds of its own membership regarding the vision for the institution or school in question (Salvaterra 1991), and to make decisions regarding the degree of influence, on the one hand, or control, on the other, which best would facilitate the accomplishment of the mission (Campbell 1995). According to DiPietro (1991), the absence of explicit clarity regarding sponsorship can lead to decisions made by individual parties that become fixed and immovable without full information or can lead to the loss of institutional presence of the religious congregation; the written policy or agreement often can serve as a way for the involved parties to commit themselves to the same stated objectives. Such policies or agreements force the parties to talk to one another and to come to an understanding and appreciation of each other's role in governance (Savage 1991). This would seem important, given that role confusion was an area of weakness expressed through the survey and in the follow-up interviews. Likewise, according to Savage, a written policy would allow the parties to focus on specific institutional issues, such as programs and the funding of those programs, and not abstract concepts, such as the "traditions of education" of a particular religious congregation (Warner 1991, 15). Whatever governance model is in place and whatever financial arrangements have been agreed upon would appear to be served best through a clear written agreement which would reduce the possibility of conflict in times of crisis.

A second implication for sponsorship from the present research re-
volves about the formational efforts aimed at the various constituencies
of the school and at the members of the religious congregation or
province. One area of weakness noted both in the surveys and in the
interviews was the question of whether or not formational efforts are
sufficient to make sponsorship work. This question does not deny the
belief expressed that lay colleagues in theory and in fact have a share in
the educational mission of the Church, as expressed in the charism of
the religious congregation and lived out in the local school. However, it
does signal an apprehension that the efforts have not been sufficient or
appropriate for the long-term continuance of the mission of the sponsored school.

Teachers, board members, and school leadership have been offered
formational opportunities in a variety of ways. However, according to
Kelly (1996), formational efforts must be built upon lived situations
where the sense of collaboration between religious and lay is genuine
and strong and where it has imprinted on the lay staff a very strong
sense of the core values of the religious congregation. Programs, though
important, are most effective when they are systematic, ongoing, and
consistent with the lived reality of the school. The data from this study
have revealed that more religious congregations or provinces with a
model in place for five to ten years offered formational opportunities
than those with a model in place for more than ten years. A question
could be raised as to reason for this: less need? what more can be done?
more ongoing local experiences than formal activities? The data also
have revealed that those religious congregations or provinces with less
than five years of having a model in place emphasize board effort. Perhaps the pressing need of having a strong organizational sense of mission and identity at the highest levels of policy-making governs this decision.

Much less has been done with parents, students, and alumni/ae. It
would seem important that religious congregations or provinces, as
well as the institutions themselves, direct attention to these other major
constituencies. Each has an important role as the school attempts to live
out its mission in concrete ways and to promote its identity and values
within a wider community. The authentic involvement of students, parents, and alums in the mission of the school in the present can also help
to assure that the mission will continue in the future with their support,

both in terms of identification with, and of financial backing for, the mission.

Finally, it would seem that religious congregations or provinces ought to insure that ongoing formation programs regarding key issues of sponsorship (identity, charism, collaboration in mission, rightful roles of the parties) are in place for their own membership. Reasons for this would be so that their members can be leaven in institutions where they are present, so that they can serve as resources to faculty, boards, and others, and so that they might be agents of encouragement and empowerment and not bearers of bad news or victims to nostalgia or myopic vision. With declining and aging numbers it would seem all the more urgent that religious congregations utilize their own membership most effectively for the continuance of mission.

A third implication for the future which can be drawn from the research is that older working models of sponsorship, as well as newer models and initiatives, must be shared among religious congregations and provinces. The finding that about half of the sponsorship resource personnel are part-time and that congregational leadership, by and large, is not involved in educational associations which would promote the sharing of ideas and models regarding sponsorship could indicate that time and other constraints might lead to some isolation in dealing with questions of sponsorship. The experiences of Catholic colleges and universities, of Catholic health care institutions and systems, and of successful sponsorship models might not be widely known. Such knowledge might promote more effective models of sponsorship. The remark of Guerra (1996) regarding the need for communication among the builders of sponsorship appears accurate and on target.

A further implication for sponsorship is that newer models will emerge to meet the new needs of religious congregations or provinces and to address new realities in Catholic schools. Models of these new forms of sponsorship for Catholic elementary and secondary schools might well be replicated from Catholic higher education and from Catholic health service institutions; other models are already being created by religious congregations or provinces and Catholic schools themselves (e.g., some of the new initiatives noted in the research).

In some cases this new model takes the form of the transfer of sponsorship from one congregation to another because it is seen that preserving a Catholic identity is more important than preserving the congregational identity (Cassidy 1995); in other cases schools which were not originally sponsored by a religious congregation have asked to be a part of a network of sponsored schools of a particular congregation, agreeing to accept the goals and criteria required by the network (Magnetti 1996); in still other cases new schools have requested a particular religious congregation to sponsor them so that they could have an identity and charism which they felt appropriate to their emerging mission.

The *tutelle* movement, the French concept of school sponsorship, provides another model. The *tutelle*, according to Welch (1994), provides orientation to the educational mission of the congregation's schools with an emphasis on the distinctive characteristics of the congregation's educational philosophy and spirituality; visitation, animation, and evaluation responsibilities fall under the *tutelle* but are performed by the congregational leadership. The merit of the *tutelle* is that it is simple and unambiguous, it is the same whether a member of the religious congregation is in charge or not, and it allows the energies of the members of the congregation and the lay colleagues to be channeled into mission effectiveness concerns.

Another model, from health services, is the merging of a religious-sponsored institution into a secular institution (Leonard and Morrison 1995). Such a model requires a sponsorship agreement and board which maintains the sponsor's interests and obligations in the integrated structure. The institution remains Catholic, and specific sponsorship components are put into place: periodic sponsorship reviews, development of sponsorship programs, and education of lay staff. The application of this model to schools might lean less toward public education and more to nonreligious, private education (established school groupings, privately managed schools, some form of charter school).

Two established models of lay sponsorship of Catholic health services are the "private association of Christian faithful," a group of persons who, with canonical recognition, have come together on their own initiative to conduct an apostolic work, and the "private juridic person," which emphasizes an organization or institution more than individual persons. According to McMullen (1996), these are not particularly good models for lay leadership since it has been found that the statutes are not sufficiently clear, that personnel feel isolated and insecure, and that they are not self-executing models. Nonetheless, they represent stages in the evolution of models of lay leadership which Catholic elementary

and secondary schools might adapt in the event religious congregational sponsorship cannot be maintained.

Still another model for religious congregational sponsorship is
cosponsorship. According to Cassidy (1996) and to the article "Cosponsorship: Are You Ready?" (1996), cosponsorship is a model of joint
sponsorship so that the religious congregations which come together
sponsor all the facilities jointly and collectively rather than merely
being involved in the ones which they individually owned, administered, and sponsored originally. Such a model requires congregational
leadership that is willing to spell out in concrete terms how the new
arrangement will strengthen the ministry and what the organizations
will be able to accomplish together that they could not achieve alone.
In addition, a model such as this allows religious congregations to address both ministry and business needs. Congregations' ownership in
cosponsorship is proportionate to the assessment of value of the institutions. One form of governance structure is a four-layered structure
with the religious congregations at one level forming a member corporation (juridic person) at a second level, which then governs the
cosponsored system (third level), that operates the specific entities or
institutions (fourth level). Such a model, growing out of a health care
viewpoint, could be adopted with some adaptation for clusters of
schools as well.

A somewhat similar model, again from health care, is the sponsorship network wherein sponsors in a region come together to discuss collaboration and explore ways to meet needs better (Gillis 1993). According to Cassidy (1994), this regional network could encompass both
ownership by and partnership with the laity.

Keith (1993) has described a Mission Integration Plan and Council
model developed to insure that the congregation's mission is being
safeguarded and extended in these newer collaborative models. The
plan puts in place a mechanism, the council, to make congregational or
Catholic values a part of decision making, direction setting, and strategic planning. The council is a forum which holds the authority for planning and implementing the mission integration strategies. In addition,
it provides a formal process for evaluating those actions in the light of
the mission statement of the institution and the core religious congregation values. Finally, it is a consultant on all major policy decisions and

policy revisions; ongoing accountability is provided for at every level of the institution.

The recent history of religious congregational sponsorship of health care institutions, and to a lesser extent of higher education, and some of the new initiatives already taken or being contemplated by religious congregations regarding Catholic schools, including use of the juridic person and some aspects of cosponsorship, point out that, even as religious congregations deal with current models of sponsorship, new models must be imagined to address new needs. These new needs include such things as coping with the continued declining numbers of members of religious congregations, dwindling congregational resources, and lay teachers and boards seeking some more concrete identity and a support system for Catholic elementary and secondary schools in which they minister and which they govern. As difficult as the future might appear for the involvement of religious congregations in Catholic education at the elementary and secondary level, current and new models of sponsorship seem to be a way that some of the unique gifts of religious congregations to Catholic schools can be maintained. The special corporate culture (Deal and Kennedy 1982) brought to schools by the religious congregations, a culture with a clear foundational history, with heroes and heroines with names and faces, with special traditions, and with special rituals, has been and still can be a source of institutional strength.

The social capital provided by the religious congregation for a school has been and still can be a source of institutional strength. Religious community sponsorship of Catholic elementary and secondary schools, a concept and practice which has arisen because of very similar realities among religious congregations but which has developed in a number of different ways that respect the traditions and unique circumstances of religious congregations and their schools, would appear to be the best hope for the continuance of the unique Catholic school that has been traditionally associated with religious congregations of women and men in the United States. Although there is no one way or best way to make sponsorship a reality, the ongoing development of both the concept and the practice of sponsorship will have a major impact on all of Catholic elementary and secondary education in the United States.

Perhaps it will be through new models of sponsorship that there will be not only a future but a bright future for Catholic schools.

References

Amos, H. 1996. "A Moral Quandary for Sponsors." *Health Progress* 77 (January–February): 20–22, 42.

Amos, J. 1996. "Public Juridic Person Offers Flexibility." *Health Progress* 77 (January–February): 31–35.

Cada, L., et al. 1979. *Shaping the Coming Age of Religious Life.* New York: Seabury Press.

Campbéll, P. 1995. "Evolving Sponsorship and Corporate Structures." *Health Progress* 76 (July–August): 35–42.

Cassidy, J. 1994. "Sponsors Envision New Directions for Health Care Ministry." *Health Progress* 75 (May): 20–24.

Cassidy, J. 1995. "Companions on the Journey." *Health Progress* 76 (May): 32–33.

Cassidy, J. 1996. "Sponsors Lead Ministry Transformation." *Health Progress* 77 (May–June): 36–37.

"Cosponsorship: Are You Ready?" 1996. *Health Progress* 77 (July–August): 32–33.

Deal, T., and A. Kennedy. 1982. *Corporate Cultures.* New York: Addison-Wesley.

DiPietro, M. 1991. "Changes in Governance of Catholic Colleges and Universities: Some Practical Observations." *Current Issues in Catholic Higher Education* 11(2): 8–13.

Duminuco, V. 1996. "Response." In *Sponsorship, Colleagueship and Service: A Conversation about the Future of Religious Communities and American Catholic High Schools,* D. McDonald, ed., 12–13. Washington, D.C.: National Catholic Educational Association.

Fichter, J. 1964. *Parochial School: A Sociological Study.* New York: Anchor Books, Doubleday.

Gallin, A. 1984. "Sponsorship as Partnership." *Current Issues in Catholic Higher Education* 4 (2): 7–10.

Gillis, V. 1993. "Sponsorship Networks." *Health Progress* 74 (April): 34–37, 41.

Gray, H. 1996. "Religious Communities and Secondary Education: Opportunities in Sponsorship and Governance." In *Sponsorship, Colleagueship and Service: A Conversation about the Future of Religious Communities and American Catholic High Schools,* D. McDonald, ed., 19–24. Washington, D.C.: National Catholic Educational Association.

Guerra, M. 1996. Introduction. In *Sponsorship, Colleagueship and Service: A Conversation about the Future of Religious Communities and American Catholic*

High Schools, D. McDonald, ed., iii–vi. Washington, D.C.: National Catholic Educational Association.

Hauke, M. 1993. "Evangelization through Institutional Sponsorship." *Health Progress* 74 (October): 48–50, 67.

Keith, J. 1993. "Mission Integration Preserves Sponsor's Values." *Health Progress* 74 (April): 38–40.

Kelly, T. 1996. "Religious Communities and American Catholic Schools: A Vision of Collaboration." In *Sponsorship, Colleagueship and Service: A Conversation about the Future of Religious Communities and American Catholic High Schools*, D. McDonald, ed., 3–11. Washington, D.C.: National Catholic Educational Association.

Leonard, D., and G. Morrison. 1995. "The Influence Model of Sponsorship." *Health Progress* 76 (June): 14–17, 22.

Magnetti, J. 1996. "Colleagueship and Leadership: Not Mine, Ours; Not They, We." In *Sponsorship, Colleagueship and Service: A Conversation about the Future of Religious Communities and American Catholic High Schools*, D. McDonald, ed., 33–37. Washington, D.C.: National Catholic Educational Association.

McCluskey, N., ed. 1964. *Catholic Education in America: A Documentary History.* New York: Bureau of Publications, Teachers College, Columbia University.

McMullen, B. 1996. "A Closer Look at Lay Sponsorship." *Health Progress* 77 (January–February): 28–30.

Mulvihill, N. 1996. "Public Juridic Person Ensures Catholic Presence." *Health Progress* 77 (January–February): 25–27.

Munley, A. 1992. *Threads for the Loom.* Silver Spring, Md.: Leadership Conference of Women Religious.

National Catholic Educational Association. 1987. *The Catholic High School Teacher: Building on Research.* Washington, D.C.: National Catholic Educational Association.

Salvaterra, M. 1991. "Catholic Identity at Risk: Case Study of Two Colleges." A paper presented at the annual meeting of the American Educational Research Association, Chicago, April 3–7.

Savage, T. 1991. "Trustees and Sponsors of Catholic Higher Education: What Should They Be Talking About Together?" *Current Issues in Catholic Higher Education* 11(2): 5–7.

The Official Catholic Directory. 1996. New Providence, N.J.: P. J. Kenedy & Sons.

Warner, R. 1991. "The Relationship between Trustees and Sponsoring Religious Congregations." *Current Issues in Catholic Higher Education* 11(2): 14–16.

Welch, M. 1994. "Sponsorship." *Bulletin on Issues of Religious Law* 10 (Summer): 1–12.

3 Leadership Given to the Religious Mission of Catholic Schools

Kathleen Carr, C.S.J.

The religious mission of the Catholic school is its proprietary strength. This religious mission establishes the relationship between culture and the Gospel and illuminates all knowledge with the light of faith (Congregation for Catholic Education 1988). As a defining characteristic, the religious mission permeates all aspects of Catholic school life. The religious mission differentiates Catholic education from public education and gives Catholic schools their unique identity. Thus, their educational goal is to "interweave reason and faith . . . bringing forth within what is learnt in school a Christian vision of the world, of life, of culture and of history" (Congregation for Catholic Education 1997).

Among the critical issues facing Catholic education at the dawn of a new millennium is the retention of Catholic identity. This concern has evolved over the course of the past twenty-five years. A key factor has been the transition of leadership. In the late 1970s, lay principals began replacing religious sisters, brothers, and priests. The decline in vocations to the priesthood and religious life in the previous decade limited the pool of sisters, brothers, and priests to fill leadership positions in Catholic schools. The trend continues today as evidenced by recent National Catholic Educational Association statistics which show that 52 percent of secondary school principals (Guerra 1994) and 51.3 percent of elementary school principals are laypersons (Kealey 1996).

The leadership transition from religious to lay principals raises obvious questions (see Jacobs, chapter 4, this volume). Can Catholic identity be sustained by lay principals who generally have not had substantive training in theology, scripture, and the Church's educational mission? Training in these areas is extensive and integral to spiritual formation programs for sisters, brothers, and priests. What impact will this difference in the leaders' background have on the religious mission of Catholic schools? Who will prepare future leaders for Catholic schools and how will these leaders become knowledgeable about and committed to the religious mission? Additional Catholic identity questions concern criteria for assessing the Catholic identity of Catholic schools. What elements are essential to a school's Catholic identity? How are criteria measured? What are the long-term effects of Catholic education on students' faith-development and behavior?

Catholic identity is being discussed at the national, regional, and archdiocesan levels. In local schools, principals and faculty examine ways the school community nurtures its Catholic character and manifests its religious mission to its publics. Participants in the national discussion include the National Catholic Educational Association and the National Conference of Catholic Bishops and Catholic universities that provide Catholic school leadership training programs and those that are establishing research centers for the study of Catholic education. Recent efforts which contribute to the discussion include the periodical *Catholic Education.* The first edition of this journal, in the fall of 1997, states that the publication commits itself to "focus on the latest research and scholarly reflection around critical issues . . . the Catholic identity of schools." In addition, the Consortium for Catholic Identity has designed a two-year program for Catholic school administrators to "preserve and protect the Catholic identity within our schools." These efforts are motivated by a desire to further the distinctive nature of Catholic education, to assist in strengthening the knowledge and developing the skills required to safeguard its religious mission and contribute to the formation of those entrusted with leadership of Catholic schools.

This year marks the twenty-fifth anniversary of the United States bishops' promulgation of *To Teach as Jesus Did.* The bishops used this document to explicate the place of Catholic education within the context of the United States Church and American society. The mind of the bishops regarding Catholic education is clear: "education is one of the most important ways by which the Church fulfills its commitment to the dignity of the person and the building of community" (National Conference of Catholic Bishops 1972). The document further states that the purpose of the Catholic school is to reveal the Gospel message of Jesus, create communities of faith, and promote service to others.

The research reported in this chapter examines the religious mission of Catholic schools from the standpoint of the school principal. The principal is responsible for providing leadership for this mission within the school community. The data reported in this chapter show how principals judge themselves in relation to the religious mission. The results add to the Catholic identity discussion and contribute specific data regarding the principal's leadership role in maintaining Catholic schools' historic goals, and factors that contribute to their effectiveness.

Theoretical Framework

In this chapter the term "spiritual leadership" refers to leadership the principal directs toward achieving the school's religious mission. This chapter will examine the Catholic school principal's self-efficacy and satisfaction derived from spiritual leadership.

Self-efficacy is the individual's belief that despite adversity, one possesses the requisite skills and abilities necessary to realize a goal (Bandura 1977a). Self-efficacy is a universal concept that may be applied to a variety of circumstances. For the purposes of this chapter, self-efficacy is applied to principals' spiritual leadership role and the abilities needed for the school community to realize its religious purposes. Self-efficacy is considered a cognitive process that requires goal identification, assessment of abilities necessary to achieve the goal, and prediction of the outcome (Stipek and Weisz 1981).

Research on self-efficacy as it relates to education deals almost exclusively with teachers in two dimensions: general teacher efficacy and personal teacher efficacy (Evans and Tribble 1986; Gibson and Dembo 1984). Teacher efficacy is the broader concept and refers to the overall relationship between teaching and learning (Ashton and Webb 1982; Brophy 1979), while personal efficacy specifically refers to an individual's belief that she or he possesses capabilities necessary to affect student learning (Ashton, Webb, and Doda 1982a; McLaughlin and Marsh 1978). The spiritual leadership self-efficacy construct in this chapter is based upon Ashton, Webb, and Doda's (1982a; 1982b) work on personal teacher efficacy and Bandura's (1977) self-efficacy construct.

Satisfaction generally refers to an individual's affective response to goal achievement (Lee, Dedrick, and Smith 1991). Job satisfaction specifically describes the overall affective orientation of individuals toward work roles they currently occupy (Kalleberg 1977). The focus of this chapter is on the principal's affective orientation toward achieving religious goals. The degree of satisfaction or dissatisfaction is a combined function of the degree of value fulfillment and the importance of the value to the individual (Mobley and Locke 1970). Research on the satisfaction of educational administrators is limited. Available data suggest moderate levels of overall job satisfaction among educational administrators.

Satisfaction theory and its application to educational settings has focused primarily on teachers. Overall satisfaction among teachers is typically due to positive teacher-student interaction and student success (Guskey 1982; Kottkamp, Provenzo, and Cohn 1986; Rosenholtz 1985). Organizational factors are also indicators of increased satisfaction and include teachers' perceived relationships with colleagues (Rosenholtz 1989; Rutter et al. 1979), and principals' high expectations for the quality of teacher instruction (Firestone and Rosenblum 1988; Litt and Turk 1985). Elementary principals are more apt to derive overall satisfaction from their work than their counterparts at the junior and senior high school levels. Among elementary principals a greater degree of satisfaction is derived from matters related to staff and a lesser degree from role-specific and occupation-related matters (Johnson and Holdaway 1990).

Conceptually self-efficacy and satisfaction are two theoretically distinct but related concepts (Lee, Dedrick, and Smith 1991; Fuller et al. 1982; Maehr 1987). Self-efficacy involves a cognitive process of goal identification, ability assessment, and judgment about effort required for goal attainment and outcome prediction (Stipek and Weisz 1981), whereas satisfaction is the affective response to goal achievement. Catholic school leaders' self-efficacy and satisfaction with their spiritual leadership are concerned with principals' judgments regarding their ability to realize the school's religious purposes and the value derived from achieving that goal.

The literature identifies several contexts in which self-efficacy and sat-isfaction are related: (a) the ways schools are organized influence job sat-isfaction by providing opportunities that foster teachers' sense of self-efficacy (Lee, Dedrick, and Smith 1991), (b) efficacious teachers report higher levels of satisfaction with teaching as a career (Ashton and Webb 1986; Trentham, Silvern, and Brogdon 1985), and (c) to the extent that proximal goals are attained, both satisfaction and self-efficacy increase. In addition, organizational members reporting a higher sense of self-efficacy portray themselves as active participants in organizational pro-cesses, more satisfied and more committed to remain in the organization than their counterparts reporting a lower sense of self-efficacy (Porter and Steers 1973). The results of the research presented in this chapter offer additional data which support a relationship between self-efficacy and satisfaction as they relate to spiritual leadership in Catholic schools.

Motivation deals with the "why" of behavior. It is the internal states of the organism that lead to the initiation, persistent effort, and direc-tion of behavior (Ferguson 1994). Motivation theory has been studied in terms of intrinsic factors and extrinsic factors (Lortie 1975; McLaugh-lin and Marsh 1978). Extrinsic motivation relates to the mechanistic model that views "behavior as determined by physiological drives and stimulus-response learning" (Csikzentmihalyi and Nakamura 1989, p. 46). Intrinsic motivation behavior is based on the individual's ca-pacity for intentional and purposeful action which is rooted in cogni-tive activity (Bandura and Cervone 1986).

A person's motivation can be influenced by previous association with or involvement in an organization. Prior employment, for ex-ample, preconditions an individual's expectation regarding work in that organization (Lawler 1973). Past experience influences how an in-dividual assesses the probability that a specific need will be satisfied. Antecedent firsthand experiences influence motivation, and informa-tion gained vicariously by means of legitimate sources also influences motivation. The sum of past experiences combine to form the basis for individual motivation (Hersey and Blanchard 1972). Motivation, then, is a function of antecedent events which influence individual behavior according to specific events which have occurred (Ferguson 1994).

Motivation, in this research on Catholic elementary school prin-cipals, is understood as antecedent to and informing one's attraction to continue working in a Catholic school. Within Catholic schools, leadership is exercised in a particular mission context and is directed toward achieving both religious and academic goals (Flannery 1988). A meaningful way to consider the motivation to continue as a Catholic school principal is in terms of mission-related motivation factors (i.e., religious goals) and professional-related motivation factors (i.e., academic goals). This chapter examines the principal's mission-related motivation as it relates to the religious mission of Catholic schools.

RESEARCH QUESTIONS

How self-efficacy, satisfaction, and motivation relate to Catholic school principals' spiritual leadership role will be investigated here. This chapter examines the characteristics of principals who are satisfied with their spiritual leadership, have high levels of self-efficacy regarding spiritual leadership, and possess a mission-related motivation orientation. A series of questions are asked in order to explore relationships among these characteristics.

METHODOLOGY

In order to measure spiritual self-efficacy, spiritual satisfaction, and mission-related motivation, an 88-item survey was sent during January 1995 to a national systematic sample of 887 Catholic elementary school principals in 156 dioceses located in the fifty states, Puerto Rico, and Washington, D.C. Overall the sample represents 12.3 percent of all Catholic elementary school principals in the United States. Approximately 70 percent of principals returned the questionnaire. The data reported here are based on the analyses of 612 survey responses. Of these, approximately 58 percent are lay principals and 42 percent are from religious communities. The respondents are primarily female (83 percent), over 50 years of age (57 percent), and Catholic (99 percent).

Among lay principals, 58 percent are under 50 years of age, whereas 22 percent of religious principals are less than 50 years old. The largest group of lay principals (45 percent) is between the ages of 40 and 49. Among religious principals the largest group (51 percent) is between the ages of 50 and 59 and the second largest (28 percent) is 60 years or older.

Religious principals are the more experienced leaders, with 24 percent having between twenty-one and thirty years school experience. The largest group of lay principals (43 percent) report from one to five years of experience as a principal. Seventy-one percent of the religious principals have more than ten years of principal experience. Lay principals are less experienced, with 74 percent reporting less than ten years of principal experience.

Principals in this sample generally hold at least a master's degree (91 percent); two-thirds of these degrees are in educational administration or education. Almost two-thirds of the principals have state certification in administration. Almost three-fourths of the principals have taken graduate courses within the past five years and 96 percent frequently participate.

Measures

The research deals with four constructs of spiritual leader self-efficacy, spiritual leadership satisfaction, mission-related and professional-related motivation, and personal religiosity. The items that assess each of these concepts are listed in table 1 (see Appendix to this chapter). The items were assessed on a 4-point Liket scale with 1 indicating "strongly disagree" and 4 indicating "strongly agree." The items were drawn from previous research on Catholic school personnel (Ciriello 1987; Deneen 1994; Tarr 1992). The items formed scales that met standard criteria for statistical reliability.

RESULTS

Findings will be presented in sections. Technical material, such as statistical analyses, can be obtained from the author. Major results are described in the text.

Spiritual Leader Self-Efficacy and Mission-Related Motivation

Scores on the self-efficacy scale were divided into high, medium, and low levels. Scores of greater than 3.6 on the 4-point scale were called *high* and were achieved by 20 percent of the principals. Scores lower than 2.9 were called *low* and were achieved by 14 percent of the principals. The remaining 65 percent were classified in the *moderate* category. The same cut-off scores were used to classify principals on mission motivation. Sixty-five percent were categorized as *high*, 7 percent as *low*, and 29 percent as *moderate.*

Table 2 reports the contingent relationship between these scales. Scores were as expected. Principals who scored high on mission motivation also scored high (26 percent) or moderate (64 percent) on self-efficacy. Simultaneously, principals who scored low on mission motivation also scored low (35 percent) or moderate (58 percent) on self-efficacy. Hence, mission motivations and self-efficacy for spiritual leadership were clearly related.

Mission-Related Motivation, Self-Efficacy for Spiritual Leadership, and Satisfaction

The groups displayed in table 2 were then compared with each other in a series of statistical tests. Principals who were high in self-efficacy and high in motivation had higher satisfaction scores than any other group.

Mission- and Professional-Related Motivation

When individual principals were divided into the categories of mission-related and professional-related, it was found that mission-related was dominant for 71 percent of the sample. This was true of religious principals (75 percent) as of lay principals (68 percent). Next, principals in the mission- and professional-related groups were compared on the other scales. It was found that mission-related principals had higher scores than professional-related principals on the self-efficacy measure (means = 3.36 and 3.24, respectively) and on the satisfaction measure (means = 3.37 and 3.20 respectively).

Mission-Motivation, Satisfaction, Experience, and State in Life

Analyses were run to determine statistical relations among these factors. Two major results were obtained. With regard to mission motivation, years of experience and state in life (religious vs. lay) predicted mission motivation. Principals with longer experience in Catholic schools and principals from religious congregations had higher mission-related scores than principals who had spent less time in Catholic schools or who were lay persons.

Similar relationships were found for spiritual satisfaction. Principals' satisfaction was high for those with longer experience in Catholic schools and those who were members of religious congregations.

Self-Efficacy for Spiritual Leadership and Spiritual Leadership Satisfaction

Table 3 reports levels on the three religiosity items according to principals' religious or lay status. Frequency of attendance at worship services was very high in both groups. However, the religious group scored considerably higher on the items assessing the importance of religion and personal relationship with Christ.

Regression analyses were then run to determine which factors best predicted self-efficacy scores. For religious and lay principals, spiritual leadership satisfaction was the strongest predictor of self-efficacy. For religious principals only, absence of a state certificate also predicted self-efficacy. And for lay principals, degree of religiosity also predicted self-efficacy.

Which factors predicted satisfaction? For both religious and lay principals, satisfaction was predicted by self-efficacy and by mission-relatedness.

Last, mission-related motivation was inspected. It was predicted by three factors for both religious and lay principals. These factors were: professional-related motivation, degree of religiosity, and years of experience as a Catholic school principal. As implied in prior results, an additional factor predicted mission motivation for religious principals. Lack of a degree in the discipline of education led to higher commitment to mission.

Interpretation

Literature on Catholic schools views the principal as responsible for furthering the religious mission of Catholic schools. Church documents and Catholic school resource material clearly and consistently delineate the role of the principal as spiritual leader. The research presented in this chapter offers insights into how principals regard their spiritual leadership, the satisfaction principals derive,the sense of self-efficacy they possess as spiritual leaders, and factors that motivate them to continue as leaders in Catholic schools.

While the focus of this chapter is on the principal's spiritual leadership, it is understood that this particular role is exercised in conjunction with educational leadership and managerial leadership. The separation of spiritual leadership from the other Catholic school leadership roles is artificial and is intended for examination purposes only. The integration of all facets of Catholic school leadership is essential for the effective exercise of leadership in Catholic schools. The Catholic school principal's leadership is a "blend of educational skill, managerial skill and a dynamism which is able to perform well and to grow spiritually and educationally" (Drahmann and Stenger 1989, p.7).

Both the academic and religious goals of Catholic school education must be realized if the Catholic school is to fulfill its mission effectively. Factors related to religious purposes are emphasized here. They are not intended to exclude the equal importance of Catholic school academic goals and the motivation to achieve these goals. The aim of Catholic schools is to integrate knowledge and faith, and to combine academic and religious formation.

The following conclusions are drawn from the research findings.

- Principals are more apt to remain as principals in Catholic schools for religious than for academic reasons. Principals tend to have slightly higher levels of mission-related motivation than professional-related motivation.
- A mission-related motivation orientation is a significant predictor of spiritual leadership satisfaction.
- Principals with a combined mission-related motivation orientation and a high sense of spiritual leadership self-efficacy have high levels of spiritual leadership satisfaction.
- Religiosity and experience as a Catholic school principal are important predictors of mission-related motivation.
- Lay principals with a high sense of spiritual leadership self-efficacy are apt to have high spiritual leadership satisfaction and attribute a high degree of value to the overall importance of religion in life and to the practice of religion.
- Lay and religious principals share similar levels of self-efficacy with spiritual aspects of leadership.
- Religious principals report higher levels of satisfaction with the spiritual aspects of leadership than do lay principals.
- Overall, the level of satisfaction and self-efficacy with spiritual leadership among Catholic school principals in this research sample is high.

- Religiosity is a critical variable that significantly influences lay principals' sense of spiritual leadership self-efficacy.
- Religiosity is a significant predictor of mission-related motivation.

The proportion of lay principals already exceeds the number of religious principals in Catholic schools. Thus lay principals will continue
to shape the course of Catholic education into the twenty-first century.
Present findings suggest that religious principals are apt to have significantly higher levels of a mission-related motivation orientation and
spiritual leadership satisfaction than their Catholic school lay principal
counterparts. It would follow that additional resources are needed to
increase the satisfaction of lay principals. Because the data suggest that
mission-related motivation increases over time, a key might be retain
lay principals in the system so that their mission motivation would
increase. Such a result calls for new structures to support retention of
effective principals within the Catholic school system.

Considerations for the Training and Support of Catholic School Leaders

The results of this study serve as a basis for the following comments
on the ongoing development of principals as spiritual leaders in Catholic schools. There are four areas of considerations dealing with Church
documents, effective schools research, personal faith life, and collaboration among Church agencies, with former leaders of Catholic schools
and among peer Catholic school leaders.

1. Church documents on Catholic education set the context for the
religious mission of Catholic schools. Leadership recruitment programs
and professional development programs should be expanded or
strengthened by incorporating Church documents on Catholic education as a substantive component. The content from the following documents should be included: *Declaration on Christian Education* (1966);
To Teach as Jesus Did (1972); *Teach Them* (1976); *The Catholic School*
(1977); *Sharing the Light of Faith* (1977); *Lay Catholics in Schools: Witnesses to Faith* (1982); *The Religious Dimension of Education in a Catholic
School* (1988); *The Catholic School on the Threshold of the Third Millennium* (1997).

A study of these documents should include the origin of each document, the historical context in which it is formulated, the main tenets
and the evolution of the Church's teaching on Catholic education and

Catholic schools. Great effort should be taken to correlate the teachings in Church documents to the daily experience of leadership in Catholic schools.

For example, principals could engage in discovering how these statements from the documents relate to school life:

- "teacher behavior and witness are considered the primary vehicles through which the distinctive character of Catholic schools is passed on in the lives of students" (*The Catholic School* 1977);
- "teachers participate in an ongoing formation process aimed to animate them as witnesses of Christ in the classroom" (*The Catholic School* 1977);
- "professional credentials are considered as important as one's character and lifestyle. All Catholic educators are not simply professionals but are considered to share in an educational ministry" (*Teach Them* 1976);
- "Catholic educators assist in the prophetic mission of Christ" (*Lay Catholics in Schools: Witnesses to Faith* 1982).

2. Programs of study should include focus on the characteristics of effective schools and relate these to the religious mission of Catholic schools. Several factors in the effective schools' literature suggest a strong relationship between effective schools and schools with a value orientation. Some of the more salient points are:

- effective schools have a strong shared-*value* system and a common purpose about the intent of education (Purkey and Smith 1983; Rosenholtz 1989);
- effective schools promote a strong sense of *community* among school members (Bryk and Driscoll 1988);
- a value-oriented set of *beliefs,* held in common by the school community tends to increase teacher efficacy (Salganik 1982);
- a hallmark of effective schools is a faculty and principal who affirm and support the school's core *mission* (Chubb and Moe 1990; Purkey and Smith 1983).

Theoretically, Catholic schools possess several of the essential elements which constitute school effectiveness. Religious beliefs and

Christian values are at the core of our mission and form the basis of Catholic school philosophy. Formation in religious, moral, and social values is at the heart of Catholic education (Benson, Williams, and Yeager 1984). Leadership in a Catholic school focuses on the meaning-inducing quality of Catholic school life. It is a deliberate aim, equally as important as the organization of instruction (Bryk and Lee 1992).

3. As important as the document teachings are, the exercise of spiritual leadership requires more than being well-versed in document content or having knowledge of the Catholic faith. They must be balanced with a growing personal relationship with God, in an active life of faith. The value of this relationship must be communicated by the leader in practical and specific terms to the school community. Opportunities should be provided for principals to share how they experience God's presence, direction, compassion in the exercise of their leadership.

One's relationship with God is personal. Catholic school principals are expected to give public witness to their personal relationship with God. They deserve the resources necessary to foster their ability to do this. These include, but are not limited to, spiritual direction, retreat time, reflection periods, meaningful liturgical celebrations, adult religious education, faith-sharing, and opportunities to discuss God's movement in their lives. Returning to the data, we find that when the religious mission of the Catholic school is realized, principals' satisfaction and self-efficacy with spiritual leadership increase.

4. Collaboration among Church agencies must continue and expand as resources allow. Catholic school leadership development is an important work essential to the Church's teaching mission. The responsibility for providing resources to assist in faith formation of Catholic school principals is not the sole responsibility of the office of the superintendent, but rather should be shared with the wider Church. Diminishing financial and personnel resources within the Catholic Church create the need to forge new partnerships and expand existing ones within the Church and beyond it. Efforts should be directed toward collaboration across diocesan agencies to maximize the potential of available resources for the nurturing, training, and development of Catholic school leaders, particularly in the area of faith formation.

Principals are resources for each other. Creative ways to tap this resource need to be explored. Some dioceses have programs in which veteran principals serve as mentors to their newer colleagues. Partnerships such as these strengthen bonds among school leaders, create networks, and promote a sense of community. The latter is a clearly stated goal of *To Teach as Jesus Did.* Before leaders are able to create a community of faith among the school community, they must know what it is to belong to such a community.

Efforts in the wider community should be directed toward colleges and universities as potential resources for the ongoing professional development of school leaders. Efforts in this regard should continue particularly at Catholic institutions of higher learning, to collaborate in the training, preparation, and ongoing development of Catholic school leaders.

Other potential resources available to Catholic school principal-formation programs include religious congregations which traditionally provided the leadership for Catholic schools. They represent a wealth of experience and a life-long commitment to Catholic education. As religious principals grow older and leave the schools, ways should be identified to involve this group in efforts to support and sustain the spiritual leadership of Catholic school principals.

The data indicate that satisfaction, self-efficacy, and motivation of Catholic school leadership increase with experience. The longer principals are in the system, the more satisfaction, self-efficacy, and motivation levels are apt to increase. Nurturing principals' spiritual leadership in its early stages of development is critical to Catholic school effectiveness. Spiritual leadership is understood to be an important indicator of Catholic school effectiveness (Convey 1992). The time, attention, and planning that is required to begin and sustain partnerships aimed at increasing longevity in the system could be well worth the investment.

APPENDIX

Table 1.   Items on the Satisfaction, Self-Efficacy, Motivation, and Religiosity Scales

---

Spiritual Leadership Satisfaction Scale Items
helping students grow spiritually
manifestations of the school's Catholic identity
recognition of my spiritual role
faith community among faculty and students
influence on the religious aspects of school affairs
helping teachers grow spiritually
implementing religious mission of Catholic education
religious philosophy of the school
ongoing spiritual formation of faculty

Spiritual Leadership Self-Efficacy Scale Items
inspire teachers regarding school's spiritual mission
integration of religious values with all of school life
religion as significant element
spiritual development of students
sustain school's Catholic character in time of adversity
help students in areas of worship and community service
provide clear description of purposes of Catholic schools

Mission-Related Motivation Scale Items
commitment to the mission of Catholic education
view of administration as my ministry
opportunity to witness to my faith
wanted to work in a Catholic environment
assist in spiritual development
God's choice for my life
religious philosophy of the school
overall importance of religion in life

Professional-Related Motivation Scale Items
my professional qualifications
social environment (discipline, caring)
help educate young people

(continued)

Table 1.   (*continued*)

interest in administration
opportunity to share my values for personal growth
  and development
academic philosophy of the school

Religiosity Scale Items
frequency of attendance at worship services
nurturing a personal relationship with Jesus Christ

Table 2.   Mission-Related Motivation by Spiritual Leadership
Self-Efficacy Level

	Spiritual Leadership Self-Efficacy Level		
Mission Motivation Level	*High*	*Moderate*	*Low*
High	25.6%	63.5%	10.9%
Moderate	13.0%	71.2%	15.8%
Low	7.5%	57.5%	35.0%

Table 3.   Religiosity by Religious and Lay Status

	Total	*Religious*	*Lay*
Frequently attend worship services	592 (98%)	255 (99%)	337 (96%)
Religion in life extremely important	474 (78%)	235 (93%)	239 (67%)
Personal relationship with Jesus Christ extremely important	440 (73%)	234 (92%)	206 (59%)

REFERENCES

Ashton, P., and R. B. Webb. 1986. *Making a Difference: Teachers' Sense of Efficacy and Student Achievement.* New York: Longman.

Ashton, P., R. B. Webb, and N. Doda. 1982a. "A Study of Teachers' Sense of Efficacy." Final report, vol I. Gainsville: University of Florida. (ERIC Document Reproduction Service No. ED 231 834.

Ashton, P., R. B. Webb, and N. Doda. 1982b. "A Study of Teachers' Sense of Efficacy." Final report, vol II. Gainsville: University of Florida. (ERIC Document Reproduction Service No. ED 231 835.)

Bandura, A. 1977a. "Self-Efficacy: Toward a Unifying Theory of Behavioral Change." *Psychological Review* 84(2): 191–215.

Bandura, A. 1977b. *Social Learning Theory.* Englewood Cliffs: Prentice-Hall.

Bandura, A., and D. Cervone. 1986. "Differential Engagement of Self-Reactive Influences in Cognitive Motivation." *Organizational Behavior and Human Decision Process* 38: 92–113.

Benson, P. L., D. L. Williams, and R. J. Yeager. 1984. "Study Assesses Quality of Catholic Schools." *Momentum* 15: 4–9.

Brophy, J. 1979. "Teacher Behavior and Its Effects." *Journal of Educational Psychology* 71: 735–50.

Bryk, A. S., and M. E. Driscoll. 1988. *The School as a Community: Theoretical Foundations, Contextual Influences, and Consequences for Students and Teachers.* Madison: University of Wisconsin, National Center for Effective Secondary Schools.

Bryk, A. S., and V. Lee. 1992. *Lessons from Catholic High Schools on Renewing Our Educational Institutions.* Symposium on Educational Choice. Washington, D.C.: Economic Policy Institute.

Chubb, J. E., and T. M. Moe. 1990. *Politics, Markets, and America's Schools.* Washington, D.C.: Brookings Institution.

Ciriello, M. J. 1987. "Teachers in Catholic Schools: A Study of Commitment." Doctoral dissertation, The Catholic University of America, 1987. *Dissertation Abstracts International* 48: 8514A.

Ciriello, M. J. J., ed. 1994. *The Principal as Spiritual Leader.* Washington, D.C.: United States Catholic Conference.

Congregation for Catholic Education. 1997. *The Catholic School on the Threshold of the Third Millennium.* Rome: Vatican Polygot Press.

Congregation for Catholic Education. 1988. *The Religious Dimension of Education in a Catholic School.* Rome: Vatican Polyglot Press.

Consortium for Catholic School Identity. 1997. *Enhancing Catholic School Identity: A Distinctly Different Approach to Excellence.* Arlington, Va.: Office of Catholic Schools.

Convey, J. J. 1992. *Catholic Schools Make a Difference: Twenty-Five Years of Research.* Washington, D.C.: National Catholic Educational Association.

Csikszentmihalyi, M., and J. Nakamura. 1989. "The Dynamics of Intrinsic Motivation: A Study of Adolescents." In C. Ames and R. Ames, eds., *Research on Motivation in Education:* vol. 3. *Goals and Cognitions* (pp. 45–71). New York: Academic Press.

Deneen, J. 1994. *Self-assessment Survey.* Washington, D.C.: United States Catholic Conference.

Drahaman, T., and A. Stenger. 1989. *The Catholic School Principal: An Outline for Action,* rev. ed. Washington, D.C.: National Catholic Educational Association.

Edmonds, R. 1979. "Some Schools Can Work and More Can." *Social Policy* 9: 28–32.

Evans, E. D., and M. Tribble. 1986. "Perceived Teaching Problem, Self-Efficacy, and Commitment to Teaching Among Preservice Teachers." *Journal of Educational Research* 80(2): 81–85.

Ferguson, E. 1994. "Motivation." In R. Corsini, ed., *Encyclopedia of Psychology* (vol. 2, pp. 429–33). New York: John Wiley and Sons.

Firestone, W. A., and S. Rosenblum. 1988. "Building Commitment in Urban High Schools." *Educational Evaluation and Policy Analysis* 10: 285–99.

Flannery, A. 1988. *Vatican Council II: The Conciliar and Post-Conciliar Documents,* rev. ed. Boston: Daughters of St. Paul.

Fuller, B., K. Wood, T. Rapoport, and S. Dornbusch. 1982. "The Organizational Context of Individual Efficacy." *Review of Educational Research* 52(1): 7–30.

Gibson, S., and M. H. Dembo. 1984. "Teacher Efficacy: A Construct Validation." *Journal of Educational Psychology* 76(4): 569–82.

Guerra, M. 1994. "Dollar and Cents: Catholic Schools and Their Finances." Washington, D.C.: National Catholic Education Association.

Guskey, T. R. 1982. "Differences in Teachers' Perceptions of Personal Control of Positive Versus Negative Student Learning Outcomes." *Contemporary Educational Psychology* 7: 70–80.

Hersey, P., and K. Blanchard. 1972. *Management of Organizational Behavior: Utilizing Human Resources.* Englewood Cliffs: Prentice-Hall.

Johnson, N. A., and E. A. Holdaway. 1990. "School Effectiveness and Principals' Effectiveness and Job Satisfaction." *Alberta Journal of Educational Research* 36(3): 265–95.

Kalleberg, A. 1977. "Work Values and Job Rewards: A Theory of Job Satisfaction." *American Sociological Review* 42: 124–43.

Kealey, R., ed. 1996. *Balance Sheet for Catholic Elementary Schools: 1995 Income and Expenses.* Washington, D.C.: National Catholic Educational Association.

Kottkamp, R. B., E. F. Provenzo, and M. M. Cohn. 1986. "Stability and Change in a Profession: Two Decades of Teacher Attitudes, 1964–1984." *Phi Delta Kappan* 67(8): 559–67.

Lawler, E. E. 1973. *Motivation in Work Organizations.* Monterey, Calif.: Brooks/Cole.

Lee, V. E., R. F. Dedrick, and J. B. Smith. 1991. "The Effect of the Social Organization of Schools on Teachers' Efficacy and Satisfaction." *Sociology of Education* 64(3): 190–208.

Litt, M. D., and D. C. Turk. 1985. "Sources of Stress and Dissatisfaction in Experienced High School Teachers." *Journal of Educational Research* 78(3): 178–85.

Maehr, M. L. 1987. Advances in Motivation and Achievement: Enhancing Motivation (vol. 5). Greenwich, Conn.: JAI Press.

McLaughlin, M. W., and D. D. Marsh. 1978. "Staff Development and School Change." *Teachers College Record* 80: 70–94.

Mobley, W. H., and E. A. Locke. 1970. "The Relationship of Value Importance to Satisfaction." *Organizational Behavior and Human Performance* 5: 463–83.

National Conference of Catholic Bishops. 1972. *To Teach as Jesus Did.* Washington, D.C.: United States Catholic Conference.

National Conference of Catholic Bishops. 1976. *Teach Them.* Washington, D.C.: United States Catholic Conference.

National Conference of Catholic Bishops. 1979. *Sharing the Light of Faith: National Catechetical Directory for Catholics in the United States.* Washington, D.C.: United States Catholic Conference.

Porter, L. W., and R. M. Steers. 1973. "Organizational Work and Personal Factors in Employee Turnover and Absenteeism." *Psychological Bulletin* 80: 151–76.

Purkey, S. C., and M. S. Smith. 1983. "Effective Schools: A Review." *Elementary School Journal* 84: 427–52.

Rogus, J. F. 1991. *Strengthening Preparation and Support for Leadership in Catholic Schools. In Leadership of and on Behalf of Catholic Schools.* Washington, D.C.: National Catholic Educational Association.

Rosenholtz, S. J. 1985. "Effective Schools: Interpreting the Evidence." *American Journal of Education* 93(3): 352–88.

Rosenholtz, S. J. 1989. *Teachers' Workplace: The Social Organization of Schools.* New York: Longman.

Rutter, M., B. Maughan, P. Mortimore, J. Ouston, and A. Smith. 1979. *Fifteen Thousand Hours: Secondary Schools and Their Effects on Children.* Cambridge: Harvard University Press.

Sacred Congregation for Catholic Education. 1977. *The Catholic School.* Boston: Daughters of St. Paul.

Sacred Congregation for Catholic Education. 1982. *Lay Catholics in Schools: Witnesses to Faith.* Boston: Daughters of St. Paul.

Salganik, L. H., and N. Karweit. 1982. "Volunteerism and Governance in Education." *Sociology of Education* 55: 152–61.

Stipek, D., and J. Weisz. 1981. "Perceived Personal Control and Academic Achievement." *Review of Educational Research* 51(1): 101–37.

Tarr, H. C. 1992. "The Commitment and Satisfaction of Catholic School Teachers." Doctoral dissertation, The Catholic University of America, 1992. *Dissertation Abstracts International*, A 53/03.

Tarr, H., M. Ciriello, and J. Convey. 1993. "Commitment and Satisfaction Among Parochial School Teachers: Findings from Catholic Education." *Journal of Research on Christian Education* 2(1): 41–60.

Trentham, L., S. Silvern, and R. Brogdon. 1985. "Teacher Efficacy and Teacher Competency Ratings." *Psychology in the Schools* 22: 343–52.

4 Contributions of Religious to U.S. Catholic Schooling

Richard M. Jacobs, O. S. A.

Overview

In 1944, Mother Francesca O'Shea posited a theological dictum to the aspirants to her religious community, all of whom were destined to teach in Catholic schools. She told those aspirants gathered before her, "Let us always keep before us the solid religious principle: 'First things first' and trust the rest to Divine Providence" (cited in Byrne 1990, 139). While many of the aspirants may have had no knowledge that Mother Francesca's dictum reflected a *Deus ex machina* worldview, her words echoed the experience of nearly ten generations of religious in the United States, especially the legions of sisters and brothers and priests who did put first things first—by sacrificing their lives to God—and, in the face of numerous obstacles, trusted the rest to Divine Providence.

In this chapter, we will first survey some of the contributions the religious[1] made during the past two centuries to U.S. Catholic schooling. To demonstrate how these generations of religious built upon and perfected the legacy entrusted by their predecessors, we demarcated these two centuries into three eras: the era prior to the third Baltimore Council in 1884; the era after Baltimore III and the close of the Second Vatican Council in 1965; and the three decades following Vatican II.

This chapter is developed from a paper originally presented at the "American Legacy at a Crossroads" symposium sponsored by a grant from the Lilly Foundation and hosted by the Life Cycle Institute at Catholic University of America (June 1997).

Following this brief survey, we will then ponder three questions these contributions raise: What lessons do the contributions of the religious teach those who will follow in their steps? Who will replace these witnesses? And: What training does the next generation of educators in Catholic schools require to assure the U.S. Catholic community that youth in the twenty-first century will receive the moral and intellectual formation to exercise their rights and responsibilities?

As the U.S. Catholic schooling faces a new era, one that according to all evidence will be characterized by lay leadership, if the laity are to extend and perfect this American legacy as the twenty-first century dawns, they too would do well—like aspirants to religious life in previous eras—to consider Mother Francesca's dictum "to put first things first and trust the rest to Divine Providence."

THE CONTRIBUTIONS OF THE RELIGIOUS TO U.S. CATHOLIC SCHOOLING

During the twentieth century, historians have subjected the emergence of U.S. Catholic schooling—an effort unparalleled in human history—to considerable analysis. One strand of analysis focuses on the nondenominational, pan-Protestant program of moral education propounded in public schools during the eighteenth and nineteenth centuries (Church 1976; Cremin 1961, 1980; Kaestle 1973; Tyack 1966, 1974). Accordingly, by the 1820s the American Catholic community—and especially its leaders—identified the need to construct separate Catholic schools, largely as a reaction to what Catholics perceived as transpiring in public schools. That is, they viewed the program of moral education as a deliberate attempt by the Protestant majority—those who controlled the schools—to indoctrinate Catholic youth in Protestantism. Some other Catholics also viewed the emerging public school monopoly as a usurpation of the rights of parents to educate their children as they saw fit.

A second strand of analysis focuses on the social context and especially the ostracism Catholics experienced due to their status as an economically disadvantaged, immigrant minority in a largely Protestant nation. This analysis highlights the scorn of nativist prejudice as well as blatant anti-Catholic bigotry. Because of this contentious social context, if parishes were to protect their members as well as the Catholic

faith, the Catholic community would need to muster its limited re-
sources to build separate schools (Buetow 1970; Burns 1912; Burns and
Kohlbrenner 1937; Dolan 1985; Ellis 1969; Gabert 1973; Gleason 1987;
Hennesey 1981; Walch 1996).

These two strands of analysis—viewing American Catholics from
outside the community and from within—examine the emergence of
U.S. Catholic schooling upon North American soil. Both analyses also
explain the origins of U.S. Catholic schooling and how, by the close of
the Second Vatican Council in 1965, "American Catholicism appear[ed]
to be a school system with churches attached" (*Newsweek* 1971, 83).

Unfortunately, the subject of these analyses is Catholic schooling,
and the contributions of the women and men who sustained U.S.
Catholic schooling are treated only peripherally. It is this aspect of the
history of U.S. Catholic schooling—the contributions of the religious
who put first things first and trusted the rest to Divine Providence—
that is surveyed here.

In the eighteenth and nineteenth centuries, the era before the Third
Baltimore Council in 1884, aspirants to the religious life from two different worlds—the Old World of Europe with its monarchical traditions and the New World of the United States with its heady experiment
in democratic self-governance—responded to the Gospel mandate to
"leave mother and father, brother and sister behind" (Matt. 19:29) by
dedicating their lives to Catholic schooling. There were some obvious
obstacles these pioneering religious, like their secular counterparts,
had to contend with. For example, the predominant culture made it imperative to Americanize immigrant children. Then, as the nation's rural
and agrarian economy transformed into a more urban and industrial
economy, the curriculum question loomed large: What educational
program would best prepare youth to participate in the newly emerging urban-industrial economy?

There were other less obvious—but equally daunting—obstacles
the religious had to contend with. For example, financing the schools,
solidifying them in a hostile environment, developing textbooks and instructional materials to support the school's religious purpose, and improving the quality of teaching (Jacobs 1998a). Likewise, the customs
and way of life suitable for religious communities in the Old World had
to be adapted to exigencies in the New World.

Because these pioneering religious did not flinch in the face of these
obstacles, the sisters and brothers and priests provided youth of all so-

cial strata, and especially poor immigrant children, an educational program making it possible for them—within a relatively short time—to exercise their fundamental rights and responsibilities as American citizens. However, of far greater consequence to the American Catholic community is how, through the agency of its schools, the religious bequeathed a vision of life integrating Roman Catholic faith and practice with the American democratic experience (Jacobs 1990).

Evidently, the example of the pioneering religious was infectious, particularly to their students, many of whom entered the religious life and priesthood. The success the religious had in founding U.S. Catholic schooling, when coupled with the increasing number of vocations, inspired a majority of the nation's bishops to conclude in 1884 that Divine Providence was bidding American Catholics to provide "a Catholic education for every Catholic child."

As the twentieth century dawned, Baltimore III put the full weight of the Church's institutional authority behind this ambitious vision, but ominous clouds portended a stormy, if not bleak, future for U.S. Catholic schooling. Financial resources were strained and schools often operated on a shoestring. The quality of education in Catholic schools was also sometimes lacking. Finally, improving professional standards proved difficult (Walch 1996).

These obstacles did not stymie the next generation of religious. During the first six decades of the twentieth century, the era following Baltimore III and prior to the close of the Second Vatican Council in 1965, these Americanized religious built upon their pioneering predecessors' legacy by providing diocesan and national Catholic educational leadership, integrating educational progressivism with American Catholic ideals, advancing the cause of women's equality, and successfully upholding parental rights in educating their children (Jacobs 1998b). Indeed, the generous response of youth in the previous generation in heeding God's call to sacrifice their lives—among whom was Mother Francesca—enabled Catholic schooling to become in the mid-1960s the world's largest private system of schools (Hunt and Kunkel 1984). In all, the religious of this generation transformed a fledgling network of parish schools into a "formidable structure" (Ellis 1969).

The apex of success came just as the Church promulgated its agenda for the modern world. Suddenly, some ecclesial institutions and traditions—and, in the United States, the parochial schools—

were called into question. Taking a cue from the documents of Vatican II, some American Catholics questioned whether a school had any place in a parish. For the critics, parochial schools depleted limited fiscal resources while reaching only a minority of youth (Ryan 1964). Others countered that the school crisis was a surface symptom of a deeper malaise besetting parishes as parishioners endeavored to renew parish life in the spirit of Vatican II (Elford 1971). Contrarians argued that the schools should be supported at any price (McCready 1981). In the ensuing polemic, reminiscent of the schooling controversy of the late 1800s, Catholic schools came under siege as American Catholics debated whether "Catholic schooling" should remain synonymous with "parish." Within three decades of the close of Vatican II, the total number of Catholic schools declined 37.9 percent. So too, total enrollment plummeted 52.7 percent (NCEA 1986, 1996). In an era punctuated by the "statistics of crisis" (McLellan 1971), some wondered whether Catholic schools were being "killed" (Herr 1984), "committing suicide" (Greeley 1973), or entering their "golden twilight" (Greeley 1989a).

Concurrently, the religious confronted another obstacle. In the three decades between 1965 and 1995, tens of thousands of religious and priests resigned from their ministries while thousands of others left the schools to serve in newly emerging ministries. What the exodus of the religious meant to their colleagues—and how it affected their students' willingness to follow in their footsteps—is a topic receiving scant scholarly attention. But the statistics depict a nadir. By 1995, the number of religious teaching in the nation's Catholic schools decreased by 85 percent (NCEA 1986, 1996). Those remaining behind advanced in age. Fewer vocations replaced those who abandoned their vows, the aged/ infirmed, and the deceased. Did the dramatic change in religious life, from an institutional ethos where the community defined the apostolate to a more personalistic ethos where individual religious defined their ministries, portend that the religious were a "vanishing species" (Greeley, cited in Weaver 1985, 86)?

To their credit, the religious who remained in the schools in the era following the Second Vatican Council not only extended their predecessors' contributions but also, in many ways, perfected the American legacy bequeathed by their forebears. With increasing numbers of lay collaborators ministering beside them, the religious promoted academic achievement, provided educational opportunity for the poor and marginalized, and renewed the identity of the Catholic school for the post–Vatican II era (Jacobs, in press). As a consequence of these efforts, what once had been unimaginable had become reality. Not only did the closing decades of the twentieth century witness the nation's political leaders calling for the public schools to imitate Catholic schools, the number of Catholic schools also increased modestly.

And so it is that over the course of two centuries, the religious did put first things first and trusted the rest to Divine Providence. By so doing, the religious contributed the sorely needed human and spiritual resources making it possible for American Catholic youth to venture forth from a self-protective, insular ghetto intended to protect a much-maligned minority community. The religious prepared their students well—through a program of Catholic moral and intellectual formation imbued in educational progressivism—to participate in and to influence the nation's social, economic, political, and moral mainstream. In the immediate three decades following the close of the Second Vatican Council in 1965, the religious completed their mission, bequeathing control of this American legacy to the laity who had labored alongside the religious since the earliest foundations of U.S. Catholic schooling (O'Donnell 1971). Now, as this legacy stands at this crossroads, it will be this new generation of post–Vatican II lay Catholics who will control the schools and chart their direction into the twenty-first century as a new era in U.S. Catholic schooling opens.

QUESTIONS THESE CONTRIBUTIONS RAISE FOR U.S. CATHOLIC SCHOOLING

Debate about the appropriateness of Catholic schooling did not terminate with the ecclesiastical legislation of Baltimore III. While it is true that the nation's Catholics never did muster the will to provide a Catholic education for every Catholic child, the Catholic community did provide a Catholic education for many of its children and some non-Catholic children as well.

Schneider attributes much of this success to *ex opere operato* (that is, "by outward acts" validly ordained ministers confect sacraments), a concept associated with medieval sacramental theology. As *ex opere operato* concerned religious life—and convent life in the nineteenth and

twentieth centuries, in particular—it also denoted the unflinching belief that religious profession would make all things possible (Schneider
1986, 7). Firm in the belief that God would favor the religious, there was
no valid reason for the religious not to confront directly any obstacle to
God's will.

As the twenty-first century looms just beyond the horizon, some in
the American Catholic community wish to extend this American legacy
by providing youth a Catholic education where feasible. But in this new
era—one swiftly bypassing the Industrial Age and entering into the
Information Age—the goal of providing youth a Catholic education
will be achieved not through the concerted efforts of the religious but
through the laity. As the contributions of the religious to U.S. Catholic
schooling demonstrate, sacrifice is the first step. Once this sacrifice is
made—"putting first things first"—the laity must not cower in the face
of the inevitable obstacles that will beset them from all sides. Why?
Again, the witness of the religious proves instructive: "trust the rest to
Divine Providence."

In light of the precipitous decline in the number of religious teaching and administering in the nation's Catholic schools and the concur-
rent increase in the number of the laity, we pose three questions: What
lessons do the contributions of the religious teach those who will follow
in their steps? Who will replace these witnesses? What training will the
next generation of educators in Catholic schools require to assure the
American Catholic community that youth in the twenty-first century
will receive the moral and intellectual formation to exercise their rights
and responsibilities?

• *What lessons do the contributions of the religious teach those who will
follow in their footsteps?*

The most significant lesson the contributions of the religious will
teach the laity who will follow in their footsteps is scriptural. This lesson is instructive about the requirements for membership in the Christian community as well as the cost of discipleship.

The contributions of the religious remind their progeny that membership in the Christian community requires disciples to leave all for
the sake of the Kingdom, including brothers or sisters, father, mother,
or children, land or houses (Matt. 19:29), by selling their possessions
and giving the proceeds to the poor (Matt. 19:21), and, even, by leaving

their very selves behind (Matt. 16:24). The pioneering religious literally did leave everything behind to minister to Catholic youth in the nascent republic. In a nation where the allure of secular ideologies and blatant materialism evidences a strong culture of death (John Paul II 1995), will the laity be as willing as the religious to put first things first by sacrificing themselves and their lives—to leave all behind for the sake of the Gospel—to provide youth the moral and intellectual formation that will liberate them from the culture of death?

In light of this scriptural lesson, the religious challenge the laity— first and foremost—to recognize that work in the nation's Catholic schools has at its core a divine purpose. That is, educating youth involves forming them intellectually and morally to exercise their rights and responsibilities as Catholic citizens, not only of this nation and the global community but of God's kingdom as well. As the legions of religious testified by their willingness to accept God's call and sacrifice their lives for the Gospel, the cost of discipleship is steep. And yet, only as lay women and men respond to God's call by allowing his will to transcend their decision-making will these disciples be able to foster the divine purpose that transforms the work of educating youth into a redemptive ministry (Jacobs 1996a).

This scriptural lesson also challenges the laity to recognize that life in the Christian community has a clear direction. It is not a matter of blind faith and mindless assent to dogma. Rather, the direction of Christian life is founded upon hope of what will be and patience with what is. St. Paul first articulated this direction in his letter to the Romans: "For by hope, we are saved: but hope that is seen is not hope: for what one sees, why does one yet hope? But if we hope for that we see not, then do we with patience wait for it" (Rom. 8:24–25).

Amidst the many obstacles that have beset U.S. Catholic schooling since its inception in the New World, very few deterred the religious from trusting in Divine Providence. Within the Catholic community, some thought it wrong-headed for Catholic children to attend school in isolation from their non-Catholic peers. Others, mainly voices from outside the Catholic community, asserted that Catholic schools threaten the unity-of-purpose believed necessary to advance the nation towards its destiny. But, for two centuries, the religious did not allow these obstacles to ferment the vice of despair. Instead, by putting first things first, the religious placed their trust in Divine Providence and hoped in the unseen. Inspired by an imperceptible vision of what could be possible in America for the Church they loved, the religious went forward despite the rising tide of negativity from within and outside the Catholic community and, in turn, won the respect and admiration of their fellow citizens. The religious also inspired many of their students to follow in their footsteps. And, the witness of this new generation of Americanized religious, in turn, sustained Catholic schooling by insuring a dependable supply of teachers and administrators.

Take, for example, Mary Claire Concannon, who, in 1931, rejected a scholarship at Seton Hill College to join the Sisters of St. Joseph of Baden, Pennsylvania. With the doors of Catholic higher education just opening to women, only a powerful inspiration would lead promising young women to forsake the allure of a college scholarship and to enter convents. According to Byrne (1990), the continued love of family, the personal warmth, and the professional excellence of the Sisters of St. Joseph of Baden exerted a powerful magnetism that drew many young women, like Mary Claire, to leave worldly considerations behind and follow in the sisters' footsteps. Reflecting upon her call to the religious life after six decades, she wrote: "I was attracted to those who were for others, and by that call to excellence—that what they did they did so well" (quoted in Byrne 1990, 123).

When authentic Christian witness—grounded in the virtue of hope in what can be and patience with what is—is presented to youth in this generation, why should any disciple believe their response will be less generous? But, if there is to be a response, there first must be witness. For two centuries, the religious provided the witness that now challenges the laity following in their footsteps to consider two notions. First: the educational ministry is not so much about pedagogical competence as it is about a relationship. While a delimited technical core of subjects, when bound up with a communal organization, decentralized governance, and an inspirational ideology, enable students in Catholic schools to achieve academically—especially impoverished inner-city youth (Bryk, Lee, and Holland 1993; Greeley 1982, 1989b; Viteritti 1996), the absolutely crucial factor is the educator's ability to engage each student's soul in an intimate conversation that molds the will and intellect so as to fashion a being of human and Christian perfection (Pius XII 1955a). Where this relationship is present, God labors through his disciples to provide the moral and intellectual formation that youth need. Without this relationship, all that educators can provide youth, at best, is competent instruction (Jacobs 1997).

Second: the witness of the religious challenges the laity to consider the notion that educators in Catholic schools should not be overly pre-occupied with financial considerations. These ministers should focus instead on developing human resources that translate the Catholic school's moral and intellectual purposes into practical learning experiences (Congregation for Catholic Education 1982). Generations of religious challenge their progeny in this generation to put worldly concerns aside, to sacrifice their lives in loving service of God and neighbor, and to be about the ministry of evangelizing youth. The most valuable resource—a generous spirit animated by love of God and neighbor—is of far greater significance than are professional credentials and degrees as well as an abundance of financial resources. The witness of the religious reminds the laity that, even with very modest financial resources, much good can be accomplished.

- *Who will replace these witnesses?*

In one of the first studies of lay teachers in Catholic schools, Quigley (1938) maintained that the Church would need to actively recruit lay teachers to sustain and expand Catholic schooling during the second half of the twentieth century. While Quigley focused on the expansion of Catholic schools—principally Catholic high schools—and its implication for staffing schools, he recognized that religious communities could not supply the number of teachers and administrators needed.

Six decades following publication of Quigley's study, it is abundantly clear that the Church cannot rely on the religious to sustain the schools it currently has as well as those now being designed and constructed. Whether God is or is not calling young women and men to embrace the religious life and priesthood, the burden of staffing and leading the nation's Catholic schools will descend upon the shoulders of the laity well into the twenty-first century.

To staff Catholic schools, McCready suggests that the Church turn to Catholic higher education as a resource for new vocations:

In the post-immigrant era, we need to develop a "teacher corps" which would allow men and women to devote all their energies to the schools for a limited duration of time. If five percent of the

Catholic college graduates in one year volunteered for this type of program we would realize more than 20,000 new teachers for parochial schools. The limited term of the commitment might enable more people to experience working in the schools, and this in turn might produce a smaller group of long-term teachers. (1989, 229)

It is not difficult to envision how to establish this teacher corps. Most Catholic colleges and universities boast campus ministry centers offering students opportunities for service learning. However, few—if any—campus ministry centers promote or offer extended-service learning experiences in Catholic schools. The basic challenge is to get Catholic college and university students into the Catholic elementary and secondary schools—preferably those in inner cities and in poor and rural dioceses—so that these undergraduates can observe and experience the ministry of Catholic educators. For these young Catholics, the opportunity to see and to work alongside Catholic educators is a salutary benefit. At the same time, some of these undergraduates may be inspired to sacrifice themselves to this ministry upon graduation, even if only for a short period of time.

In conjunction with this specialized-service learning and following the lead of the Alliance for Catholic Education (ACE), the nation's Catholic colleges and universities could learn from ACE's success and develop similar opportunities for their graduates. Their idealism and energy would not only inspire their colleagues and students. An additional benefit would accrue when, after earning professional certification, some of these young women and men would elect to commit themselves to the ministry of Catholic education.

One neglected source of potential vocations for the nation's Catholic schools are the children of the laity who already minister in Catholic schools. While the generalization is not true in every case, educators do tend to be children of educators, in much the same way that Protestant ministers tend to be children of ministers. In light of this, the nation's Catholic leaders might think creatively about how they can stimulate the children of the laity serving in the nation's Catholic schools to follow in their parents' footsteps.

Might it not be in the best interests of the nation's dioceses to establish scholarship foundations for Catholic educators and to enter into collaborative arrangements with the nation's Catholic colleges and universities to offer one tuition scholarship to a child of anyone teaching or administering in Catholic schools for each ten years of service? This would not only be a powerful manifestation that diocesan authorities and the Catholic community care about, value, and are committed to the laity serving in Catholic schools. In addition, a scholarship program would provide a financial incentive for lay educators to remain in Catholic schools (Jacobs 1991). Furthermore, a scholarship foundation would offer deserving Catholic youth, whose parents have given up much, the opportunity to further their Catholic education in a Catholic college or university. It is a truly sad irony that many educators in Catholic schools cannot afford the "luxury" of a Catholic education for their own children because of the financial constraints they must accept to minister on behalf of other parents whose children are enrolled in Catholic schools.

The concept of encouraging the laity to offer their lives in the service of Catholic schooling is not new. In fact, it was an objective the nation's first bishop identified in his pastoral letter of 1792. The nation's Catholic leaders must take Bishop Carroll's lead and promote this vocation as a necessary witness, one that the Catholic community absolutely needs if it is to build upon and perfect the contributions of the religious in previous generations.

But, it must be asked: How often do American Catholic leaders proclaim what the vocation of the Catholic educator is truly about—a sacrifice of one's life, a renunciation of secular ideologies and blatant materialism—a form of religious idealism that views the transformation of this world as a sublime use of one's God-given talents? How often, for example, do teachers and principals in Catholic schools, pastors in their parishes, and bishops when they preach the homily at Confirmation, challenge young Catholics to consider dedicating their lives to the ministry of Catholic education? Were youth to be inspired by the proclamation of these noble ideals, there is more than a faint glimmer of hope that they will respond generously. And, when young women and men do express an inchoate interest in devoting their lives to Catholic schooling, where might they find information describing this ministry as well as personal guidance about pursuing their interest further?

This obstacle raises a question about whether the nation's Catholic leaders, in particular the bishops and the administrators of the nation's Catholic colleges and universities, possess the courage to muster their will to provide the support needed by those who are willing to sacrifice their lives to minister in Catholic elementary and secondary schools. It is by no means overstating the case to say that any failure in this regard will lead ultimately to the dissolution of Catholic schooling as *Catholic* in the twenty-first century.

- *What training will the next generation of Catholic teachers require to assure parents, parishes, and the Church that youth of the twenty-first century will receive the moral and intellectual formation they will need to lead the U.S. Catholic Church?*

The training required to teach and administer in Catholic schools is two-dimensional: *professional* training, which attends to state certification requirements, and *vocational* training, which attends to the Church's purpose for sponsoring schools (Congregation for Catholic Education 1988). While the former is readily available at most colleges and universities, the latter is not. With the laity now comprising more than 90 percent of educators in Catholic schools (NCEA 1996), it is all the more imperative that they receive an integrated program of professional and vocational training that will enable them to extend and perfect this American legacy.

The professionalization of those who teach and administer in the nation's Catholic schools, an elusive goal just one century ago, is nearly complete. Most new educators in the nation's Catholic schools meet (or are in the process of meeting) state certification requirements. Further, as research data attest, educators in Catholic schools are at least as effective as their public and private-school peers in communicating the school's program of intellectual formation (Bryk et al. 1993; Coleman, Hoffer, and Kilgore 1982; Coleman and Hoffer 1987; Greeley and Rossi 1966; Rossi and Rossi 1961). And most dioceses as well as many Catholic schools provide in-service professional development programs. Where continuing professional formation is attended to, this achievement will not only be preserved, the American legacy that now stands at a crossroads will also be perfected—at least insofar as its program of intellectual formation is concerned—well into the twenty-first century.

Yet, the professionalization of Catholic schooling—important as that is—is but one dimension of the Catholic educator's vocation. What the religious received as a regular part of their formation, what they lived and breathed in their communities, and expressed in the apostolate—what might be termed "vocational training"—is something lay educators do not ordinarily receive and, until fairly recently, has not been a regular part of continuing in-service education (Jacobs 1996b). This failure does not bode well for U.S. Catholic schooling or its students, if only for the reason that unformed or ill-formed educators in Catholic schools may unwittingly propound a program of moral formation that has little, if any, referent to the school's fundamental purpose, that is, its Catholic identity (Heft 1991; McCready 1989).

For much of the history of U.S. Catholic schooling, religious communities provided vocational training for their members (Murphy 1976). Ideally, this training enabled the religious to understand Catholic educational thought and the community's traditions as well as what this implied for the role of the Catholic educator. Meanwhile, professional training—undertaken through the auspices of the diocesan schools offices or at local religious or secular colleges or universities—equipped the religious with the professional knowledge and skills they needed not only to be effective educators but also to perfect the schools.

During the first six decades of the twentieth century, Catholic colleges and universities lent their assistance by establishing training programs which integrated formative and professional training. The outcome was unmistakable, if the anecdotal stories about Catholic schooling in the 1940s, 50s, and 60s are anywhere near the mark. Where the religious received an integrated program of vocational and professional training, a Catholic ethos permeated curriculum, instruction, and administration in Catholic schools and, as a consequence, students received a distinctly Catholic education. Perhaps these decades embody the zenith of U.S. Catholic schooling—its "golden era"—where professional training augmented vocational training. Sadly, however, most of these programs were terminated in the 1970s and 80s with the consequences now being recognized nationwide.

One especially pronounced consequence is that the laity who serve in the nation's Catholic schools—some of whom are not Catholic—and who desire or need the requisite vocational training to function effectively in Catholic schools, have fewer opportunities to receive the training previously available. In light of this, it is entirely possible that the laity who serve and will serve in the nation's Catholic schools are professional and will be professional. Further, they will capably achieve their professional purposes, as standardized test scores will corroborate. All the while, however, many of these educators may also be inexperienced or uninformed about—if not antagonistic to—the substantive religious, theological, and spiritual mission of Catholic schooling (Harkins 1993; Kushner and Helbling 1995).

A second consequence—less pronounced but more extensive because of its impact upon Catholic educational thought—is that serious scholarly study of U.S. Catholic schooling has also diminished. Perhaps 1976, the year *The Notre Dame Journal of Education* ceased publication, marks the watershed. Since 1976, there has been a twenty-year dearth of scholarly investigation and research into the substantive issues relating to U.S. Catholic schooling. In those all too few instances where scholars have initiated serious research projects, these have emanated from secular research institutions. Moreover, much of what is published promotes secular themes adapted for consumption by Catholic educators. The sad truth is that, at least in the United States, there has been little original research into, and thought about, education from a distinctively Catholic perspective since the close of the Second Vatican Council. In an era when Catholic educational philosophy offers a prophetic critique of the deleterious consequences of educational programs devoid of a moral formation, research is inadequate and literature promoting Catholic educational philosophy is scarce.

For the diocesan superintendents, these two consequences only compound the difficulties associated with providing adequate training for Catholic educators. With the dearth of vocations to the religious life and the priesthood, now more than ever there exists an increased need for vocational training—perhaps even basic catechesis—for the laity who are replacing the religious in the nation's Catholic schools. Where are superintendents to turn for assistance in providing vocational training, if not to their colleagues in Catholic higher education?

In light of the need to staff the nation's Catholic schools with adequately trained teachers and administrators, it is time for Catholic higher education to direct its attention once again toward Catholic elementary and secondary schooling and to focus, first, upon identifying those who may be willing to serve in Catholic schools, and second, upon providing the training that will extend and perfect the legacy of U.S. Catholic schooling. Administrators of the nation's Catholic colleges and universities should realize that the consequence of any failure in this regard will be deleterious, not only for youth and the American Catholic community, but for Catholic higher education as well.

Providing vocational training for teachers in the nation's Catholic schools is a formidable endeavor, as recent experience has shown.[2] Vocational training requires both pre-service and in-service continuing education experiences, steeped in adult learning theory (Boone 1992; Knowles 1988). The goal in providing this training is to enable those who serve in Catholic schools to grow in their knowledge of and appreciation for the Catholic faith as well as to know exactly what the Church expects of them as ministers (Ciriello 1996) so that the school's Catholic purpose and identity—its "grammar of Catholic schooling" (Jacobs 1997)—will be made explicit.

Without vocational training, it makes little sense for bishops, superintendents, and pastors to expect educators in Catholic schools to be effective in counteracting the prevailing secularist, materialist, and anti-religious Zeitgeist and to hold the educators accountable for not enabling their students to overcome its pervasive influence. In the face of this challenge, bishops, superintendents, and pastors must provide educators in Catholic schools with the vocational training they need to enable their students to be the light to the nations (Vatican Council II 1965) who effect the social reconstruction of all things in Christ (Pius XII 1955a).

Offering educators in Catholic schools an integrated program of professional and vocational training would concretely demonstrate Catholic higher education's solidarity with the Church and its educational apostolate. In addition, programs like these would translate rhetoric about the Catholic identity of Catholic higher education into concrete action, for example, a commitment to social and economic justice on behalf of those who minister in the nation's Catholic elementary and secondary schools. Furthermore, a commitment to provide training for those who serve in the nation's Catholic schools would be an exemplary way for Catholic higher education to fulfill its institutional mission, that is, to be of service not only to the Church but to society as well (John Paul II 1990). In addition, providing training for educators in Catholic schools would be a tangible expression of gratitude to those who provide the moral and intellectual formation for graduates of Catholic schools who attend Catholic colleges and universities. And lastly, a self-serving reason: by training the laity who will extend and perfect Catholic schooling in the twenty-first century, the nation's Catholic colleges and universities will continue to have a dependable pool of students who possess the moral and intellectual formation that will enable them to engage in and to benefit the most from a Catholic undergraduate experience.

A Closing Thought

With the close of the twentieth century drawing near, the world's largest network of private schools—some call it "an American legacy"—is positioned at a significant crossroads. The baton is passing from the hands of the religious—those who built and sustained this legacy for nearly two centuries—to the hands of the laity—those entrusted with its future.

For the American Catholic community of the twenty-first century, this transfer of control is not simply a matter of replacing teachers and administrators and providing them training adequate to the mission of evangelizing youth. More significantly, this transfer portends momentous consequences; as Joseph Salzmann opined as the battle for control of the schools reached a fever pitch in the late nineteenth century, "the future belongs to him that controls the schools" (quoted in Heming 1895, 172).

The direction the laity will chart for Catholic schools by translating the school's Catholic identity into concrete educational practice will shape how many of the next generation's American Catholic laity will not only perceive the Roman Catholic Church but also their membership in it. Failure in this regard has moral implications and not only for Catholic education. Without a well-formed laity, there will be fewer Catholic women and men capable of confronting, challenging, and transforming the culture of death now threatening to destroy the moral fiber of the nation.

Notes

1. Throughout this chapter, the phrases "religious sisters and brothers and priests," "religious women and men," "the religious," and "religious" are used inter-

changeably to refer to the religious (the "sisters and brothers") as well as the priests (the religious and secular "fathers") who devoted their lives to U.S. Catholic schooling.

2. Some of the nation's Catholic colleges and universities as well as the USCC Department of Education and the NCEA have attempted, over the years, to sponsor vocational formation programs for Catholic school principals and teachers. Unfortunately, most of these initiatives have derailed, for numerous reasons.

What offers great promise are diocesan efforts where the schools office and superintendent make a long-term commitment to provide resources for vocational formation. The effectiveness of these programs does take a few years, though, as principals gradually learn to talk with one another about their vocation and work as well as how they might foster formative faculty development in their schools.

References

Boone, E. J. 1992. *Developing Programs in Adult Education*. Prospect Heights, Ill.: Waveland Press.

Bryk, A. S., V. E. Lee, and P. B. Holland. 1993. *Catholic Schools and the Common Good*. Cambridge: Harvard University Press.

Buetow, H. A. 1970. *Of Singular Benefit: The Story of Catholic Education in the United States*. New York: Macmillan.

Burns, J. A. 1912. *The Growth and Development of the Catholic School System in the United States*. New York: Benziger Brothers.

Burns, J. A., and B. J. Kohlbrenner. 1937. *A History of Catholic Education in the United States*. New York: Benziger Brothers.

Byrne, P. 1990. "In the Parish but Not of It: Sisters." In J. P. Dolan, R. S. Appleby, P. Byrne, and D. Campbell, eds., *Transforming Parish Ministry: The Changing Roles of Catholic Clergy, Laity, and Women Religious*, pp. 109–200. New York: Crossroad.

Church, R. L. 1976. *Education in the United States: An Interpretive History*. New York: The Free Press.

Ciriello, M. J., ed. 1996. *Expectations for the Catholic School Principal: A Handbook for Pastors and Parish School Committees*. Washington, D.C.: United States Catholic Conference.

Coleman, J. S., T. Hoffer, and S. Kilgore. 1982. *High School Achievement: Public, Catholic and Private Schools Compared*. New York: Basic Books.

Coleman, J. S., and T. Hoffer. 1987. *Public and Private High Schools*. New York: Basic Books.

Congregation for Catholic Education. 1982. "Lay Catholics in Schools: Witnesses to the Faith." In A. Flannery, ed., *Vatican Council II: The Conciliar and Post-Conciliar Documents*, vol. 2, rev. ed., pp. 630–61. Northport, N.Y.: Costello.

———. 1988. *The Religious Dimension of Education in a Catholic School*. Washington, D.C.: United States Catholic Conference.

Cremin, L. 1961. *The Transformation of the School*. New York: Vintage Books.

———. 1980. *American Education: The National Experience, 1783–1876*. New York: Harper and Row.

Dolan, J. P. 1985. *The American Catholic Experience*. New York: Image Books.

Elford, G. 1971. "School Crisis—or Parish Crisis? Perhaps the parish school crisis is only a surface symptom of a deeper malaise that besets the parish itself." *Commonweal* 93 (17, January 29), 418–20.

Ellis, J. T. 1969. *American Catholicism*, 2d ed., rev. Chicago: The University of Chicago Press.

Gabert, G. 1973. *In hoc signo? A Brief History of Catholic Parochial Education*. Port Washington: Kennikat Press.

Gleason, P. 1987. "The School Question: A Centennial Retrospect." In *Keeping the Faith: American Catholicism Past and Present*, pp. 115–35. Notre Dame: University of Notre Dame Press.

Greeley, A. M. 1973. "The Catholic Schools Are Committing Suicide." *New York Times Magazine* 123 (42,273, October 21), 40–65.

———. 1982. *Catholic High Schools and Minority Students*. New Brunswick: Transaction Books.

———. 1989a. "Catholic Schools: A Golden Twilight?" *America* 160 (5, February 11), 106, 108, 116–18.

———. 1989b. "My Research on Catholic Schools." *Chicago Studies* 28 (3, November), 245–63.

Greeley, A. M., and P. H. Rossi. 1966. *The Education of Catholic Americans*. Chicago: Aldine Publishing Company.

Harkins, W. 1993. *Introducing the Catholic Elementary School Principal: What Principals Say about Themselves, Their Values, Their Schools*. Washington, D.C.: National Catholic Educational Association.

Heft, J. 1991. "Catholic Identity and the Future of Catholic Schools." In P. Seadler, ed., *The Catholic Identity of Catholic Schools*. Washington, D.C.: National Catholic Educational Association.

Heming, H. H., ed. 1895. *The Catholic Church in Wisconsin from the Earliest Time to the Present Day*, vol. 1. Milwaukee: Catholic Historical Publishing Company.

Hennesey, J. 1981. *American Catholics: A History of the Roman Catholic Community in the United States*. New York: Oxford University Press.

Herr, D. 1984. "Stop Killing Catholic Schools." *U.S. Catholic* 49 (October), 13–18.

Hunt, T. C., and N. M. Kunkel. 1984. "Catholic Schools: The Nation's Largest Alternative School System." In J. Carper and T. C. Hunt, eds., *Religious Schooling in America*, pp. 1–34. Birmingham: N.p.

Jacobs, R. M. 1990. "Agenda semper recogitanda: The Americanist Catechetical Agenda and the National Catholic Educational Association, 1904–1984." Dissertation, The University of Tulsa.

———. 1991. "A Modest Proposal: A Catholic Educator Recruitment and Retention Policy." *Momentum* 22 (3), 58–61.

———. 1996a. *The Vocation of the Catholic Educator.* Washington, D.C.: National Catholic Educational Association.

———. 1996b. "Focusing on Catholic Identity: One Principal's Successful Efforts." *Momentum* 27 (2), 61–64.

———. 1997. *The Grammar of Catholic Schooling: A Practical Philosophy of Catholic Education.* Washington, D.C.: National Catholic Educational Association.

———. 1998a. "The Future Belongs to Those Who Control the Schools: Part I—Contributions in the 18th and 19th Centuries." *Catholic Education: A Journal of Inquiry and Practice* 1 (4, June), 364–89.

———. 1998b. "The Future Belongs to Those Who Control the Schools: Part II—Contributions in the First Six Decades of the 20th Century." *Catholic Education: A Journal of Inquiry and Practice* 2 (1, September), 4–23.

———. In press. "The Future Belongs to Those Who Control the Schools: Part III—Contributions Following Vatican II." *Catholic Education: A Journal of Inquiry and Practice.*

John Paul II. 1990. *On Catholic Universities (Ex corde ecclesiae).* Washington, D.C.: United States Catholic Conference.

———. 1995. *The Gospel of Life* (*Evangelium vitae*). Boston: Pauline Books and Media.

Kaestle, C. 1973. *The Evolution of an Urban School System: New York City, 1750–1850.* Cambridge: Harvard University Press.

Knowles, M. S. 1988. *The Modern Practice of Adult Education: From Pedagogy to Andragogy.* Englewood Cliffs: Cambridge Book Company.

Kushner, R., and M. Helbling. 1995. *The People Who Work There: A Report of the Catholic Elementary School Teacher Survey.* Washington, D.C.: National Catholic Educational Association.

McCready, W. C. 1981. "Let's Support Catholic Schools at Any Price." *U.S. Catholic* 46 (November), 12–17.

———. 1989. "Catholic Schools and Catholic Identity: 'Stretching the Vital Connection'." *Chicago Studies* 28 (3, November), 217–31.

McLellan, J. 1971. "The Statistics of Crisis: Discussion of the Parochial Schools' Trouble Is Taking on a New Precision." *Commonweal* 93 (17), 421–23.

Murphy, J. F. 1976. "Professional Preparation of Catholic Teachers in the Nineteen Hundreds." *Notre Dame Journal of Education* 7, 123–33.

National Catholic Educational Association. 1986. *1986 Data Bank Historical Data.* Washington, D.C.: National Catholic Educational Association.

————. 1996. *United States Catholic Elementary and Secondary Schools, 1995–96: The Annual Statistical Report on Schools, Enrollment and Staffing.* Washington, D.C.: National Catholic Educational Association.

Newsweek. 1971. "The Catholic School Crisis." *Newsweek* 78 (14, October 4), 83–84.

O'Donnell, H. J. 1971. "The Lay Teacher in Catholic Education." *Notre Dame Journal of Education* 2, 84–96.

Pius XII. 1955a. "The Catholic Teacher." In the Benedictine Monks of Solesemes, *Education: Papal Teachings,* A. Robeschini, trans., pp. 512–21. Boston: St. Paul Editions.

————. 1955b. "Redemption and Education." In the Benedictine Monks of Solesemes, *Education: Papal Teachings,* A. Robeschini, trans., pp. 500–503. Boston: St. Paul Editions.

Quigley, T. J. 1938. "The Lay Teacher in the Catholic School System." Thesis, Catholic University of America.

Rossi, P. H., and A. S. Rossi. 1961. "Some Effects of Parochial Education in America." *Daedelus* 90 (Spring), 300–28.

Ryan, Mary Perkins. 1964. *Are Parochial Schools the Answer?* New York: Holt, Rinehart, and Winston.

Schneider, M. 1986. "The Transformation of American Women Religious: The Sister Formation Conference as a Catalyst for Change." *Cushwa Center for the Study of American Catholicism Working Paper Series 19* (1, Spring), 7. Notre Dame, Ind.: University of Notre Dame.

Tyack, D. 1966. "The Kingdom of God and the Common School: Protestant Ministers and the Awakening in the West." *Harvard Educational Review,* 33, 447–69.

————. 1974. *The One Best System: A History of Urban Education.* Cambridge: Harvard University Press.

Vatican Council II. 1965. "Pastoral Constitution on the Church in the Modern World." In A. Flannery, ed., *Vatican Council II: The Conciliar and Post-Conciliar Documents,* vol. 1, rev. ed., pp. 903–1014. Northport: Costello.

Viteritti, J. P. 1996. "Stacking the Deck for the Poor." *The Brookings Review,* 14 (3, Summer), 10–13.

Walch, T. 1996. *Parish School: American Catholic Parochial Education from Colonial Times to the Present.* New York: Crossroad-Herder.

Weaver, M. J. 1985. *New Catholic Women: A Contemporary Challenge to Traditional Religious Authority.* San Francisco: Harper and Row.

5 Promises and Possibilities

THE CATHOLIC ELEMENTARY
SCHOOL CURRICULUM

Merylann J. Schuttloffel

This study describes those characteristics that distinguish Catholic elementary school diocesan curricula. Two dimensions emerge as unique qualities of these curricula. First, sample Catholic elementary school curricula demonstrate a continuum of diocesan centralization. The continuum illustrates two extremes: on one end, formalization and centralization; on the other, those curricula that are loosely coupled to the diocesan structure. Second, these curricula illustrate their Catholicity in the content areas more or less explicitly. Three common philosophical tenets also emerge that explicitly support a curriculum's Catholicity: (1) the importance of acquiring Catholic faith knowledge, (2) the opportunity to practice Catholic faith experiences within the school community, and (3) a holistic approach to the student that recognizes multiple needs. Ultimately the role of teacher emerges as significant in determining the implementation of a Catholic elementary school curriculum that supports academic achievement and faith formation. The study recommends further research in related areas.

Funding for this study was provided by the Lilly Foundation within the project, *The Future of Catholic Education*, Life Cycle Institute, The Catholic University of America, Washington, D.C.

Catholic education is enjoying a renaissance that often brings its schools to the center of educational reform. The Lilly Foundation Project, *The Future of Catholic Education,*[1] integrates into a single discussion the many individual topics that intersect to form Catholic education. The segment of Catholic education under examination here is the current state of the Catholic elementary school curriculum. Reform movements that consider the attributes of Catholic schools transferable to public schools may seem laudable, but secular educators often miss the fundamental difficulty with this transference. What makes Catholic schools *Catholic* is precisely that which is *not* transferable. This study searches the elementary school curricula of various Catholic dioceses for answers to questions about those features that make the curricula Catholic.

The study of curricula for the purpose of identifying the *Catholic* in Catholic education presents a quagmire of difficulty. In an attempt to unravel this question, this chapter begins with a brief review of curriculum orientations. With this knowledge in hand it is possible to detect why curricula should be an artifact of Catholic education. In the final analysis, the study also describes why curricula do not give a complete answer to what makes Catholic education *Catholic,* but does uncover two characteristic dimensions of Catholic elementary school curricula: centralization and explicit Catholicity.

This study answers two questions specific to the Catholic elementary school curriculum: What does the Catholic elementary school curriculum look like? Why is the curriculum coherent (or incoherent) with the mission of Catholic education? Each of these questions leads to a response that broadens our understanding of the role of curriculum in Catholic education.

A REVIEW OF CURRICULAR ORIENTATIONS

Curricular orientations provide a distinct flavor and focus for an individual curriculum. An orientation suggests clues to the purpose for study in a particular subject area. The following five curricular orientations portray different philosophical underpinnings (Eisner 1985) and give a brief background for understanding a Catholic elementary school curriculum today. First, the *development of cognitive processes* orientation promotes the concept of process over content. Cognitive processes are perceived like muscles; if challenged and strengthened, these cognitive processes are capable of dealing with new or unfamiliar problems. A curriculum with this orientation emphasizes the importance of problem solving, the transfer of learning, and mental discipline. *Academic rationalism* is a second curricular orientation related to a classical or essentialist view of schooling. The curriculum of academic rationalism directs all students to study the fundamental knowledge groups from an early age. An educated person is someone who understands the great issues and questions of life. The third orientation is *personal relevance.* Personal relevance is based on the concept that learning takes place when the curriculum is meaningful to the learner. The student educated by personal relevance learns through a natural growth progression and becomes increasingly capable of functioning as an adult in our society. *Social responsiveness* has two veins in its orientation. Social adaptation is a single strain with its fundamental focus the observation of the needs of society followed by building an educational response. Social reconstructionism, the second type, creates a curriculum that examines society's needs for the purpose of reconfiguring society to eliminate the needs. Though different in purpose, these two veins fall under the same orientation because they both scrutinize the needs of society to form the basis for curriculum. Finally, *curriculum as technology* is an orientation reflecting the influence of behaviorism in education. Behavioral objectives state the required learning results. When the student reaches the objective, learning has taken place.The assumption within this orientation is that the curriculum as a technology proposes to be value-neutral or scientifically objective. The other four orientations declare clearly what each values. This belief in value neutrality shows the high value placed upon the scientific quality of behavior objectives and their measurable outcomes.

This brief approach to these five curriculum orientations draws clearly the connection between philosophy and curriculum. Each orientation has a distinct purpose for students interacting with the curriculum. Each orientation affects how the teacher implements the curriculum. And each orientation implies a vehicle for evaluating the success of the curriculum. If the curriculum transmits the values espoused by the school community, the development of the curriculum requires a clear understanding of those values the community desires to communicate to its learners.

A values dilemma plagues the nation's public schools system in a pluralistic society. Whose values should dominate the curriculum? The public school response has been an effort to appear value-neutral, shifting closer to the *curriculum as technology* orientation each year. In essence, responding in this manner creates a larger problem. There are values the community wants to transmit, and their denial leads to confusion for educators and students. Teaching is not a value-neutral activity, even when operating within a technically based curriculum. Recent research by Goodlad et al. (1995) verifies the moral nature of teaching. Herein lies the advantage held by Catholic elementary schools compared to their counterparts in the public schools. Catholic schools have the opportunity to explicitly promote specific values through the curricula.

Eisner's (1985) curricular orientations represent particular philosophical beliefs and purposes for education. This study investigated the Catholic elementary school curriculum in search of those qualities that make it a distinctly Catholic-orientated curriculum. A description of the study's sample and methodology focuses on how these qualities were identified.

Sample and Methodology

A primary objective in this study was to yield credible findings. The collection of appropriate data was key to meeting this objective. To provide the data for the study, thirty-four dioceses in the United States were contacted by letter. These dioceses represented a large proportion of Catholic school enrollment. The dioceses also represented a geographical cross section of the United States. Each diocesan Catholic school office was asked to provide a complete copy of their elementary school curriculum. The dioceses were informed that these curricula were data for a research study. The dioceses listed in figure 1 (see Appendix to this chapter) provided complete copies, summary copies, descriptive letters, and telephone conversations about their curricula. Standard qualitative data collection methods were used. These were the qualitative data for the study.[1] This methodology follows the tradition of Wolcott (1995) and Eisner (1991). Qualitative research methodology is often used when quantification is less instructive than qualitative descriptions.

ANALYSIS OF THE DATA

The ability to clearly define curricula eludes researchers and practitioners alike. Many practitioners grow disenchanted with the ambiguity of curriculum work. Typically this represents a lack of understanding for the work's importance and purpose. The frustration associated with curriculum work stems from its unfinished quality, as practitioners continually search for the curricular description best suited to portray their priorities. In response, numerous curricular categories or descriptions have emerged from research (Eisner 1985; Glatthorn 1995, 1994).

This study focused on the written curriculum (Glatthorn 1995) through an examination of diocesan curricular documents. There will be a later argument for the need to study other dimensions of the Catholic elementary school curriculum, but the written curriculum, because it represents an official diocesan school document, was the starting point. The term "written" will convey the same meaning in this study as an explicit curriculum (Eisner 1985). The written curriculum is that which is acknowledged by the school as leading to specific learning objectives.

First, a form was created that indicated the various content areas in a typical elementary school curriculum. Then a diocesan curriculum was throughly examined for the usual elementary school content areas. Next, the philosophy of education for a subject area was read and any references that clearly indicated Catholicity (see sample data later) was noted. After analyzing each curriculum for themes and characteristics, each was reviewed again. The second examination was motivated by a desire to include items that may have surfaced in later documents that were overlooked during the initial reading. If there were any questions, or there was some confusion in the coding, a representative of the diocesan staff was called for clarification. In most cases, the curricula spoke for themselves.

WHAT DOES THE CATHOLIC ELEMENTARY SCHOOL CURRICULUM LOOK LIKE?

It is important to begin any discussion of this study's findings with a disclaimer: The Catholic elementary school curriculum *does not exist.*

Catholic schools function within a tradition of local schooling. The local Catholic elementary school, typically associated with the local Catholic parish, reflects the culture and mission of that parish community. Catholic school parents have the opportunity to strongly influence the nature of the curriculum within their school. Although each school community intends for their children to benefit from recent trends in education, individual schools may hold values particular to that context.

The study's findings point to two important dimensions of the Catholic elementary school curriculum. These dimensions are polar points on two continua that provide a framework for understanding the curricula. The first continuum describes the centralized or decentralized quality of diocesan curricula.

Centralization presents itself uniquely in dioceses that do not impose any kind of diocesan curriculum, instead recommending curriculum-writing guidelines that shape the intent of local curriculum development. A diocese may choose to provide only direction to the local school through a broad curriculum framework. In these cases then, the written curriculum emerges from the local school through a process described and encouraged within diocesan guidelines. This local school independence of curricula contradicts most public school trends toward increased curricula centralization. There is direct renunciation of a bureaucratically designed and implemented curriculum. Little evidence exists of diocesan school offices emulating their public school counterparts by creating diocesan staff roles designed to write curricula. Most curricula arises from the hard work of teachers during off hours from the school schedule.

There are also diocesan curricula, particularly those written within the last five years, which have a distinctly technical quality (Glatthorn 1995). These curricula address specific areas of current curriculum practice and state performance-testing criteria. The extent of the detailed direction within the curricula reflects the diocese's fundamental philosophy toward centralization. Centralized curricular decisions have several advantages. A more centralized curriculum offers continuity for an increasingly transient student body moving between the various school sites. There is also the potential insurance of broad minimum-content standards coverage. These centralized curricula model curricula of public school counterparts.

From diocesan philosophy, then, evolves two different approaches to the Catholic elementary school curriculum. One approach bases its curricular framework on a loosely delivered set of diocesan guidelines or curricula (archdiocese of Chicago). This approach has a local flavor and responds to local student needs. It functions with heavy direction from in-house teachers and local parents' expectations. It is generative in the sense that local teachers generate their own curriculum that represents their school's clientele and requirements. The intent of this approach is to draw the written and taught curriculum close together with the methodology, the "how" of teaching addressed by their harmony.

The second approach is a clearly defined curriculum. This approach attempts to guarantee accountability in all schools for high-performance curricular standards (archdiocese of Philadelphia). Beyond that, the curriculum gives specific direction to its implementation. While local school input is important within the process, clear direction comes from the numerous specifically directed behavioral outcomes or instructional objectives. The second approach intends to leave little room for discrepancy or misunderstanding between the written and taught curriculum. Within the second approach teaching becomes a technical activity designed to produce results. The "how" of teaching is clearly articulated through results outcomes.

There is no distinct distribution of dioceses between these two approaches in Catholic school curricula; the reality is also a graduated continuum. Various dioceses fall somewhere between the two end points, often displaying characteristics of both approaches. Even a diocese with a detailed curriculum may emphasize the need for local schools to implement their curricular standards within the most appropriate local means (diocese of Tulsa). Many dioceses state that the curricula are currently under revision or are incomplete due to changing diocesan or accreditation requirements. The written curriculum is a moment frozen in time that rarely lasts very long.

There are advantages to each curriculum approach. The question then becomes one of delineating how much curricular freedom, or how much curricular conformity, is beneficial for student learning.

Informally, diocesan-level practitioners solve the centralization dilemma by trusting the good will of their local principals and faculty to mediate the most useful interpretation of the curriculum. "Teachers within the Archdiocese endeavor 'To teach as Jesus did.' The power of a teacher can never be underestimated; what is done in a classroom affects what is accomplished by the students. . . . The power of a teacher is far-reaching; what is done in the classroom influences the student for life" (archdiocese of Baltimore). The acknowledged high performance of Catholic school students tends to reinforce the belief that the Catholic school curriculum has been successfully mediated within the school.

Within both approaches for the Catholic elementary school curriculum, there are identifying components. As the Tyler (1949) curriculum model suggests, the key component of the written Catholic elementary school curriculum is the educational philosophy which screens it. Educational philosophy often seems removed from the daily issues of teachers and principals. How does philosophy connect with the broken copier or the absent student? The answer is that responses to the routine issues of daily life in Catholic schools build directly on the philosophical foundation of the institution. Catholic educational philosophy motivates the actions of the participants in Catholic schools. The philosophy of the Catholic school states what it values, what its purpose is, and how it intends to accomplish the goals.

WHY IS THE CATHOLIC ELEMENTARY SCHOOL CURRICULUM COHERENT WITH THE MISSION OF CATHOLIC EDUCATION?

A coherent curriculum describes a curriculum held together by a large common purpose. For the Catholic elementary school the larger purpose is the mission of faith formation within its students (National Conference of Catholic Bishops 1973). Theoretically each piece of the curriculum contributes to reaching this goal. The obvious implication of coherence is that it should be possible to find evidence of Catholicity within the entire curriculum.

As the discussion of educational philosophy indicates, philosophy and curriculum connect in important ways. A school's philosophy determines the primary orientation of the curriculum. Samples of Catholic elementary school curricula demonstrate consistent philosophical themes. These philosophical statements typically appear before the curriculum of a specific content area. The more clearly curriculum writers articulate the Catholic school philosophy as it relates to the specific content area, the more clearly the curriculum's stated objectives are consistent with the Catholic school's mission. This is shown by a quote from the language arts curriculum of the diocese of Cleveland:

> The communication of the gospel message by word and witness is central in Catholic education. A Graded Course of Study in Language Arts makes a unique and important contribution to the attaining of these goals of Catholic education. This philosophy envisions our schools motivating students to grow academically, culturally and socially in an atmosphere "designed to celebrate and practice love of God and neighbor."

The curriculum document goes on to state more explicitly the goals of the study of language arts. Note the clear connections drawn between Catholic faith practice and the content area.

How many diocesan curricula verbalize their Catholic school mission? The integration of Catholicity into content area curricula is a visible maneuver to communicate the fundamental Catholic nature of the elementary school. And perhaps more importantly, the integration is an effort to state clearly that faith formation is not an activity isolated within religious education classes. Another diocesan curriculum (Kansas City, 1996) draws together neatly the content area and its relationship to Catholic faith practice.

This sample math curriculum statement in Figure 2 succeeds in integrating faith formation into the entire Catholic elementary school experience.

As the discussion of educational philosophy demonstrates, philosophical orientations do affect daily life in schools within the explicit written curriculum. When teachers answer the question, "Who do we teach and why?" the response indicates the "what" (instructional content, learning activities) and the "how" (interactions, methodology) of schooling. Catholic school curricula also spring from a philosophical foundation for education. By examining a school's curriculum it is possible to determine the dominant philosophical orientation. One purpose of this study is to see whether the sample curricula of Catholic dioceses communicate a Catholic educational philosophy and its values.

Several key ingredients shape the framework of a Catholic school philosophy. First, Catholic schools describe themselves as transmitters of faith knowledge. Religious education curricula state instructional objectives that require knowledge of the tenets of Catholic faith. This knowledge base rests on scripture, Church documents, and tradition, most recently articulated within the *Catechism of the Catholic Church* (Commission of Bishops 1994). An example of the key concepts of a religious education curriculum is contained in Figure 4.

An important feature of these religious concepts is their integration of the other subject content areas. It is this integration of the students' relationship with God into the entire educational experience that makes faith formation possible for students within the Catholic school.

First, evangelization of non-Catholic students also presents an opportunity to witness the Catholic faith and demonstrate knowledge of the faith. Students have many informal opportunities to explain their Catholic traditions and practices to non-Catholic peers. Knowing about the Catholic faith is an important feature for students in becoming adult Catholics with fully developed consciences capable of right judgment.

Second, the Catholic school creates an environment that promotes the nurturing of the faith and its practice. During school liturgical services students perform leadership roles that prepare them for adult ministry. The Catholic school community bridges the student's transition into adult participation in the parish community. Samples of community building activities for students may include becoming a pen-pal for a senior citizen for a primary student, reading the bulletin to look for an activity to join in the parish for an intermediate-level student, collecting clothing for a needy family in the middle-school grades. These activities promote an emphasis on the development of a faith learning community, including parents and parishioners, that assists faith formation. Within the context of the Catholic school students learn that the lived faith is not only a vertical relationship with God, but a horizontal relationship within their faith community.

Third, Catholic schools identify with a holistic approach to education. The following quote from the Visual Arts Philosophy of the diocese of Phoenix (1995) states this belief:

"We believe Art Education is the means to develop the whole person by promoting the spiritual, moral, physical, creative and intellectual development of each student." The needs of the student beyond academic achievement require service and support. The changing support structures for families require Catholic schools to aggressively fill the gaps (Garanzini 1995). Catholic schools offer extracurricular programs, before and after school child-care, and parent education programs. The Catholic school recognizes the student as a child with multiple needs and makes an effort to provide appropriate services. Students are valued in their individuality with an emphasis on their creation in the image and likeness of God. These holistic values reappear in each diocesan curriculum with little variation in language and a consistent meaning. In another example, "Catholic schools strive to educate the whole person by promoting the spiritual, moral, physical and intellectual development of each student in a value-centered environment" (diocese of Cincinnati, 1994).

And, in another philosophy of education statement,

> Affirmed, treasured, and supported by the loving witnesses of Christian faith communities, the child continues a lifelong response to God's love by growing and excelling through responsible involvement in the academic, cultural, and civic concerns of daily life. (diocese of Cleveland, 1993)

An opportunity to learn faith knowledge, a community where students live the faith, and a holistic approach that shapes the student are three common threads found in Catholic elementary school curricula. The common philosophical threads of the Catholic school represent an integration of the curriculum orientations present within the Catholic educational philosophy. For example, many Catholic elementary school curricula emphasize what is characterized as a "back to basics" education. There is an emphasis on the fundamental knowledge necessary to be considered an educated person within our society. This represents the academic rationalism orientation. At the same time, Catholic elementary school curricula place a profound importance on developing the whole child. This holistic orientation is consistent with those who believe in the personal relevance orientation. Even though Catholic schools have traditionally minimized student choice, students are aggressively prepared to make choices of right judgment. The most recent phenomenon present within Catholic elementary schools is the cognitive development orientation. The focus of students' work is on the process of learning rather than narrowly on the content. This movement is more advanced within specific Catholic schools dependent upon local and diocesan leadership. The advantage of incorporating the cognitive development orientation into Catholic elementary schools is that it serves as a balance to the technical, accountability-focused orientation.

The technical orientation, with its focus on management and skills, is so common within state curricula that Catholic schools who model curricula after a state curriculum framework (often done in preparation for performance testing) risk losing the value-laden strength of the Catholic school curriculum. The Catholic school's fundamental purpose contradicts a dedicated technology orientation. Teachers within a Catholic elementary school may work from a curriculum written with the curriculum as technology orientation, but even then, Catholic values infuse the curriculum. A technically orientated curriculum within the Catholic school does not remain value-neutral. A particular Catholic elementary school may be within a diocese that has organized the curriculum in a very technology-orientated manner. The teacher who implements that curriculum accepts the curriculum's operational standards, but at the same time reconciles it with the pervasive Catholic values of the school philosophy. These larger, pervasive Catholic values represent some other curricular orientations, most importantly the faith formation curriculum. The diocese of Cleveland, for example, attempts to create balance within the curriculum by including the positive features of various curricular orientations. Those dioceses with recent revisions to their curricula often are very explicit in the Catholic dimension in order to balance the technical orientation in subject content areas.

Media stories that expose the lack of moral behavior by adults and young people create an urgency to tie public school curricula to a fundamental value system. Educational researchers focus on the implicit values already communicated within the public educational system (Goodlad et al. 1990; Jackson et al. 1993). Catholic schools have the advantage of a clear tradition of gospel values. These external educational pressures challenge Catholic school leaders to promote a strong moral tone within the Catholic elementary school curriculum.

WHAT QUESTIONS REMAIN?

The formalizing of the Catholic elementary school curriculum is a process that is highly developed in some dioceses and under renewal in others. Those who undertake the monumental task of curriculum writing have the advantage of the work already completed by others (Kealey 1985). For example, the archdiocese of New Orleans credits the archdiocese of Cincinnati for its curriculum guides. Catholic elementary school curricula often reflect the various educational orientations present within public school curricula. The challenge for Catholic school curriculum writers is to represent the faith formation curriculum within the instructional goals and objectives across the curriculum content areas.

All schools search for a meaningful curriculum. From a clear mission statement develops a meaningful curriculum. The assumption that a useful curriculum helps students "make meaning" out of their learning experiences, requires a Catholic elementary school curriculum to make faith formation a meaningful experience for students. Following this logic, the Catholic elementary school curriculum should clearly reflect the Catholic elementary school's mission of faith formation. Enhancing the mission of faith formation within the written curriculum helps to bring Catholic values into all areas of school life. From this perspective the Catholic elementary school curriculum moves beyond the routine academic requirements to educate the whole student. The faith formation curriculum creates a special faith-lived meaning in every school activity.

Is this permeation of faith life found within the written content curriculum? Possibly not. It is this complicating factor that makes a study of the Catholic elementary school curriculum more than an examination of curricular documents for pertinent data. Often a Catholic school curriculum does not explicitly state faith formation goals beyond the area of religious education, even though the assumption would be that the Catholic school does integrate these goals. There exists a qualitative difference between the Catholic school's curricular documents, the explicit or written curriculum, and the messages students learn within the Catholic elementary school, the implicit curriculum ((Bransford, Vye 1989; Eisner 1985). The ability or inability to capture this enveloping translation of the Catholic elementary school's mission inhibits the thoroughness of this study. Critics of Catholic education suggest there is nothing special going on within these schools except high academic expectations and strict discipline (McNergney, Herbert 1995). Additionally, it is pointed out that Catholic schools have selective student bodies and unique parent constituents. In contradiction, there are those public school reformers who speak as proponents of Catholic schooling. They recognize the uniqueness of the Catholic school mission and its effect on the environment of the school (Goodlad et al. 1990; Jackson et al. 1993; Sergiovanni 1994). These individuals explain the impact of a unique student-teacher-community relationship and acknowledge the power of the implicit curriculum.

Teaching is fundamentally mindful decision-making (Zumwalt 1989). Teaching is the essential ingredient in the effectiveness of a written curriculum. Catholic school teachers emerge as critical players in the Catholic elementary school curriculum-instruction-learning equation (Ross et al. 1993; Jones et al. 1988). The Catholic school teacher's ability to make the curriculum a living document requires an understanding of teaching that goes beyond curriculum objectives. Teaching within the Catholic elementary school is special and unique as a faith teaching-learning experience. The Catholic school teacher potentially brings gospel values into all areas of classroom life. The implicit faith formation curriculum of a Catholic school is powerful. Those who teach and are principals within Catholic schools recognize their influence on students. They acknowledge that other interactions within the Catholic school also have a profound effect on students, for example, coaches, resource personnel, and school staff. These interactions speak to the entire values formation experience students witness within the Catholic school.

Two key qualities of the Catholic elementary school curriculum were described by this study's data. First, each of the sample Catholic elementary school's curricula represents a diocesan organizational philosophy falling on a continuum from a more centralized approach to a more decentralized approach. Second, each sample curriculum is more or less explicit in stating its Catholicity in the content areas. These two dimensions of Catholic elementary school curricula, centralization and Catholicity, portray a system of parochial schools steeped in the parish school tradition. These two dimensions also describe the transition of these elementary schools into structured diocesan systems.

The data describing the elementary Catholic school's written curriculum received attention from this study, but other important questions about the Catholic elementary school faith formation curriculum and instruction require future research. The quality of teaching that transforms the written curriculum into the learned curriculum, the modeling of Catholic faith and values implicit within life in the classroom, and the interactive influence of the Catholic school and family, each warrant study for their contribution to the learning experience within the Catholic school. Potentially these studies will explain more thoroughly how the Catholic elementary school serves in faith formation for the Church.

APPENDIX

Figure 1.   Participating Dioceses

Diocese of Arlington
Archdiocese of Baltimore
Archdiocese of Boston
Archdiocese of Chicago
Archdiocese of Cincinnati
Diocese of Cleveland
Diocese of Kansas City
Archdiocese of Newark
Archdiocese of New Orleans
Archdiocese of New York
Archdiocese of Philadelphia
Archdiocese of Phoenix
Diocese of Providence
Diocese of Rockville Centre
Archdiocese of Saint Louis
Diocese of Toledo
Diocese of Tulsa
Archdiocese of Washington

Figure 2.   Concepts in Math Education

CONCEPT: DIGNITY OF THE HUMAN PERSON

The Dignity of the Human Person calls us to reason and problem
solve.

TOPIC #

1   Problem Solving
4   Estimation and Reasoning
7   Data Analysis, Probability and Statistics
8   Patterns, Relationships and Functions
9   Algebra

CONCEPT: CALL TO A SPECIFIC HISTORY

The value of mathematics calls us to understand the roots in its
history and gives shape to the present and the future. Math
throughout history has affected human development, and will
continue to do so in the future.

TOPIC #

5   Measurement
6   Geometry and Spatial Sense

CONCEPT: CALL TO LIFE IN A COMMUNITY

We are called to become confident in our own unique abilities,
and to share these abilities with our community.

TOPIC #

2   Math as Number Sense, Numeration, Number Systems,
         and Number Theory
3   Relationships, Computations, Operations
10   Communication

(Diocese of Kansas City, 1996)

Figure 3.   Graded Course of Study in Language Arts

The Graded Course of Study in Language Arts endeavors to attain the goals
of Catholic education by forming Christians who:
—work cooperatively in a spirit of mutual service
—cultivate their intellectual growth and determine their aesthetic
standards
—appreciate and enjoy a constantly widening scope of literature
and the language in which it is communicated
—become aware of important historical and literary elements of
our cultural heritage
—relate the ideas, feelings and experiences derived from
literature and communicate them effectively to others
—use knowledge gained from reading to make sound judgements
based on Christian principles
—realize that the effective and responsible use of the English
language is crucial to becoming a Catholic influence in
contemporary social justice and moral issues
—are encouraged to broaden their reading interests
—make choices in leisure reading and viewing activities
grounded in literary discretion and moral judgements
—possess the tools of language necessary for critical evaluation of
media, propaganda, news and advertisements
—integrate and apply language arts activities to all aspects of the
curriculum (pg. 9)
(Diocese of Cleveland, 1993)

Figure 4.   Concepts in Religion

KEY UNIFYING CONCEPTS IN RELIGION

Concepts which mark the tradition of theological statements of papal, episcopal, and scriptural writings that direct religious education are:

1. Presence of God

God is the author and creator of all life. God took the form of a human in the person of Jesus Christ. The Spirit of God permeates all we are and all that we are called to do. In accepting the mystery of the Trinity, Catholics believe that God is transcendent as well as incarnate.

2. Dignity of the Human Person

The human person is the clearest reflection of the presence of God in the world. Each person is a reflection of God. Each person is an expression of the creation of God and the meaning of the redemptive ministry of Jesus Christ. Every human life is sacred.

3. Call to Life in Community

Each person is called to live in and build a faith community: in the home, in school, in parish, in their neighborhoods, in the workplace, in society, indeed in the world. While each person is a unique gift from God, people are called to work together to strengthen their faith life and live that life in harmony with their brothers and sisters.

4. Reverence and Stewardship of the Planet

All of life is sacred. Catholic Christians believe that we are one with all of creation. We are called to revere and protect nature and natural life. As people grow in awareness of the causes and effects on ecosystems, Catholics are called to promote life forms and to confront the forces of evil which threaten the preservation of those forms.

5. Call to a Specific History

Each person is born into a particular historical period—in their families, in the church and in the world. The present context has roots in a history of the past which gave shape to the present. Knowledge of history and traditions help shape future life and work to continue building the reign of God.

These concepts provide the framework for determining all knowledge, values, skills, and experiences in the present and future lives of students. Each religion unit and course connects to one or more of these basic concepts.

(Diocese of Kansas City, p. 1)

Figure 5.   Tenets of a Catholic Educational Philosophy

1. An opportunity to learn faith knowledge
2. A community where the faith is lived
3. A holistic approach to the student

NOTE

1. The ability of this document to support Catholic elementary education, in both research and practice, rests on the unselfish contributions of diocesan superintendents, diocesan curriculum staff, and practitioners nationwide. Their willingness to provide the needed information made this work possible. One fundamental strength of Catholic education is the collaborative benevolence of those within Catholic school organizations in sharing their work. Without the generous understanding of scholarship displayed by many dioceses, this project would have lacked a practical foundation.

REFERENCES

Bransford, J. D., and N. J. Vye. 1989. "A Perspective on Cognitive Research and Its Implications for Instruction. In L. B. Resnick and L. E. Klopfer, eds., *Toward the Thinking Curriculum: Content and Cognitive Research*, 173–205. Alexandria: ASCD.

Commission of Bishops. 1994. *Catechism of the Catholic Church.* New York: William Sadlier.

Eisner, E. W. 1985. *The Educational Imagination: On the Design and Evaluation of School Programs.* New York: Macmillan.

Eisner, E. W. 1991. *The Enlightened Eye: Qualitative Inquiry and the Enhancement of Education Practice.* New York: Macmillan.

Garanzini, M. J. 1995. *Child-Centered, Family-Sensitive Schools: An Educator's Guide to Family Dynamics.* Washington, D.C.: National Catholic Educational Association.

Glatthorn, A. A. 1994. *Developing a Quality Curriculum.* Alexandria, Va:. ASCD.

Glatthorn, A. A. 1995. *Content of the Curriculum.* Alexandria, Va.: ASCD.

Goodlad, J. I., R. Soder, R. and K. A. Sirotnik, eds. 1990. *The Moral Dimensions of Teaching.* San Francisco: Jossey-Bass.

Jackson, P. W., R. E. Boostrom, and D. A. Hansen. 1993. *The Moral Life of Schools.* San Francisco: Jossey-Bass.

Jones, B. B., A. S. Palincsar, D. S. Ogle, and E. G. Carr. 1988. *Strategic Teaching and Learning: Cognitive Instruction in the Content Areas.* Alexandria, Va.: ASCD.

Kealey, R. 1985. *Curriculum in the Catholic School.* Washington, D.C.: National Catholic Educational Association.

McNergney, R. F., and J. M. Herbert. 1995. *Foundations of Education: The Challenge of Professional Practice.* Neelhan Heights, Mass.: Allyn and Bacon.

National Conference of Catholic Bishops. 1973. *To Teach as Jesus Did.* Washington, D.C.: USCC Office for Publishing and Promotion Services.

Ross, D. D., E. Bondy, and D. W. Kyle. 1993. *Reflective Teaching for Student Empowerment.* New York: Macmillan.

Sergiovanni, T. J. 1994. *Building Community in Schools.* San Francisco: Jossey-Bass.

Tyler, R. W. 1949. *Basic Principles of Curriculum and Instruction.* Chicago: University of Chicago Press.

Wolcott, H. F. 1995. *The Art of Fieldwork.* Walnut Creek: AltaMira Press.

Zumwalt, K. 1989. "Beginning Professional Teacher: The Need for a Curricular Vision of Teaching." In M. C. Reynolds, ed., *Knowledge Base for the Beginning Teacher,* 173–84. New York: Pergamon Press.

Religious Knowledge and Belief of Lay Religion Teachers in Catholic Elementary Schools

6

Paul Galetto, O.S.A.

In no small way, the future of Catholicism is dependent upon those who teach the faith to the young members of the Church. The ideas presented, the impressions given, and the lessons taught will mold young boys and girls who in time will become the leaders of the next generation. What can be said about those who are doing the teaching today? What do they know about Church teachings? To what degree do they believe the teachings of the Church? How can the Church assist the teachers and catechists in their preparation and presentation of the teachings and beliefs of Catholicism?

A review of practices in fifteen dioceses throughout the United States reveals a diversity of approaches to the task of certifying teachers of religion. Three dioceses have no program in place although each claimed to be in the process of developing one. Some dioceses are more demanding than others in the number of clock hours they require for certification. Some dioceses have levels of certification (e.g., high school, elementary school, parish program, or Master, Intermediate, Beginner) while others offer blanket certification. Some dioceses work their certification in conjunction with local Catholic colleges while others have video programs. Some have regular updates at three-year intervals while a few offer a one-time forever certification. The only consistent element throughout is the diversity of approaches.

In reading the literature that dioceses publish, it appears obvious that not only theological concerns are at work but also geographic, cultural, and (for lack of a better term) indigenous factors. There are no apparent references to socio-logical or statistical studies to support the approaches that are taken. Instead, there is a general "seat-of-the-pants" approach. Overall, the programs might benefit from research that illustrates the relationship of various factors and what the participants know and believe about Catholic Church teachings.

To answer the questions that this information raises, we must ex-amine knowledge and belief and then what factors affect them. Both knowledge and faith are two parts of a rather complex construct known as religiosity.

The Construct of Religiosity

One of the most significant studies of religiosity is by Rodney Stark and Charles Glock (1968). Although previous researchers had been fa-miliar with conceptualizing religiosity as a multidimensional phe-nomenon, Glock (1962) observed that most prior religious research tended to focus on only one or two particular dimensions to the ex-clusion of the others. Glock theorized that religiosity consisted of five measurable dimensions: experiential (feeling, emotion, and personal piety), ritualistic (religious behavior such as church attendance and communal prayer), ideological (religious beliefs), intellectual (reli-gious and biblical knowledge), and consequential (the personal effects of religion in the secular world). It seems that the original titles used by Glock caused some confusion and needless argument. In the inter-ests of clarity, Stark and Glock (1968) later revised the titles of Glock's five dimensions to include: experience, practice, belief, knowledge, and consequences. They later expanded the original five dimensions to include four secondary aspects of religiosity: ethicalism, devotion-alism, the communal, and friendship. Stark and Glock's work has served as a basis for much of the subsequent research in the measure-ment of religiosity. (For further discussion on the topic of religiosity, see Galetto 1995).

Knowledge and Belief

Stark and Glock (1968) defined the knowledge dimension as having to do with "the expectation that the religious person is informed and knowledgeable about the basic tenets of his or her faith and its sacred scriptures" (p. 16). One must know teachings before one can accept them and integrate them into his or her life.

The belief dimension, according to Stark and Glock (1968), was constituted by "expectations that the religious person will hold to certain beliefs" (p. 14). Every religion sets some minimum of beliefs that its adherents must confess if they are to be considered a member of that faith. Belief is different from knowledge. One may know what his or her faith teaches, but might not accept that particular tenet of faith.

Church Documents

Based on the above description of religiosity, there are comparable dimensions in Catholic Church literature that define the characteristics and role of the catechist. The comparable concepts to knowledge and belief are, respectively, knowledge of Church teachings and fidelity to the Magisterium.

Knowledge of Church Teachings

The Second Vatican Council's *Declaration on Christian Education* (1965) stated that: "[Teachers] should therefore be prepared for their work with special care, having the appropriate qualifications and adequate learning both religious and secular" (no. 8). This statement recognized that catechists must be sufficiently prepared to meet the demands placed upon them as teachers and people of faith. The Congregation for the Clergy (1971) in the *General Catechetical Directory* observed: "That a strong doctrinal heritage must be acquired is self-evident. This must always include adequate knowledge of Catholic doctrine together with a degree of scientific theology obtained at higher catechetical institutes. Sacred Scripture should be as it were the soul of the entire formation" (no. 112).

The American hierarchy addressed this issue of knowledge of Church teachings in several places. In a paper entitled *A Report on the State of Catechesis in the United States* the United States Catholic Conference (1990) stated: "From their [the bishops'] comments it is clear that catechist formation is a high priority for many bishops, and that they are concerned about the quality of catechists in their diocese" (p. 33). It is apparent that to be a qualified catechist, one must have an adequate knowledge of Church teachings. The United States Catholic Conference issued two policy statements that address this particular concern: *Teach Them* (1976) and *Sharing the Light of Faith* (1977).

Teach Them (1976), a statement by the bishops on the importance of Catholic schools, specified that all who are in the school are responsible for its religious atmosphere. The document suggested that "doctrine" be a part of the educational approaches used to initiate new teachers in the schools. When teachers are aware of the faith and its importance in their own lives they will carry out: "the commitment of handing on the faith to the next generation, not merely preserved, but more glorious, more efficacious, more valued by those who in their turn will take up the charge to 'go and teach'" (no. 5).

The United States Catholic Conference (1977) issued *Sharing the Light of Faith* (*SLF*) as the application of the *General Catechetical Directory* to the local Church in the United States. Chapter nine of the text was dedicated solely to catechists and most especially their qualities, roles, and preparation. Addressing the desirable characteristics of the catechist, *SLF* stated: "As important as it is that a catechist have a clear understanding of the teaching of the Christ and His Church, this is not enough. He or she must also receive and respond to a ministerial call, which comes from the Lord and is articulated in the local Church by the bishop" (no. 213). With respect to the formation process of the catechist, *SLF* noted that knowledge of religious teaching was essential. It called for "instruction in theology and scripture" as well as "continuing in-service educational opportunities." Throughout the document, passing references were made to the cognitive aspects of religious education.

In summary, whether overtly or not, it seems clear from the position of the hierarchy of the Church that it is a requisite quality of catechists that they be well informed about the teachings of the Church if they are to be effective teachers of religion. With respect to the Stark and Glock model of religiosity, the obvious comparison is with the dimension of knowledge—the basic understanding one must have of the tenets of his or her faith.

Fidelity to the Magisterium

The essence of good catechists is that they concentrate the content of their teaching on what is found in the Magisterium of the Church. In a talk that Pope John Paul II (1992) gave to the American bishops on the topic of Catholic elementary schools in the United States and the lay teachers in them, he said: "In regard to the content of religion courses, the essential criterion is fidelity to the teaching of the Church" (p. 179). In an earlier document of the Congregation for Catholic Education (1983), *Lay Teachers—Witnesses to Faith,* this same issue was addressed. In talking about the school community, of which the teacher is a part, the document stated that being a member of the community "involves a sincere adherence to the Magisterium of the Church [which offers] a presentation of Christ as the supreme model of the human person" (no. 38).

Documents of the United States Catholic Conference have also addressed this issue. The clearest statements of this position were found in *SLF* (1977), where it stated that one of the primary characteristics of the catechist is that he or she exhibits commitment to the Church.

> One who exercises the ministry of the word represents the Church, to which the word has been entrusted. The catechist believes in the Church. . . . The catechist realizes that it is Christ's message which he or she is called to proclaim. To insure fidelity to that message, catechists test and validate their understanding and insights in the light of the gospel message as presented by the teaching authority of the Church. (no. 208)

Fidelity to the Magisterium of the Church is similar to Stark and Glock's conception of belief. They define the belief dimension as the expectation that the religious person will hold to certain beliefs as a member of the religion.

METHODOLOGY

Population and Sample

During the 1993–94 academic year, there were some 112,199 teachers at the 7,114 Catholic elementary schools in the U.S. Of this number, 89.5 percent (100,400) were lay teachers (Brigham 1994). This population was broadly defined as all teachers of religion in Catholic elementary schools in the United States. This was the population used for this study and analyzed through use of cluster sampling. (It must be noted that not all elementary school teachers teach religion. Those who do not teach religion were excluded from consideration.)

A random cluster sample of 10 percent (n=714) generated by the National Catholic Educational Association from its list of U.S. Catholic schools (including schools in the Bahamas, the Virgin Islands, and Puerto Rico) was taken from this population. Of the 714 schools who received a letter requesting their participation, 442 schools volunteered to be a part of the study.

In April of 1994, surveys were mailed to the 4,375 lay and religious teachers of religion in these schools. A total of 2,578 valid surveys from 419 schools were returned in the confidential preaddressed envelopes provided. Of these, 2,291 (89%) were from lay teachers of religion and were used in this study. The valid response rate was 59 percent for potential respondents and 95 percent for the schools that agreed to participate in the survey.

Measures

The first section of the survey gathered demographic information on gender, race, age, religious status, and education. The next section dealt with the respondent's teaching situation including locality of the school, percentage of Catholic students, years of teaching, religious education, certification status, and description of students. Then, the respondent was given twenty-five theological and moral issues to consider. The issues represented three major areas: general Christian belief, Catholic dogma, and Catholic moral teaching. Each issue was followed by several statements reflecting divergent positions on it. An example follows:

1. God's existence
   A. God is a supreme, omnipotent Being.
   B. God is fallible and subject to change.
   C. God does not exist.

The respondent was asked first to identify the statement that came closest to the Church's position on the particular issue (the Knowlege of Church Teachings measure) and, second, to identify the statement that came closest to his or her own position on that same issue (the Personal Belief measure). Items were dichotomously scored such that each contributed either a zero (for an incorrect answer) or a 1 (for a correct answer) to a possible total score of 25 for Knowlege of Church Teachings.

In a parallel fashion, for each item where the respondent chose as a personal position the correct answer under Knowledge of Church Teachings, that item contributed one point toward the Personal Belief measure, also scored out of 25.

Results

Two levels of analysis were conducted. First, dependent measures and demographic variables were examined to look for patterns in the data. Second, personal belief and knowledge scores were regressed on relevant predictors.

Tables 1, 2, and 3 present summary data describing the characteristics, credentials, and teaching situation of the respondents. The teachers were overwhelmingly female and white. Almost all were Catholic with 88 percent being Catholic from birth and an additional 8 percent having converted to Catholicism. Thirty-nine percent of the teachers were age forty-five and over. In terms of education, the majority (75%) of respondents had some graduate credits beyond a bachelor's degree. However, three-quarters had no graduate credits in theology. About one-third of the teachers had between nine and twelve years of formal religious education through parish or Catholic school with another 38 percent reporting more than twelve years. Over 90 percent of these lay teachers had no experience of religious formation such as that provided in a convent or seminary.

The majority of respondents (56%) had been certified to teach religion either by the diocese or through college courses taken. The most common means of preparation for those certified was to take formal noncollege credit courses such as those in a program sponsored by the diocese (40%).

Most teachers had taught ten or fewer years in Catholic schools (59%) and were teaching religion to classes of students who were at least 90 percent Catholic (79.0%). Students were typically white (82%) and from middle-class families (96%). Two-thirds of respondents were teaching first through sixth grades. Some 46 percent were working in what they termed suburban schools.

On the 25-item instrument, the average score for knowledge of Church teachings was 16.49 out of a possible 25 (with standard deviation of 2.90) and the average score for personal belief of Church teachings was 15.13 (with standard deviation of 3.25). Table 4 lists the issues that were used in the instrument with the percentage of teachers correctly indicating the Church's position on the issue and the percentage holding that position as their personal belief. For complete results see *Building the Foundations of Faith* (Galetto 1996).

There was broad variation among the items on knowledge and personal belief. Therefore, regression analyses were conducted to determine the factors accounting for differences on each scale. Several predictor variables were included: (1) age of the teacher (coded as 44 and under versus 45 and older); (2) method of certification (scaled values); (3) if the teacher had been a convert to Catholicism; (4) educational level of the teacher (scaled values); (5) number of years of formal religious education of the teacher (scaled values); (6) experience of religious formation in a convent or seminary (coded as none versus some); (7) number of years teaching religion (scaled values); (8) certification status (scaled as certified, in process, or not certified); (9) number of graduate theology credits (coded as no credits versus some credits); (10) grade level taught (scaled values); (11) locality of the school (coded as suburban versus other); (12) percentage of Catholic students in class currently taught (scaled values); (13) social class of the majority of students taught (scaled values); (14) race of the majority of the students taught (coded as white versus nonwhite and used for personal belief analysis only).

Tables 5 and 6 summarize the results of the two stepwise regressions. It is noted that the technique of stepwise regression maintains only significant predictors in the final equation. Therefore, only those predictors adding unique capacity to account for variance on the dependent measures are reported.

The two analyses yielded similar results. Predictors of knowledge of Church teachings accounted for 19 percent of the variance on this measure ($R^2 = .19$). Twenty-two percent of the variance on personal belief of Church teachings was accounted for by the predictors ($R^2 = .22$). Teacher age, formal religious education, and method of certification were the strongest predictors of each measure. In each analysis, grade level taught was a less potent but still significant predictor. The regression findings differed only in that the percentage of Catholic students being taught predicted knowledge scores, whereas race of students predicted belief scores. The nature of the associations detected in the regression analyses is elaborated upon below.

The older the teacher, the greater the likelihood that he or she knew and personally believed what the Church teaches. In both regressions, age was an important conceptual variable. The correlation coefficient between age and years teaching religion was .558. This would suggest that individuals who continue to teach in Catholic schools are knowledgeable about the Church's teachings and tend to agree with these teachings.

The number of years that a teacher was educated in Catholic schools also significantly predicted knowledge and beliefs. In the original form in which this question was asked, formal religious education was meant to include both Catholic school as well as parish religious education programs. However, when asked to break down their educational experience, the vast majority of teachers had their formal religious education in a Catholic school (73 percent went beyond eighth grade in a Catholic school).

The manner in which teachers are certified is a third predictor of knowledge and belief. The more formal the certification process, the higher were the scores on both measures. Teachers whose certification consisted mostly of college credit courses scored highest, followed by those with noncollege credit programs (such as those sponsored by a diocese). Those who had informal programs such as in-service days or watching videos scored slightly better than those who underwent no certification process at all.

The higher the grade level taught, the more likely the teacher knew and believed the Church's teachings. This variable was a stronger predictor of knowledge than of personal belief. Teachers who taught the junior high level (grades 7 and 8) scored highest of any group. They were followed by those who taught grades 4 through 6. Teachers in Pre-K and Kindergarten scored only slightly higher than those teaching in grades 1 through 3.

In most of the Catholic schools in our sample, over 90 percent of the students attending religion classes were Catholic. Nonetheless, the higher the percentage of Catholics, the more likely that the teacher knew the teachings of the Catholic faith. There is a caveat here, however. Non-Catholic teachers teaching religion in the Catholic school system were more likely to be found in schools with lower percentages of Catholic students. Non-Catholic teachers scored lower than Catholic teachers with respect to knowledge of Church teachings.

The variable of race was entered only in the personal belief regression and proved to offer some predictive quality. In several areas (Asians, Hispanics, American Indian/Alaskan, African-American) the number of cases was too small to make any inferences. Because of this fact and its nature as a nominal variable, its entrance into the regression was reconfigured into whites vs. non-whites.

It must be remembered that we are dealing with the personal belief of teachers and the race of the students they teach. This variable cannot be dealt with in isolation because when it entered the regression it controlled for other variables in the model. Teachers who instructed classes that are majority white scored higher than teachers in any other group. These breakdowns into various racial groups were defined by the teachers themselves.

INTERPRETATION

The medley of major predictors concerning the knowledge and belief of the teachings of the Catholic Church by Catholic lay teachers of religion in Catholic elementary schools helps direct the efforts to establish effective training programs. The age of the teacher, the number of years of formal religious education, the method of certification, and the grade level taught are factors that should be considered in the planning of the religion program.

A key finding here is that the more formal religious training possessed by the teacher, the more thorough was her knowledge of Catholic teachings and the more consistent was her personal belief with them. This was true both for teachers who had more years of formal religious education in Catholic institutions before the age of twenty-three and for those whose preparation to teach religion consisted of formal courses in colleges or other settings. This suggests that those concerned with the preparation of teachers of religion should focus on providing them with formal religion courses rather than informal in-service sessions or the viewing of videotapes.

These data gathered here are preliminary. John Convey, in his 1992 work on Catholic education, noted that Catholic elementary schools are ripe for study. More research is needed before any long-range solutions are found. However, this does not undercut the value of what is here. These data are an important first step in establishing how better to serve the teachers of religion in our Catholic schools.

First, age by itself is difficult to interpret as a factor and is better viewed in combination with other factors. The medley of predictors suggests that, for lack of a better term, exposure and the manner of exposure to Church teaching are what is important. It follows that faculty retention should be a goal of catechetical programs. It is in the best interest of Catholic elementary schools to have established faculties where the teaching of religion is done by competent and experienced teachers. Retention can be encouraged through better pay, improved working conditions, fostering the sense of commitment that exists in teachers, or appealing to their sense of ministry. As Buetow (1988) states in referring to the *General Catechetical Directory:* "The selection of religion teachers must, therefore, receive the greatest of care. Only those who are distinguished by ability, learning and spiritual life are to be chosen for so important a task" (p. 256).

Second, these predictors together offer several approaches to the issue of effective training for teachers of religion.There is no good substitute for a full-hearted approach to the certification process. Over and over again, the indications are that college credit courses are the best means for certifying teachers. The formal setting, for whatever reason, has a positive impact on those attending. One strategy is to coordinate diocesan schools with local Catholic institutions of higher learning. Where possible, a diocese should take advantage of these local colleges and universities and make arrangements with them for certification classes for catechists. Arrangements for tuition and credit are problems that will arise, but it is in the best interest of both the diocese and colleges to accommodate one another. An important finding of this present research is that certification by itself is not the answer; it is the method of certification that is most important to knowledge and belief in the teachings of the Church.

Third, there is an immeasurable value to Catholic schools. Those who attend these schools are better able to know and to believe what the Church teaches. This would seem to indicate that the process of certification needs to be long-term. We as a Church cannot think of the faith development of a person in the short term. This would appear to indicate that formation as a catechist should be ongoing. A one-time forever method does not seem to be effective. As a Church we need to realize the importance of educational experiences in the faith life of people. This present research and the research of others, most especially Andrew Greeley's (1989), confirm that Catholic schools do make a difference in people's lives. We should acknowledge that and be proud of it. Ignorance of the Church's teachings benefits neither the Church nor its people. Catholic schools are a financial investment that is well worth the cost because ignorance of faith is too high a price to pay. Clergy and laity must be willing to make the sacrifices of time and money that are needed to keep these institutions of religious formation alive.

Fourth, grade level as a predictor of knowledge and belief suggests that discussing one's faith with others is important. Those who teach more advanced grades are more likely to be engaged with their students in dealing with particular points of interest. It is this interaction that is itself an educational experience. Also, some of this present research indicates that those who teach across grade levels are the most likely to score higher in both knowledge and belief. As a Church we need to engage people, especially teachers and catechists, in an active discussion, one that is instructional rather than confrontational.

We need to make available more opportunities for learning about the faith. Priests, religious, and master catechists need to offer their expertise in matters of Church doctrine in a manner that will facilitate a better grasp of what the Church teaches. Most of today's teachers of religion are married and have children living with them at home. The time these teachers have to dedicate to the preparation of religion classes needs to be optimized. Resource books that contain the necessary information that will help teachers be more effective must be made available; for example, articles on how children acquire and assimilate religious concepts. Easy-to-read material needs to be provided also for new teachers of religion since there is such a high turnover rate in Catholic schools. We need to compensate for the lack of experience and familiarity with the material among these new teachers.

The traditional Catholic was steeped in doctrine and structured in an ethos that teachers with religious vocations nourished. These schools are no longer the norm. Today's teachers of religion are lay persons, often young, and not necessarily with Catholic school backgrounds. This change is most productively seen as a challenge that, when confronted properly, can only improve the schools and help them achieve their primary aim of sustaining the faith through informed and committed people of God.

Table 1.   Background Characteristics of Teachers

Characteristic	Percent of Respondents
Gender	
Female	95
Race	
White	94
Age	
Under 25	6
25–34	24
35–44	30
45–54	29
55 or older	10
Faith	
Catholic	88
Convert	8
Non-Catholic	4
Educational level	
College	25
College with graduate credits	52
Master's degree	12
Master's with graduate credit or doctorate	11

Table 2.   Proportion of Teachers with Various Credentials

Credential	Percent of Respondents
Graduate credits in theology	
None	76
1–12	18
13–plus	6
Years of formal religious education before age 23 (parish or school)	
None	8
1–8	20
9–12	34
More than 12	38
Experience of religious formation	
No religious formation	91
Certification to teach religion	
Certified by the (arch)diocese	45
Certified through college courses taken	11
Teaching while attending certification courses	21
Teaching without having undergone a certification program	22
Preparation for certification to teach religion	
Never taken any informal or formal courses	9
Majority of preparation was informal instruction (e.g., local in-service program, watching videos)	32
Majority of preparation was formal noncollege credit courses (e.g., program sponsored by the diocese)	40
Majority of preparation was formal college credit courses	18

Table 3.   Proportion of Respondents in Various Teaching Situations

Characteristic	Percent of Respondents
Locality of the school	
Inner city	8
City	31
Suburban	47
Rural	15
Percentage of Catholic students	
90–100%	79
60–89%	13
Less than 60%	8
Years of teaching religion	
0–5	38
6–10	24
11–15	16
Over 16	22
Economic status of majority of the teacher's religion students	
Poor	2
Lower middle	13
Middle middle	61
Upper middle	21
Wealthy	1
Ethnicity of majority of the teacher's religion students	
Asian/Pacific Islander/American Indian/Alaskan	2
Black, non-Hispanic	5
Hispanic	5
White	82
No majority	4

Table 4.   Knowledge of Church Teaching and Personal Beliefs
on Particular Issues

Issue	% who correctly identify Church's position	% who identify Church's position as their own
1. God's existence	99.8	97.5
2. Divinity of Jesus	93.5	90.5
3. Role of faith and good works	87.3	83.4
4. Real presence in the Eucharist	86.5	63.4
5. Male priesthood	71.6	32.5
6. Human and divine authorship of the Bible	24.5	19.3
7. Establishment of the Hierarchy of the Church	48.7	41.4
8. Afterlife	87.2	74.4
9. Infallibility of Pope	34.8	26.5
10. Elective abortion	77.2	26.3
11. Church moral teaching	30.7	27.6
12. Artificial birth control	80.8	10.2
13. Role of Mary in salvation	79.3	72.2
14. Existence of Devil	83.3	74.1
15. Resurrection	94.2	87.2
16. Predestination	49.2	48.1
17. Who can be saved	44.0	43.6
18. Role of suffering	79.8	77.0
19. Indissolubility of marriage	88.8	54.4
20. Euthanasia	34.3	31.3
21. Discrimination	96.8	91.8
22. Homosexuality	42.9	41.9
23. Premarital Sex	99.0	60.5
24. Reception of Communion by non-Catholics	17.4	13.2
25. Sacramental forgiveness of sins	17.3	12.9

Table 5. Summary of Stepwise Regression Analysis for Variables
Predicting Knowledge of Church Teaching ($N=2,106$)

Variable	$\underline{B}$	Beta
Age	.68	.26*
Formal religious education	.53	.22*
Method of certification	.41	.13*
Grade level taught	.31	.11*
Percent Catholics taught	.15	.05*

Note: $R^2 = .19$, Only significant predictors are included in the table.
* $<.01$

Table 6. Summary of Stepwise Regression Analysis for Variables
Predicting Personal Belief of Church Teachings ($N=1,995$)

Variable	$\underline{B}$	Beta
Age	.90	.31*
Formal religious education	.53	.19*
Method of certification	.60	.16*
Race of students	1.0	.10*
Grade level taught	.21	.07*

Note: $R^2 = .22$, Only significant predictors are included in the table.
* $<.01$

<h1 style="text-align:center">REFERENCES</h1>

Benson, P., and M. Guerra. 1985. *Sharing the Faith: The Beliefs and Values of Catholic High School Teachers.* Washington, D.C.: National Catholic Educational Association.

Brigham, F. H., Jr. 1994. *United States Catholic Elementary and Secondary Schools 1993–1994: Annual Statistical Report on Schools, Enrollment and Staffing.* Washington, D.C.: National Catholic Educational Association.

Buetow, H. 1988. *The Catholic School: Its Roots, Identity, and Future.* New York: Crossroad.

Congregation for Catholic Education. 1983. "Lay Teachers: Witnesses to Faith." *The Pope Speaks,* 28, 45–73.

Congregation for the Clergy. 1971. "The General Catechetical Directory." In B. L. Marthaler, ed., *Catechetics in Context.* Huntington, Ind.: Our Sunday Visitor.

Convey, J. J. 1992. *Catholic Schools Make a Difference: Twenty-five Years of Research.* Washington, D.C.: National Catholic Educational Association.

DeJong, G. F., J. E. Faulkner, and R. H. Warland. 1976. "Dimensions of Religiosity Reconsidered: Evidence from a Cross-cultural Study." *Social Forces,* 54, 866–89.

Galetto, P. W. 1995. "An Analysis of the Knowledge, Beliefs and Sense of Efficacy of Lay Teachers of Religion in Catholic Elementary Schools." [CD-ROM]. Abstract from ProQuest: Dissertation Abstracts Item: 9519791.

———. 1996. *Building the Foundations of Faith.* Washington, D.C.: National Catholic Educational Association.

Glock, C. Y. 1962 "On the Study of Religious Commitment." *Religious Education, Research Supplement,* 42, 98–110.

Greeley, A. 1989. "My Research on Catholic Schools." *Chicago Studies,* 28 (3), 245–63.

John Paul II. 1992. *The Pope Speaks to the American Church.* San Francisco: Harper Collins.

Stark, R., and C. Y. Glock. 1968. *American Piety: The Nature of Religious Commitment.* Berkeley: University of California Press.

United States Catholic Conference. 1976. "Teach Them." *Origins,* 6, 1–7.

———. 1978. *Sharing the Light of Faith.* Washington, D.C.: United States Catholic Conference.

———. 1990. *A Report on the State of Catechesis in the United States: Findings and Conclusions.* Washington, D.C.: United States Catholic Conference.

Vatican Council II. 1965. *Declaration on Christian Education.*

7 Creating Information for Catholic Educational Leaders

George Elford

The later decades of the twentieth century have been called the Information Age. Information technology in this period has been characterized by almost daily advances. Information at the disposal of leaders in most fields has increased exponentially. Ironically, it was the banking industry, long thought to be the most staid and conservative, that led the way in the use of computer and information technology to increase services to clients. In contrast to other fields, educational management has not been a field that has been transformed by the Information Age.

An adage in business management in the Information Age is that "You cannot manage what you cannot measure." Information technology has been at the heart of the management process in most fields. In terms of current practice, educational leaders, including those in Catholic education, would likely view this adage as something of an overstatement. Most educational leaders would, however, likely agree that this adage does point in the right direction. Classic descriptions of leadership and the management process have long focused on information as the driving element in the process. An often cited description of the management process[1] has the leader involved with: (1) decision-making, (2) programming, (3) communicating, (4) controlling, and (5) reappraising. Reappraising restarts the cycle with further decision-making. Information provides the basis for this reappraising. Effective management thus depends on information which is the basis for this reappraising. The leader must have in place and effectively use an "information system" for providing this information for internal management.

This chapter will discuss the information requirements and possibilities for leaders in Catholic education. Catholic education describes education in the Catholic faith and tradition that occurs in various settings including Catholic schools.[2] Leaders in Catholic education include those managing Catholic schools and programs at the local and regional or diocesan levels and also national leaders. The goals of Catholic education as defined by this faith and tradition are in the cognitive, affective, and behavioral domains. This chapter will address information requirements and possibilities for Catholic educational leaders in both school and parish programs, while giving more attention to Catholic school leadership in keeping with the focus of this book.

Leaders can use information in two ways. They can use it externally to promote the school and publicize its success in the marketplace. External uses of educational information are the uses of information designed to reach various publics and stakeholder groups. They can use it internally in the management of the school as described in the decision-making cycle cited above. Internal uses of information are designed to enable school and program staff, especially the leaders, to work with the students and make improvements in their programs. The term "educational information" as used in this chapter will describe information relating to instructional processes and outcomes.

CREATING AND USING INFORMATION: LESSONS FROM J. D. POWER AND ASSOCIATES

The automobile industry provides a valuable example of the creation and use of information that is instructive for present purposes. While the goal of the automobile industry is to make a profit, an essential instrumental goal is customer satisfaction that can be documented. In 1968 in a suburb of Los Angeles called Agoura Hills, J. D. Power III pioneered what became an internationally recognized system of information for the automobile industry. This system addresses the industry's instrumental goal. J. D. Power and Associates[3] established an owner satisfaction continuum which measures customer satisfaction over the first five years of ownership. This firm publishes syndicated studies such as the Sales Satisfaction Study, Initial Quality Study, and

Customer Satisfaction Study. These industry-supported studies were created in response to intense competition and especially international competition. J. D. Power and Associates now have nine offices in six countries. The primary uses of this customer-response information are external; the results are valuable to the leading companies in the competitive car market. Power, in addition, provides training and consulting services within the industry to manufacturers, distributors, and retailers, which would represent internal uses for this same information. Power enables automobile companies to both improve customer satisfaction and to be recognized publicly for these improvements.

Could something analogous to this service ever come to be in American elementary and secondary education, public or Catholic? Rather than attempting an answer to that question, a more useful task for the present is to examine the lessons demonstrated for educators by the J. D. Power and Associates phenomenon. These lessons would include the following:

Information for Public Use is the Product of Some Form of Standardized Measurement

Information in this context is characterized by objectivity. Powers uses customer surveys that are carefully designed and field-tested to accurately capture the views of customers. The key to creating publicly useful information is standardization. Everyone is asked the same carefully worded questions under the same conditions.Thus, most of what is referred to as information in this chapter comes from well-designed surveys and standardized assessments.

Standardization can be implemented in several ways. The range of possible sources of standardized information goes well beyond multiple-choice standardized tests. Such tests have been widely administered in U.S. schools for decades, although not used with anything approaching effectiveness. For example, among the standardized assessments in use are rating scales used by teachers observing the skills of primary grade children. These kinds of standardized ratings deserve much broader use. Teacher ratings, if standardized, could be effectively used at all grade levels. Teachers are an almost totally neglected source of valuable data. In recent years, standardization techniques have been applied to the assessment of written work and portfolios of student work. ACT has recently developed standardized portfolio assessments for use at the high school level, which ultimately depend on the "standardized" judgments of teachers.

The creation of information in this sense requires additional effort and professionalism within the educational enterprise. Information as described above goes beyond personal impressions and the results of conversations and casual observation. Anecdotal information and grades are widely used to describe what is being accomplished. These fall short of being information in the sense used here. In fact, most of what is contained in school records is not information in this sense. Even those items checked off on the "right side" of the students' report cards, describing teacher's judgments about deportment and effort, are not based on a standardized rating scale. Without standardization, this information cannot be interpreted accurately without some knowledge of the persons involved.

*Information Created Either for Internal or External Use
Often Turns Out to be Used for Both Purposes*

Information as described here is a valuable asset and tends to be given multiple uses. The Power case shows how a system that first and foremost generates information for use in the marketplace soon developed internal uses in the management of companies. As noted above, the Power group provides training and consulting services to companies in the automotive industry. In education, information created for use in the college admissions process, for example, becomes information used by real estate agents in the marketplace as they actively promote a kind of real-estate-based "choice system" even within public education. Major urban newspapers now utilize state assessments and other data, originally collected for internal uses, to generate online report cards for individual public schools to inform the public as well as the real estate agents. (Currently, Catholic schools are not included in these "report cards.")

Competition Fosters the Creation of Information

Power prospered by providing information in a highly competitive field. Had the industry been a monopoly, he might not have prospered. American elementary and secondary education is dominated by a government monopoly, with nine out of ten students in public schools. This monopoly and the absence of competition could account for the low priority given to the creation of information in the sense used here. Catholic schools have somewhat mirrored the practices of public schools though they are outside the bounds of the protected monopoly. Catholic school leaders have not taken full advantage of the competitive advantages they could enjoy by creating information and effectively using information.

The thrust for "accountability" in public education in response to widely held views about a crisis in education has caused states and large districts to create information systems. This press for accountability is ultimately driven by the notion of international economic competition as affected by education. The state-developed accountability systems now produce information that can be used in the competition between Catholic and public schools. This competition tends to be different depending on the Catholic school's location. Where public schools are most "competitive academically" in more affluent suburban areas, Catholics tend to select Catholic schools more for religious and value reasons than for academic reasons. In lower-income urban areas, Catholic schools are sought out by Catholic and non-Catholic families for academic reasons in direct competition with public schools.

Confidence is a Condition that Disposes Leaders to Create and Use Information

J. D. Power and Associates created a system that favors different companies in different ways. Companies cooperate because they are confident that sooner or later the results will show them as winners. Confidence is a key element in their willingness to participate.

Confidence is likewise an important element for Catholic educational leaders in their creation and use of information. Confidence in turn begets confidence. Supporters and clients draw confidence in the programs offered when the leaders are confident about creating and using information. Supporters and clients are, in turn, disheartened by leaders who show reluctance about dealing with information. As shown later in this chapter, both Catholic school leaders and leaders in parish catechetical programs have reason to be confident concerning the results they are likely to see.

The Creation and Use of Information Should be Focused on Basic Goals

J. D. Power focused on customer satisfaction that could be documented. This is clearly important in a competitive marketplace.

Documented customer satisfaction is also important in education, especially in the free market that Catholic schools serve. A more fundamental goal in education, however, is learning which translates into growth or maintenance in knowledge, skills, and desirable practices that can be documented. The concept of maintenance is important here; it does little good for schools to teach students knowledge and skills that they lose very quickly. At present, there are no school reports describing these basic goals of student growth and skill maintenance. There is no instructional balance sheet enabling educators to see for themselves or to report to others the state of their enterprise in terms of growth. In this information age, this is evidence of an unfinished agenda in education concerning the creation and use of essential information.

An important product of the current press for accountability in U.S. schools is that some have begun to focus on assessing growth in education. A leading example is the Tennessee Value-Added Assessment System developed by William L. Sanders.[4] This system uses state assessment results to monitor the progress of students year by year. Sanders looked at students' performance in math using this state-level system with teachers identified on a scale from "high growth" to "low growth." Sanders found that students who had comparable skills at grade two were dramatically better skilled by grade five if they had high-growth as opposed to low-growth teachers. With today's information technology, it is clearly possible to set up an information system for individual schools and school systems that monitors an individual's growth or maintenance in knowledge and skills. Setting up such an information system does require a confidence and commitment that may be in short supply among educational leaders in all schools. Confident leaders are the ones likely to respond to this challenge and opportunity.

INFORMATION FOR CATHOLIC SCHOOL LEADERS

Catholic schools are unique. As McDermott has pointed out,[5] the Catholic school is a religious community within an academic community. An information system for Catholic schools must serve both communities, even though one component of the system might address one or the other community. Some components might address both. For example, a "customer satisfaction" survey of students and parents would address both the religious and academic aspects of the school. A survey service following the Power model could offer valuable information to Catholic school leaders in looking at the perceived effectiveness of both communities. Such a service would show both present perceptions and trends over time. A national service would enable the local leader to identify local strengths and challenges in reference to the patterns encountered in general by Catholic schools and other schools. Like the Power example cited above, these results could be used both for internal and external purposes.

Information for the Academic Community

Catholic schools suffer from the same paucity of educational information that characterizes all of elementary and secondary education. Today's information technology, including assessment technology, is available to create an instructional "accounting system," focused on growth that would generate an instructional balance sheet for managing successful schools. There is no such balance sheet today. This balance sheet could describe two dimensions, the present status (where the students are now) and patterns of growth (how much they have grown to reach this point). Currently used assessment reports, as a rule, cover only the students' present status.

An information system envisioned for the future describing both the present status and student growth might include additional sources of data such as standardized portfolio assessments[6] and structured teacher ratings of students' knowledge and skills. Keyed to performance standards, these teacher observations or ratings would be entered into the system (say) quarterly.

Current standardized achievement testing results could contribute better within a school's information system if the tests were administered in connection with classes or courses so that they would count in the students' grades. Grades are the chief motivators of student effort. It is difficult to use the results of "no stakes" testing where the motivational level of the test-takers is uncertain at best.

These current standardized achievement tests have scaled scores which are sophisticated statistics making possible the reporting of growth over time. These scores could play an important role in a well-designed school information system that was focused on growth.

From this instructional information system, it would become possible to describe schools in growth terms. A report, for example, could describe the school in each curricular area in terms of:

- the percentage of students showing exceptional growth
- the percentage of students showing targeted growth (based on test norms)

- the percentage of students showing less than targeted growth
- the percentage of students with poor growth patterns

This same system would also produce group data that could be associated with teachers and instructional approaches. Teacher data would best be used only for confidential feedback within the internal management plan. Occasionally teachers could be publicly recognized and rewarded if their students consistently showed exceptional growth. Most teachers would see themselves as successful if their students consistently attained the targeted pattern of growth. Criteria would evolve for describing the "growth school" in which a designated percentage of the students attained the targeted growth level or better.

For Catholic schools, such an information system would be valuable for the internal management of the school and for external uses as well. Very quickly, the schools' various publics would become accustomed to and dependent on this instructional balance sheet. Without such an instructional balance sheet, educational management remains a matter of playing the game without a scoreboard.

INFORMATION FOR THE RELIGIOUS COMMUNITY

Since 1977, when the National Catholic Educational Association (NCEA) launched a program for the assessment of religious education outcomes covering faith knowledge, attitudes, and practices, a number of Catholic school leaders have generated information relating to the religious community dimension of the school. The use of this kind of assessment, however, has been less than universal. At present, there are two such programs. The NCEA program, developed prior to the publication of the *Catechism of the Catholic Church,* offers only group results for program evaluation. A newer program, based on the *Catechism,* offered by the Catechetical Assessment Program, Inc (CAP), provides both group and individual faith knowledge results for both program evaluation and individual recognition purposes. Both of these programs assess students at three grade levels. The newer program, however, has introduced scaled scores in both faith knowledge and Catholic values that make possible for the first time comparisons across the three levels as shown below. This CAP program also includes catechists on the same (1–100) scale, with a score of 100 representing an expert catechist. A new national program being developed by the archdiocese of

Indianapolis will offer in 1999 a scaled four-level student assessment program developed in conjunction with a *Catechism*-based course of study.

PATTERNS IN FAITH KNOWLEDGE
AND CATHOLIC VALUES

The introduction of scaling across levels, with one of the levels including catechists, has provided new information on the landscape of Catholic education. An earlier study[7] had collected information describing Catholic adults who were nominated by their pastors as representing the desired outcomes of Catholic catechesis. These nominated Catholics were indeed outstanding in comparison to more typical active Catholics. This same study looked at catechists and found they were virtually identical to the nominated Catholics. It was apparent that catechists come from the ranks of the more committed Catholics. This finding about catechists also shows up clearly in the values data presented below.

Table 1 and table 2 (see Appendix to this chapter) present the patterns in faith knowledge and Catholic values across the four levels based on the CAP 1995–96 results from some 10,000 persons across twenty dioceses. This population, while not biased in any identifiable way, was a self-selected as opposed to a random national sample. Faith knowledge is reported on the 1 to 100 scale mentioned above. Catholic values are reported in terms of group average scores on a scale of 1 (low) to 5 (high) in which 3.0 would represent a completely neutral or undecided response. The Catholic values composite score was generated from the aggregate of the nine specific scales, which covered such dimensions as Catholic identity, valuing Eucharist, social concern, discipleship, etc. The individual reliability of both the knowledge and value scores reported here was approximately .90.

The information presented in these two tables points out the following:

1. Catholic school students consistently score better to a significant degree on faith knowledge than do parish program students. The distribution in the scores of these groups does, however, overlap. The earlier study showed this overlap to persist even with controls for students moving from one program to the other. *Both Catholic schools and parish programs show instructional success, each in their own way.* Other data, not presented in these tables, has shown that students who participate in either program for several years show higher average scores than do students who recently entered the program. Students completing these assessments were asked how long they were in their present program.

2. *Catholic school leaders should pay more attention to the values dimension when making their case for support from the Catholic community.* The differences favoring Catholic schooling are dramatic in the realm of Catholic values as shown in table 2. Students in parish programs at grades 10–12 represent an elite group who have stayed with the program well after the more typical students have stopped coming. This makes the contrast in the values picture at this level even more dramatic. Close to twice as many Catholic school students (25%) have very high Catholic values in comparison to the parish program students (13%.) Most (60%) of these older parish program students, despite their faithfulness to the program, were below the 3.5 point on the values scale. From grade 5 to grades 10–12, the percentage of Catholic school students with high values dropped from 89 percent to 65 percent, a drop of 26 percent. The parish program students over the same interval showed a comparable drop of 46 percent.

3. *Catholic schools and parish programs serve both a growth and maintenance function in faith knowledge.* The rate of growth across levels is not dramatic in comparison to the difference between (say) the average beginning (uncertified) catechist and the average certified catechist. In many ways, the curriculum for Catholic high schools addresses more specialized areas such as social issues and marriage and the family with less emphasis on the basic catechetical message. This could explain the absence of growth in faith from grade 8–9 to grade 11–12 as shown in table 1.

4. *Catechists do indeed represent the elite of the Catholic world especially on the values dimensions.* Virtually all catechists showed up as "High" on the Catholic values scale, with most also showing up as "Very High." In terms of their faith knowledge results, average scores across the different categories of catechists from "novice" to parish directors appear close to likely expectations. Individual results for catechists even in the middle two-thirds of the group overlap other categories. Novice catechists, for example, often score as high as certified catechists and sometimes as well as some directors.

5. *Student results from school and parish programs and student and catechist results overlap.* Table 1 reports the range of scores for the middle group or the middle 66 percent in each group of students and

catechists. At each grade level, some students in the middle group of parish program students scored above the average for the comparable Catholic school group. Also, some Catholic school students at grades 10–12 scored above the average of beginning catechists and within the middle two-thirds of the certified catechists.

The religious community or catechetical dimension of the Catholic school, as well as the parish catechetical programs, are likely to be well served by these present and planned assessment offerings to which they have access. Nonetheless, the information age offers even more possibilities.

Better Information to Serve the Religious Community

Today's scaled paper-and-pencil assessments of faith knowledge create the raw material for computer-based assessments that will enable accurate reports to be generated with fewer questions. These computer-based assessments also would enable individuals to obtain personal feedback on their Catholic values, which is not possible from paper-and-pencil assessments for reasons of confidentiality. Expanded uses of computer-based assessments will lead to assessments being offered for a number of purposes on the Internet. Persons interested in serving as catechists, for example, could, via the Internet, check on their readiness and identify their strengths and weaknesses, all within the privacy of their own homes. Parents could monitor their own and their children's development in faith knowledge by asking them to complete an Internet quiz, in which they themselves would also complete.

New methods for scoring portfolio assessments could be applied with the introduction of well-designed portfolio assessments in catechesis. These would add an entirely new and rich dimension to the assessment of faith knowledge and development. These assessments could be completed online, thereby gaining access to online scorers in a national network. This would allow individuals to gain valuable feedback on their work from more expert catechists than might be available within their own school or parish.

Today's information age and expanded assessment opportunities can offer new information and insights to foster growth in the understanding and practice of the Catholic faith. The technology is ready and at hand; it needs only to be exploited by interested catechetical leaders.

Table 1. Faith Knowledge Scaled Percent of Mastery (1–100) by Students in Catholic Schools and Catechist Groups

	Grade 5/6		Grade 8/9		Grade 10/12		Catechists		
	School	Parish	School	Parish	School	Parish	Novice	Certified	Directors
Number	3,151	1,263	2,745	1,519	853	1,366	780	604	78
Mean or average	55%	45%	57%	46%	57%	48%	71%	75%	84%
Range: middle 66%	43–66%	31–58%	45–70%	31–61%	45–72%	32–64%	59–83%	65–86%	72–97%

Source: CAP 1995–96 results

Table 2. Percent of Students in Catholic Schools and Catechists Scoring High or Very High on Composite Catholic Values Scale (Scale: 5 high to 1 low)

| Program | Grade 5/6 | | Grade 8/9 | | Grade 10/12 | | Catechists |
	School	Parish	School	Parish	School	Parish	All Levels
Number	3,085	1,263	3,415	1,469	1,560	1,279	1,815
Very high (over 4.0)	51%	29%	37%	26%	25%	13%	80%
High (over 3.5)	89%	74%	79%	64%	65%	40%	98%

Source: CAP 1995–96 results

NOTES

1. Edward H. Litchfield, "Notes on a General Theory of Administration," *Administrative Science Quarterly* 1, no. 1 (June 1956), 3–29.

2. John Pollard, "The Meaning of 'Catholic Education,'" *Momentum*, 26, no. 3 (August–September 1995), pp. 10–12.

3. See <www.jdpower.com>

4. Lynn Olson, "A Question of Value," *Education Week* (May 13, 1998), p. 27ff.

5. Edwin J. McDermott, *Distinctive Qualities of the Catholic School* (Washington, D.C: National Catholic Educational Association, 1997).

6. Mark Rekase, "Overview of the ACT Portfolio Assessment System," Paper presented at the 1996 Annual Meeting of the National Council of Measurement in Education, New York, New York.

7. George Elford, "Toward Shaping the Agenda" (Washington, D.C.: Educational Testing Service, 1994).

8 The Religious Education Curriculum in Catholic Schools

Catherine Dooley, O.P.

The story is told that in 1954 when Sister Maria de la Cruz Aymes Coucke, S.H., a supervisor in the Religious Education Office in San Francisco, visited the various parishes and noted the poor quality of the religious education materials available, she said to herself, "I can do better than that!" And she did.[1] In 1958, Benziger Publishers approached two Chicago parish priests, Fathers James Killgallon and Gerard Weber, about writing a seventh-grade textbook to replace the one currently in use in the archdiocese of Chicago and in many other areas as well. The two priests, who had coauthored a popular adult catechism, *Life in Christ,* decided that they would not only do the seventh-grade book but a whole series of textbooks as well. The work of these three people and their collaborators was a turning point in the development of religion curriculum in the United States.

The purpose of this chapter is to look at the role of the religion curriculum in the Catholic character of Catholic schools. The first section will survey the shifts in emphasis in religious education in the United States from the Second Vatican Council (1962–65) to the present.[2] The religion curriculum published by W. H. Sadlier and Benziger, two companies with a long, distinguished tradition of publishing religious education materials, will be used to illustrate the way the major developments took concrete form in text materials. Part two will consider the implications of these developments with regard to the Catholic character of Catholic schools.

PRE–VATICAN II DEVELOPMENTS

The *On Our Way* series developed by Sister Maria de la Cruz and published by W. H. Sadlier in 1956 "became the prototype of today's religion texts in Catholic Schools."[3] It moved beyond a single text of questions and answers, children and classroom, to a complete program, which included pedagogical and theological background for catechists, notes for parents, music, detailed lesson plans for teachers, and children's workbooks. It was the first religion series to be based on the kerygmatic approach. Although the kerygmatic movement was initiated in 1936 by the publication of Josef Jungmann's *Die Frohbotschaft und Unsere Glaubensverkundigung* (translated into English in 1961 as *The Good News and Our Proclamation of Faith)*,[4] it was not until the 1950s, primarily through the efforts of Johannes Hofinger, a student of Jungmann, that the movement took hold in the North American countries.

Jungmann, professor of theology at the University of Innsbruck, inspired by the dynamism of the preaching in the early Christian Church, advocated reclaiming the *kerygma,* the "good news" of Jesus Christ, as the content of catechesis. The kerygmatic renewal called for a cohesive and unified presentation of the Christian faith by an integration of the sources or "four signs" of revelation: liturgy, scripture, Church teachings, and the witness of Christian living. Jungmann affirmed developments in methodology such as the "Munich Method"[5] but believed that a change in method alone would not bring about renewal. He advocated a return to the essential elements of the Christian message, the proclamation of the good news of salvation in Jesus Christ, which calls for a lived faith response. "The child must be taught to put into practice what he learns, so that he may be a 'doer' of the word and not merely a 'hearer.'"[6]

These graded texts, beautifully illustrated in four colors, were adapted to the abilities of the learner and contained prayer and "paraliturgies," various activities, songs, and stories that connected with the children's lives. The underlying premise was that the child learns more easily and more quickly by active involvement. The content of the texts reflected a spiral approach to learning; that is, each year had a particular doctrinal focus, but other elements of the message were not only reviewed but presented from another perspective. The revised *Baltimore*

Catechism was used, but the questions and answers were memorized only after the children understood the content. The teacher guides, written primarily for the volunteer teachers who had little training, were soon used in parochial school classrooms as well. The child's text contained parent pages which suggested ways in which the parent might help the child understand the lessons but also explained the background of the lesson to the parent. Parent involvement was a major innovation.

In the fall of 1958, Benziger began the preliminary discussion of a new series with the principal authors: James Killgallon, Gerard Weber, and Sister Mary Michael O'Shaugnessy, O.P. *Word and Worship*, published in 1963, was written while the Second Vatican Council was in session and was one of the first texts to put forth the conciliar teachings on the nature of the Church in the modern world. The series incorporated some aspects of the kerygmatic approach but constructed the curriculum around the needs and developmental stages of the students, the insights of recent biblical scholarship, doctrine, and Catholic social teaching.[7] The solid theological background material in the manuals, particularly the biblical notes, was a primary means of updating for teachers and for parents.

Both *On Our Way* and *Word and Worship*, written before or during the Second Vatican Council, had widespread influence. The series focused on the learner as well as the text, on catechist/teacher formation, on the need for what was taught at school to be reinforced in the home, and emphasized Christian witness.

Vatican II Developments

The 1965 Vatican document, The Pastoral Office of Bishops in the Church (*Christus Dominus*), offers a foundational description of catechesis (no. 14): Catechesis is to develop in believers a living, explicit, and active faith enlightened by instruction.[8] Catechesis is an integrated process based on scripture, tradition, liturgy, and the teaching authority and life of the Church and is imparted not only to children and adolescents but also to young people and even adults. The direction to include all ages, especially adults, in catechesis is immensely significant and represents a radical shift from an exclusive focus on children. In this same document, the council also mandated that bishops should take steps to reestablish the adult catechumenate (no. 14) and to compile a special directory containing the fundamental principles for the catechetical instruction of the Christian people (no. 44). This paragraph remains a milestone in the development of the catechetical movement.

The Dogmatic Constitution on Divine Revelation, *Dei Verbum,* described catechesis as ministry of the word (no. 24). This description moved catechesis from the context of instruction to the context of an ecclesial ministry of the word and is therefore the responsibility of the whole community.

This ecclesial view of catechesis is supported by other documents such as The Declaration on Christian Education, *Gravissimum Educationis* (1965) [*GE*], which also marks a shift in the perception of the Catholic school, that is, from the school as institution to the school as community. "Every one directly involved in the school is a part of the school community. . . . Parents are central figures . . . and the community also includes the students, since they must be active agents in their own education" (no. 15). *Ad Gentes* (1965) elucidates the Church's missionary activity and responsibility, stressing the importance of the formation of community in this endeavor (no. 33). The Dogmatic Constitution on the Church, *Lumen Gentium* (1964), defines the Church primarily in terms of the people of God and asserts that the laity have the vocation of building up the Church because they are at once the witness and the living instrument of the mission of the Church itself (no. 33).

Cumulatively, these few sentences found in the Vatican II documents with regard to catechesis affirm that catechesis as a ministry of the word is a formative process that takes place in and through the Christian community. Catechetical instruction is given with a view to initiation into the fullness of Christian life. Catechesis, directed to all peoples and all cultures, impels Christians to service and forms Christians responsible to a world community. These are the themes that will be expanded and explored in future catechetical and pastoral documents.

POST–VATICAN II

Religion programs after the council attempted to incorporate the insights of Vatican II, the changes in the liturgy, the new understandings in scripture, and a response to social issues permeating society. It is a truism to say that the 1960s were a time of unparalleled change. The reality of dissent and diversity was seen in the civil rights movement, the war in Vietnam, a Catholic president, and various political movements. The creativity and enthusiasm that followed the Second Vatican Council quickly turned to discontent and dissatisfaction. The mass in the vernacular, the revision of the rubrics, the increased participation of the laity, mitigation of fasting and abstinence laws, ecumenical dialogue and openness to religious pluralism, questioning of traditional teaching and values were obvious signs of a Church in transition and of issues yet to be resolved. Religious education/catechesis, which implemented many of the liturgical changes and reflected current thinking in biblical studies and Vatican II theology, became the focal point of the backlash. "Crisis" and "polarization" were words frequently used to describe the reaction to the "new catechetics."[9]

Catechetical Directories

The *General Catechetical Directory* (*GCD*)[10] mandated by the Second Vatican Council and published in 1971 by the Congregation for the Clergy warned that the renewal was entering "a period of crisis." It listed a number of concerns including the inability of many people "to understand the depth of the proposed renewal as though the issue here were merely one of eliminating ignorance of the doctrine which must be taught" (no. 9). In this viewpoint, the remedy would be more frequent catechetical instruction. On the other hand, the crisis was being fanned by those who reduced the gospel message to their own efforts in promoting justice and reconciliation. The *GCD* brought balance to the situation by noting that renewal in the ministry of the word, particularly in catechesis, can in no way be separate from a general pastoral renewal. The task of catechetical renewal is the responsibility of the entire Christian community.

Under the broad umbrella of ministry of the word, the *GCD* includes evangelization, catechesis, liturgy, and theology. These elements can be differentiated because each has its own nature and purpose, but in the concrete pastoral situation they are interconnected. The purpose of evangelization is to awaken initial faith; catechesis enables faith to become living, active, and conscious through the light of instruction; liturgy celebrates, proclaims, and hands on the same faith; and theology serves catechesis by the systematic treatment and the scientific investigation of the truths of faith (no. 17). The purpose of the ministry of the word is to proclaim God's saving actions in history that were fulfilled in Christ but at the same time, in the light of God's self-revelation, "interprets human life in our age, the signs of the times and the things of this world, for the plan of God works in these for the salvation of humankind" (no. 11).

The *GCD* affirmed the insights of the modern catechetical movement, outlined the content and the methods appropriate for catechesis, and provided a blueprint for national directories such as *Sharing the Light of Faith* (*SLF*), the national catechetical directory for the United States published in 1979.

The first religion program to be produced after the publication of the *GCD* was Benziger's *The Word Is Life* (1971–73, revised in 1977–78). The books were solidly doctrinal and integrated the doctrine with insights from the behavioral sciences. The texts were built around three key characteristics of the life process: dimensions of individuation, belongingness, and availability. The authors believed that the gospel is concerned with essentially these same human dimensions but evokes a deeper meaning. The doctrinal outline for the texts was taken from the *General Catechetical Directory* (no. 43). The books were unique among religion texts in their use of stories, not only from scripture and the lives of the saints, but from talking animals, fairy tales, and other children's stories.

TO TEACH AS JESUS DID

In 1973, the U.S. Catholic bishops published two documents that had relevance for religious education/catechesis. The first was *To Teach as Jesus Did* (*TTJD*), a pastoral message on Catholic education. The document was a development of a statement issued in 1967 on the importance of Catholic schools in which the National Conference of Catholic Bishops (NCCB) stated their intention of applying the perspectives of the Vatican II Declaration on Christian Education (*Gravissimum Educationis*) to the situation in the United States. *TTJD* was the result of a long and extensive process of consultation and collaboration.[11] It was both a prophetic document and a practical one that gave hope and encouragement to fairly demoralized Catholic educators facing the crisis of lack of staff and finances to maintain Catholic schools.[12] The document identified education as part of the Church's mission, discussed the various agencies that were identified with this mission, and set out a plan for action. *TTJD* stated that the educational mission of the Church is an integrated ministry with three interlocking dimensions: message, community, and service. Doctrine was presented as not merely a matter for the intellect but as the basis for a way of life (no. 20). "Community is at the heart of Christian education not simply as a concept to be taught but as a reality to be lived" (no. 23). The experience of Christian community impels to service. The concepts of community and service as aspects of the meaning of Catholic educational ministry in *TTJD* was a major contribution to the developing understanding of catechesis and a framework which gave a new identity to Catholic schools.[13]

BASIC TEACHINGS FOR CATHOLIC RELIGIOUS EDUCATION

The second document published by the U.S. bishops in 1973 was *Basic Teachings for Catholic Religious Education* (*BT*) which aimed to set down the principal elements of the Christian message that are to be stressed in the religious formation of Catholics of all ages and in every type of religious education.[14] *BT* was an interim document, read in the light of the *General Catechetical Directory* and later subsumed into the National Directory which was then in process. It was an effort to address the polarization taking place throughout the country and provided the framework for the doctrinal content of all the textbooks being developed during the late 1970s.[15]

W. H. Sadlier published *The Lord of Life* (1976–78) series which was organized around *To Teach as Jesus Did*. "Each book in the *Lord of Life* Program is concerned with the threefold ministry of the Church: to form community, to proclaim the message of Christ, to carry out the role of service to the Church and to the whole human community." The foreword stated that "the content of the program is in accord with the *National Catechetical Directory*, the *General Catechetical Directory*, the pastoral letter *To Teach as Jesus Did*, and the directive from the Synod on Catechesis for Children and Youth, Rome, 1977."[16] The catechetical process was a "life-centered approach" consisting of three movements: life experience, faith development, and faith response. The "life-centered approach" in all text materials was/is a continuing area of concern on the part of those who fear that revelation is reduced to human experience, that teachers use activities that consume class time but do not deepen faith, or that teachers fail to make the link between faith and experience. The end of the 1970s was again a time of dissatisfaction with many elements in Church and society, and again a lens was focused on the religion materials.

CATECHESIS IN OUR TIME (1979)

The religion programs of the 1980s attempted once again to address the "lack of content" criticism, and gave more attention to teacher formation, to deeper integration of the four tasks of catechesis, and to a renewed concern for methodology or models for catechesis. The materials of this decade were particularly influenced by the publication of the Apostolic Exhortation of Pope John Paul II in 1979, *Catechesis Tradendae* (*CT*), which affirmed the work of the 1977 synod of bishops on "Catechesis in Our Times" and discussed the nature and needs of catechesis. John Paul II describes catechesis as an activity of the whole Church that has many dimensions. It is formation, education, initiation, and instruction. The primary object of catechesis is the "mystery of Christ," and the pope exhorts all catechists to transmit by their instruction and behavior the teaching and life of Jesus. This teaching is not a body of abstract truths but the "communication of the living mystery of God" (no. 7). Catechesis is intimately bound up with the whole of the Church's life and is the shared but differentiated responsibility of the entire community.

Catechesis Tradendae affirmed the direction taking place in the catechetical renewal. With regard to the controversy concerning the role of experience in catechesis, Pope John Paul II noted that it is useless to play off orthopraxis against orthodoxy; Christianity is inseparably both. Opposition can not be set up between a catechesis taking life as its point of departure and a traditional, doctrinal, and systematic catechesis (no. 22). He reaffirmed the relationship of liturgy, catechesis, and justice. That the Church's social teaching should find a place in catechesis echoed the 1971 document of the synod of bishops, *Justice in the World*, which stated that justice was a constitutive element of preaching the gospel.

CT outlines several criteria which apply to the development of curricula but can also be applied to the life of the school:

1. Catechetical texts must be linked to the real life of the generation to which they are addressed, showing understanding of the anxieties and questions, struggles and hopes of that generation.
2. Texts must be written in a language comprehensible to the generation in question.
3. They must present the whole message of Christ and the Church, avoiding distortion and highlighting what is essential.
4. Texts must aim to give to those who use them a better knowledge of the mysteries of Christ, for the purpose of fostering true conversion and a life more in conformity with God's will (no. 49).

CT is a remarkable document that not only synthesizes postconciliar deliberations but gives direction to the ministry of catechesis.

SHARING THE LIGHT OF FAITH (1979)

The National Catechetical Directory, *Sharing the Light of Faith,* in general follows the same outline as the *GCD* but addresses the catechetical needs of the Church in the United States in concrete terms. Some outstanding characteristics that made the document unique and appropriate for the American Church are the role of the ecclesial community in catechesis ("all members of the community of believers are called to share in this ministry" [no. 204]), emphasis on social justice as a constitutive element in catechesis, adult catechesis as normative, the ecumenical dimension of catechesis, and the delineation of the four tasks of catechesis—to proclaim Christ's message, to participate in efforts to foster and sustain the Christian community; to lead people to worship and prayer, and to motivate them to serve others.[17] These characteristics, reflective of preceding developments, became the criteria for the development of catechetical programs.

RELIGION TEXTS OF THE 1980S

W. H. Sadlier published a series in the early 1980s called *God With Us,* which was then revised in 1988 as *Coming to Faith.* The approach underlying the series was shared Christian praxis,[18] which involves "enabling people to live humanly and freely by interpreting and living their lives through the paschal event of Christ in history."[19] The method was adapted for use in the Sadlier program, and the lesson plans used five movements: looking at one's own experience in relation to the theme of the lesson; understanding the meaning and implications of the experience, presenting tradition and teachings of the Church which speak to that experience, seeing what this faith of the community means in one's life, and, lastly, making a decision to live that faith.

The content of the 1988 revision responded to the criticisms of the time. The scope and sequence remained basically the same, but the language and terminology were more explicitly reflective of the Catholic tradition. Although the praxis format was retained, the focus was less on the life of the student and more on the elements to be taught. Biblical material was given pride of place and strong emphasis was placed on the Church's social teachings.

Benziger published *In Christ Jesus* (1981–82) in a Catholic School edition and one for parish religious education programs. The program components included graded activity books, teacher resource books, testing programs, family handbooks, music programs, catechist enrichment books, Hispanic resource books, posters, and recommended media. The program took direction from *Catechesis in Our Time* and the catechetical directories. The series was revised in 1986 and the introduction clearly stated that this was a Catholic program that presents at each grade level the "complete content of Catholic teaching in the amount and language suitable to the age."[20] The focus was placed on fostering Catholic identity. It is obvious that the series was responding to the wave of current criticism on the textbooks, but in the presentation of the content the authors continued to keep the age-appropriate criteria. Many traditional devotions such as the Rosary and the Way of the Cross were included and special attention was given to the lives of the saints and the liturgical year. Definitions, chapter questions, and reviews were other elements found in the lessons. The four signs of catechesis were woven throughout the various levels in order to communicate to young people the religious knowledge, attitudes, and behavior proper to their age. The teacher manuals offered practical material on classroom management as well as theological formation.

GUIDELINES FOR DOCTRINALLY SOUND
CATECHETICAL MATERIALS (1990)

The bishops of the United States, while affirming the catechetical renewal initiated by Vatican II, again responded to the dissatisfaction of some in the Catholic community by publishing *Guidelines for Doctrinally Sound Catechetical Materials* (1990).[21] In view of the quantity and diversity of the materials available, the bishops drew up criteria for the selection of suitable materials for catechesis. They offered two basic principles of doctrinal soundness: materials are to present the Christian message authentically and completely in a balanced awareness of the interrelatedness of the parts of the Christian message; secondly, the mystery of faith is incarnate and dynamic, and the content of all catechetical materials should be informed by biblical, ecclesial, liturgical, and natural signs outlined in the *National Catechetical Directory.*

CATECHISM OF THE CATHOLIC CHURCH

The long-awaited publication of the *Catechism of the Catholic Church* (*CCC*) in 1992 was a major event in the history of catechesis. The text is written in narrative form and has four main parts or "pillars": the Apostles' Creed (faith professed); the sacraments (faith celebrated); virtues, beatitudes, and commandments (faith lived); and prayer, particularly the Lord's Prayer. Although this content follows the traditional pattern, it is written to respond to the questions of the present time.[22] This organization of the content aims to show the organic unity of God's mystery and of God's saving plan, and the centrality of Christ's presence in the Church, particularly in the sacraments. This organic unity requires that the catechism be read as a whole.

The *Catechism of the Catholic Church* serves several important functions:

1. It is an organic synthesis of the foundations and essential content of Catholic doctrine of faith and morals in the light of the Second Vatican Council and the whole of the church's tradition.
2. It is a point of reference for catechisms or *compendia* to be composed in various countries.
3. It is a positive, objective, and declarative exposition of Catholic doctrine.

4. It is intended to assist those who have the duty to catechize, namely Bishops and their collaborators.[23]

In part two, on the liturgy, the *Catechism* notes that the liturgy is the privileged place for catechizing the people of God (*CCC*, no. 1074) and speaks about the importance of liturgical catechesis. This emphasis on liturgical catechesis reinforces the themes found in the *Rite of Christian Initiation of Adults* (1974, 1988). The *Catechism* states that

> Liturgical catechesis aims to initiate people into the mystery of Christ (It is "mystagogy.") by proceeding from the visible to the invisible, from the sign to the thing signified, from the "sacraments" to the "mysteries."[24]

Liturgical catechesis is an integrated process, rooted in rites, symbols, and biblical and liturgical signs in the context of the community within the framework of the liturgical year. The purpose is to lead communities and individual members of the faithful to maturity of faith through full and active participation in the liturgy, which affects and expresses that faith and elicits a conscious living out of a life of justice. Liturgical catechesis aims to uncover the meaning of the words and actions so that catechumens and believers may gradually realize that when they participate in the sacramental actions they are actually participating in the saving action of Christ which the sacrament signifies.

The *Catechism of the Catholic Church* is a primary source for publishers in determining the content of text materials. In 1994, the United States bishops appointed an ad hoc committee to oversee the use of the *Catechism*. Three of the objectives of the Office of the Catechism are pertinent for the question of development of text materials. The office has the responsibility to supervise the use of the copyright for the *CCC* on behalf of the Holy See, which includes reviewing manuscripts quoting the *Catechism* to determine their consistency with it and to withhold or grant copyright permission based on that review. Second, the office has the responsibility to review catechetical materials voluntarily submitted to the ad hoc committee as to their conformity with the *CCC*. Third, the office is to study the feasibility of a national catechism/catechetical series based on the *CCC*. The reviews of this office are available to the bishops of the United States, who are free to determine the texts which will be used within their own diocesan schools and parishes.

The most recent document of importance in catechesis is the *General Directory for Catechesis* (*GDC*) (1997), which is a revision of the 1971 directory. The 1997 directory seeks to balance two constitutive elements. The first is the contextualization of catechesis as a "remarkable moment" within the process of evangelization (*CT*, no. 18; *GDC*, no. 5). The second element is the appropriation of the content of the faith as presented in the *Catechism of the Catholic Church* (*GDC*, no. 7). Evangelization is understood as a whole process whereby individual and social life is transformed in the light of the gospel. Evangelization includes three phases: missionary activity directed toward nonbelievers and those indifferent to the Gospel, proclamation to those who are unchurched and alienated, initial evangelization of the catechumen and continuing evangelization of individuals and communities who strive for an ever deeper conversion to life in Christ (*GDC*, nos. 49, 58). Catechesis, as an essential moment in evangelization, receives from evangelization a missionary dynamic. In this context, catechesis is described as "a fundamental ecclesial service for the realization of the church's missionary mandate of Jesus" (*GDC*, no. 59).

Catechetical Curriculum of the 1990s

Benziger's *Come Follow Me* (1991–92, revised in 1996–97) was the first program to reflect the direction and emphasis of the *Catechism of the Catholic Church.* The series combines developmental and thematic approaches, all based on the proclamation of the kingdom of God. Each of the grades deals with the idea of the kingdom but from a different perspective and in accord with the developmental level of the students. Activities, practices, and prayers foster Catholic identity. The format of the texts also changed in many ways. Points to remember or to memorize were emphasized. Additional material was put in sidebars. Many planning helps and resources are included for teacher formation. Family magazines with Spanish versions are ways of involving and instructing parents to share in the child's formation.

W. H. Sadlier published a new edition of *Coming to Faith* (1995–96), which "promotes a continuing commitment to religious literacy and the religious imagination of children in their Catholic faith practice."[25] The texts are correlated with the *Catechism of the Catholic Church* and teachers/catechists are urged to use the *Catechism* as a resource. Reference to the pertinent *Catechism* paragraphs are included for each lesson. A particular emphasis is placed on fostering the spirituality of the students. The content follows the general scope and sequence of the *Catechism* and is correlated with the elements listed in the protocol of the Office of the Catechism.

Through the directives of the catechetical directories *Catechesis Tradendae, Catechism of the Catholic Church* and the guidelines offered by the United States Bishops Conference, the Catholic community in the United States in the 1990s has come to what Bernard Marthaler has termed, "Curriculum by Consensus."[26] Curriculum in Catholic schools and parish religious education programs is based on the catechism tradition of creed, sacraments, commandments, and prayer. It embodies sound pedagogical principles and is consonant with the age and abilities of the learners. The tasks of catechesis outlined in the directories are aspects woven through the series. In the standard scope and sequence of religion texts, grade one generally gives an overview of God's saving history in creation, Jesus, sending of the Spirit, Church and expectation of the coming of the kingdom. Textbooks for grade two make the celebration of the sacraments of reconciliation and Eucharist the main focus. Third-grade texts center on the Apostles' Creed and often review the content of grades one and two. Grade four considers the commandments, formation of conscience, sin, and the role of the Holy Spirit in Christian life. Grade five studies sacraments, and the entire grade six is in general devoted to a study of scripture. The seventh grade is given over to the person and teaching of Jesus, and grade eight is often a recapitulation of doctrine, sacraments, and moral principles. Some publishers offer modules for seventh and eighth grade that focus on morality, scripture, sacraments, social teachings. All publishers have analyzed their materials in terms of faithfulness to the guidelines and documents provided as directives in the publication of catechetical materials.[27]

CONTRIBUTION TO THE CATHOLIC CHARACTER OF CATHOLIC SCHOOLS

What can be learned from this historical survey that might give insight into the contribution of the religion curriculum to the Catholic character of Catholic schools?

The historical overview indicates that there is both a consistency and a continuity in the development of catechetical programs. The catechism was the basis for graded textbooks, which used the catechism order of creed, sacraments, commandments, and prayer as the organizing format of the content. The catechisms developed into programs that encompassed more than children, classrooms, and instruction. Religion programs in turn fostered the transition from the school as an institution to the school as community (*GE*, no. 6). Parents have long been recognized as the primary educators of their children, and the religion programs encouraged a strong partnership between the school, the family, and the parish. The document on "The Religious Dimension of Education in a Catholic School" (RDE)[28] states that everyone connected with the school belongs to the school community, "including students since they must be active agents in their own education" (RDE, no. 31). The strong focus on community in the religion programs gives insight into the nature of the Church as developed by the second Vatican Council.

Vatican II articulated a renewed understanding of ecclesiology, liturgy, social justice, evangelization, and ecumenical relationships. This renewal took place as part of a larger movement of change within society. The world of the Catholic ethos in which the catechism was supported and reinforced by the interrelationship between parish, family, and school in shaping religious identity was no longer a given. In its place was a new world of competing socializations. The challenge following Vatican II was to incorporate into the religion programs a new critical synthesis of faith and culture that did not subordinate faith to culture and yet did not isolate one from the other. Catholic schools perform a specific pastoral function as a mediator between faith and culture (RDE, no. 31). Schools not only bring faith, culture, and life into harmony, but students are also encouraged to develop a critical sense that enables them to "recognize and reject cultural counter-values which threaten human dignity" (RDE, no. 52). In the process of catechesis the message of the Good News of salvation

> is probed unceasingly by reflection and systematic study, by awareness of its repercussions on one's personal life—an awareness calling for ever greater commitment—and by inserting it into an organic and harmonious whole; namely, Christian living in society and the world. (*CT*, no. 26)

Organic unity, coherence, harmony, entirety, and synthesis are words that are used over and over again in the catechetical documents of the last thirty years and indicate that this faith which is believed, celebrated, lived, and prayed is to be seen as one, all of a piece. Students "have the right to learn with truth and certainty the religion to which they belong" (*GDC*, no. 74). The contribution of the religion programs is that the instruction given in the context of the Catholic school is part of and completed by other forms of the ministry of the word (*GDC*, no. 74).

In constructing the curriculum around the age, ability, and developmental level of the children, Catholic schools integrate religious formation and human development. For those who believe in Christ, human and Christian perfection are "two facets of a single reality" (RDE, no. 34).

The historical overview also indicates that the construction of a religion curriculum conscientiously follows the doctrinal guidelines offered by Roman documents and the guidelines of the National Conference of Catholic Bishops. The religion texts are a major way in which the official Church documents are communicated to and implemented in the Catholic community. Publishers follow these directives in order to safeguard the integrity of the Catholic faith and to communicate it effectively by a comprehensive curriculum, an age-appropriate scope and sequence, textbooks, and catechist guides.

The "background for the teacher" in teacher manuals has been a major source of catechist/teacher formation, and now the *Catechism of the Catholic Church* is an authentic reference text for teachers. *The General Directory for Catechesis,* however, recognizes that the formation of catechists/teachers (*GDC,* nos. 234–245) is imperative. The *GDC,* moreover, places teacher formation within the context of the whole community. It reaffirms the words of Pope John Paul II that catechesis is intimately bound up with the whole of the Church's life and is the shared but differentiated responsibility of the entire community.

Religious education/catechesis since the Second Vatican Council has been like a tapestry with certain strands of thread becoming brighter as the pattern emerges. Evangelization is the mesh that underlies the entire weave. Catholic schools are a place of evangelization by their very nature, that is, their work of educating the Christian person (RDE, no. 33). The *GDC* offers a direction for the future in terms of an evangelizing catechesis, which has certain characteristics:

1. Evangelization is not possible without the action of the Holy Spirit (*EN,* no. 75).
2. Evangelization is the work of the whole Church. The first means of evangelization is the witness of an authentically Christian life (*EN,* no. 41) so that the Church may be seen as an instrument and sign of the presence of Christ in the world. Authentic Christian life flourishes in the context of a community that strives to be one in Christ. Ultimately it is the faith of the Church which evangelizes and catechizes through liturgy and ritual, through service that tends to human needs, through actions that demand justice and the transformation of social structures.
3. Catechesis must present a coherent and vital synthesis of the faith, organized around the mystery of the Most Holy Trinity, in a christocentric perspective (*GDC,* no. 114).
4. Evangelizing catechesis must take into consideration the actual situation of the people, their language, their signs and symbols, and their questions (*EN,* no. 63; *GDC,* no. 59).
5. Dialogue, both ecumenical and interfaith, is indispensable in a pluralistic religious and cultural world (*GDC,* nos. 193–201). Many students within Catholic schools are not Catholic; not all are Christians. Dialogue is an invitation to share one's faith; it is in and through systematic study and discussion that one gains the ability to articulate convictions and to have sufficient knowledge and understanding of the beliefs and practices of other religions to be able to appreciate their significance. It is in a context where there is respect for the freedom and dignity of each person that such dialogue can take place.
6. Catechesis must incorporate action on behalf of justice and implement the social teachings of the Church.
7. Evangelizing catechesis will be given life and substance by a liturgical-sacramental orientation. The baptismal catechumenate is the model for all catechesis (*GDC,* no. 59). Drawing its inspiration and principles from the catechumenate, catechesis is gradual and ongoing; takes place in and through the Christian community in the context of the liturgical year, and is solidly supported by celebrations of the word. This formation which brings together scripture, liturgy, and doctrine leads to a deeper and deeper relationship with Christ. Ultimately it leads to a change of outlook and conduct that is manifested in witness and service.

The *General Directory* marks out an agenda that is in continuity with the past, provides the fundamental principles of the Church's magisterium, particularly those inspired by the Second Vatican Council, and responds to the questions of a new era. The Catholic school has an essential part in the implementation of this agenda. The religious environment, community, and instruction in a Catholic school gives students a worldview that challenges them to contribute in a significant way to the Catholic faith community and to the larger society. This worldview enables them to have a sense of their own integrity and a deep respect for the dignity of all human persons in the pluralistic world in which they now live.

NOTES

1. Francis J. Buckley, "Woman of the Church: Sister Maria de la Cruz Aymes, S.H.," *PACE* 25 (September 1995): 3.

2. For an overview of the developments in religious education in the early part of the century, see William J. McGucken, "The Renascence of Religion Teaching in American Catholic Schools," in *Essays on Catholic Education in the United States,* ed. Roy J. Deferrari (Washington, D.C.: Catholic University of America Press, 1942), 329–51.

3. Berard L. Marthaler, "The Modern Catechetical Movement in Roman Catholicism," in *Sourcebook for Modern Catechetics,* ed. Michael Warren (Winona: St. Mary's Press, 1983), 283.

4. Josef Jungmann, *The Good News and Our Proclamation of the Faith,* trans. William A. Huesman (New York: W. H. Sadlier, 1962). For a short biography of Jungmann, see J. Hofinger, "J. A. Jungmann (1889–1975): In Memoriam," *Living Light* 13, no. 3 (Fall 1976): 350–59.

5. For a description of the Munich Method, see J. A. Jungmann, *Handing on the Faith* (New York: Herder and Herder, 1962), 174–93. The Munich Method initiated by a group of catechists in Munich in the early 1900s applied educational principles to religious education in an effort to include the child's life-experience in the instruction.

6. Sister Maria de la Cruz and Sister Mary Richard, *With Christ to the Father,* Teacher's Guide, Grade One (New York: Sadlier, 1958), 6.

7. Gerard P. Weber, "Some Recollections of and Reflections On the Writing and Editing of the Benziger Religious Education Programs: 1958–1994," (unpublished paper, 1996), has provided valuable background for material on the Benziger series.

8. The revised Code of Canon Law (1983) incorporates this definition into C. 773 but adds "the experience of Christian living" ("per doctrinae institutionem et vitae christianae experientiam") as a constitutive element of the definition.

9. Groups such as the John Birch Society, militant crusaders against communism, regarded the Church's social teachings in the text materials as subversive attempts to

introduce socialism. Other groups reacted to the inclusion of pictures and references to Martin Luther King and to the injustices and poverty suffered by minority groups in the United States. The picture of Martin Luther King with the caption, "Martin Luther King Is like Jesus" was in the third-grade text of the Benziger *Word and Worship* series. Gerard Weber recalls that when Father Killgallon spoke at a parish on Chicago's South side, he needed police protection to leave the parish hall. The authors were accused of being heretics and communists.

Charges of doctrinal deviation came from individuals but most came from highly organized national groups such as CREDO (Catholics for the Restoration of Education Doctrinal Orthodoxy), POPE (Parents for Orthodoxy in Parochial Education), and CUF (Catholics United for the Faith). Others in opposition to the textbooks were conscientious people who were concerned about the issues and the problematic changes in Church and society. They perceived that all that they had held dear and sacred in their own religious education was now trivialized or dismissed. Religious education became the focus of the controversy. See Marie Aimee Carey, "Are Religion Textbooks Teaching Heresy?" *Catholic School Journal* 30 (January 1970): 16–19.

10. Sacred Congregation of the Clergy, *General Catechetical Directory*, English translation (Washington, D.C.: Publications Office, United States Catholic Conference, 1971). For notes and commentary on the Directory, see Berard L. Marthaler, *Catechetics in Context* (Huntington, Ind.: Our Sunday Visitor Press, 1971).

11. For a description of the process, see Berard L. Marthaler, "A Pastoral on Catholic Education: The Process and the Product," *Living Light* 28, no. 2 (1992): 101–13.

12. Jay P. Dolan notes that an obvious reason for the decline of the parochial school was the declining birth rate, the questioning of the value of educating children in separate denominational schools, and the problem of finances due to hiring more lay teachers and increased salaries. Dolan states that laypeople had already begun taking up teaching positions in the 1950s but the virtual disappearance of women religious in the late 1960s–70s accelerated the trend. See Dolan's *The American Catholic Experience* (Garden City, N.Y.: Doubleday, 1985; rpt. Notre Dame: University of Notre Dame Press, 1992), 442.

13. A criticism which surfaced immediately was a lack of attention in the document to the relationship of liturgy and catechesis. The need for individual and communal prayer was a consistent theme throughout the document but worship was not listed as one of the explicit goals along with message, community, and service.

14. National Conference of Catholic Bishops, *Basic Teachings for Catholic Religious Education* (Washington, D.C.: Publications Office, United States Catholic Conference, 1973). For background to the document, see Charles C. McDonald, "The Background and Development of the *Basic Teachings* Document," *The Living Light* 11 (1973): 264–77.

15. Although the *GCD* had given strong direction to catechesis, criticism against the textbooks increased. In 1969, the U.S. bishops established and commissioned the Division of Research and Development in Religious Education at the United States Catholic Conference to develop criteria and devise an instrument for evaluating textbooks. *Evaluative Reviews of Religion Textbooks* was published in 1970 and the evaluation was completed in 1971. Many bishops felt that the evaluation would not solve the controversy because they believed many teachers no longer used textbooks. The proposed

solution was to prepare a statement of irreducible doctrinal principles that would serve as guides to publishers and religious educators. See McDonald, *Living Light* 11 (1973): 267.

16. Sr. Maria de la Cruz Aymes, S.H., and Rev. Francis J. Buckley, "Jesus Gives Joy," *The Lord of Life Program* (New York: W. H. Sadlier, 1978), 2.

17. These characteristics are taken from Mary Charles Bryce, "Sharing the Light of Faith: Catechetical Threshold for the U.S. Church," in *Sourcebook for Modern Catechetics,* ed. M. Warren (Winona: St. Mary's Press, 1983), 268–71.

18. Shared Christian praxis is an approach to Christian religious education developed by Thomas H. Groome. See his *Christian Religious Education: Sharing Our Story and Vision* (San Francisco: Harper and Row, 1980).

19. Thomas Groome, "Christian Education for Freedom: A 'Shared Praxis' Approach," in *Foundations*, ed. P. O'Hare, 10–11.

20. Gerard P. Weber, James J. Killgallon, and Michael O'Shaughnessy, *In Christ Jesus,* second edition, Grade Six Teacher's Edition, CCD (Encino: Benziger, 1986), CR 8.

21. *Guidelines for Doctrinally Sound Catechetical Materials,* in *The Catechetical Documents: A Parish Resource,* ed. Martin Connell (Chicago: Liturgical Training Publications, 1996), 575–88.

22. John Paul II, Apostolic Constitution *Fidei Depositum* (October 11, 1992), no. 2.

23. Prologue, CCC, nos. 11–12; see the summary of the "Informative Dossier," Editorial Commission of the *Catechism of the Catholic Church* (October 27, 1992) in the *Living Light* 29 (Summer, 1993): 82–84.

24. See Catherine Dooley, "Liturgical Catechesis: Mystagogy, Marriage or Misnomer?" *Worship* 66, no. 5 (September 1992): 386–97, and Catherine Dooley,"From the Visible to the Invisible: Mystagogy in the Catechism of the Catholic Church," *Living Light* 31, no. 3 (Spring 1995): 29–35.

25. *Coming to God's Word,* Grade Six, Teacher's Annotated Guide in *Coming to Faith* (New York: W. H. Sadlier, 1996), T 6.

26. Berard L. Marthaler, "Curriculum by Consensus," *Living Light* 33, no.2 (Winter 1996): 4–5.

27. For example, see the *Sadlier Sourcebook: Guidelines for Doctrinally Sound Catechetical Materials, The Catechism of the Catholic Church, Criteria for Development,* and the *New Edition of the Coming to Faith Program,* Grades K–6, directed by Dr. Gerard F. Baumbach (New York: William H. Sadlier, 1996).

28. Congregation for Catholic Education, "The Religious Dimension of Education in a Catholic School," (1988) in *The Catechetical Documents,* ed. Martin Connell (Chicago: Liturgy Training Publications, 1996).

9 The Past Before Us

THREE TRADITIONS AND
THE RECENT HISTORY
OF CATHOLIC EDUCATION

Timothy Walch

Catholic education is very much in vogue these days. Throughout the educational establishment—public as well as private—unqualified admiration is expressed for all that parish schools have accomplished in educating their students. More important, the hallmarks of contemporary parochial education—decentralization, moral purpose, small class-size, and emphasis on basic academic skills—have become popular among public school educators once again. The current national campaign for charter schools is a reflection of the implicit admiration for what has been accomplished by parish schools.

What is rarely acknowledged, however, is that the success of Catholic schools today is built upon three traditions that extend back more than two centuries. The importance of tenacity, adaptability, and community is very evident in the history of Catholic schools over the past three decades. In fact, it is not too much to say that these three traditions have been and continue to be vital elements in the character of Catholic education from colonial times to the present day and will help secure these schools in the future.

This is not to say that the history of Catholic education has followed some sort of grand plan. The beginnings of Catholic education in this country were modest to say the least. There was no fanfare—not even an episcopal blessing—when Philadelphia Catholics established what is thought to be the first Catholic parish school in the United States in 1783, a school that continues to the present day.[1]

But this largely unnoticed event began one of the most ambitious social movements in American history. Over the next two centuries, Catholic parochial schools would educate tens of millions of American citizens without direct governmental assistance.[2] By the middle of the 1960s, when the Catholic parochial school movement had reached its high point, there were more than 4.5 million children in parish elementary schools—fully 12 percent of all of the children enrolled in the United States at that time.

At the heart of the American Catholic parochial school movement over the past two centuries has been the unwavering belief that the education of children is a primary responsibility of the family and the Church, not the government. Until the middle of the nineteenth century, this also was the prevailing view of most American citizens.

But rapid industrialization and urbanization, in concert with the arrival of millions of immigrants from Ireland and Germany, made many Americans fearful of social and political unrest, and common public schools were seen as an important tool in the campaign to preserve social order. Public schools would mix together children of various social classes, nationalities, and creeds to inculcate the proper values for success in American society. The children would become patriotic, law-abiding, deferential, and diligent American citizens. Community leaders argued that the state had both a right and a responsibility to provide such education as a means of preserving order in the Republic.[3]

Catholic leaders opposed these public schools not only because these institutions usurped the traditional role of the Church in the educational process, but also because the curriculum of the early common schools included heavy doses of Protestant instruction and anti-Catholic propaganda. The early movement to establish Catholic schools was, above all else, an effort to prevent Catholic children from abandoning their religious faith.[4]

In this manner the competition for the hearts and minds of Catholic children and their parents began in the middle of the nineteenth century and continues to the present day. Catholic parents in the 1990s face educational choices similar to those faced by their great-grandparents a hundred years ago: Can I afford to send my children to the parish school? Is the Catholic school curriculum just as good as the public school curriculum? Will my children be better Catholics if they go to parish schools? Will my children lose their faith if they go to public schools? Each generation has answered these questions a little differently, and how they answered these questions deeply affected the development of Catholic schooling.

At the heart of the Catholic school movement was a tradition of tenacity. A core group of parents, pastors, and prelates in every generation showed a remarkable determination to keep Catholic schools alive no matter what the cost. It started with the English missionaries who struggled to sustain their small flock of colonial Catholics in the face of a hostile Protestant majority for more than 150 years. In fact, it was not clear until the 1820s that Catholicism in general, and Catholic schools in particular, would survive in this country.[5] Catholic schools exist today because of the determination of our ancestors to pay any price and overcome any obstacle to sustain faith-based education for their children. The tradition has been passed on from generation to generation.

A second tradition has been adaptability. The success of parochial education has been assured by the willingness of Catholic educators in each generation to change and revise the parochial school curriculum in response to changes in the public school curriculum and the desires and aspirations of Catholic parents. Catholic educators realized that a rigid, doctrinaire curriculum would force Catholic parents to choose between their religious faith and their children's future. By incorporating many of the elements of public schooling into the parish school curriculum, Catholic educators promised to secure both the faith and the future of its children.[6] That tradition of flexibility and openness continues to the present.

A third tradition has been community. Perhaps the greatest asset of parochial schooling—even to the present day—is that these schools reflected the goals, aspirations, and even the prejudices and fears of the neighborhood Catholics who supported them. Public school teachers often lived outside the neighborhoods where they taught, and the curriculum was established by a school superintendent or a school committee downtown.

But parish schools have always been community-based in every sense of the word. Many immigrant groups established their own "national" parishes with their own ethnic Catholic schools. Parents had a sense of involvement in these schools. To be sure, these immigrants deferred to their pastors and to the nuns in the classrooms, but pastors and teachers alike were well aware that parental support was vital if parish schools were to thrive.[7]

These three traditions—tenacity, adaptability, and community—provided moral strength to Catholic educators as they struggled to sustain their schools from the time the first parochial school was established in St. Mary's parish in Philadelphia more than 200 years ago. And these traditions were of vital importance during the generation of crisis in American Catholic education over the past thirty years.

The rapid decline in the number of Catholic schools and Catholic school enrollment during those years must have caused faint-hearted Catholic educators to wonder if Catholic education would, in fact, survive. In a way these three traditions were something of a safety net that insured that Catholic schools would continue in the next century.

But this metaphorical safety net was not evident to Catholic educators in the midst of the crisis. In the years up to and including 1965, the demand for parochial education and the enrollment of children in those schools increased each year without fail. In the mid-1960s, for example, Catholic elementary schools enrolled almost 4.5 million children. It was an extraordinary achievement.

But like a skydiver in free fall, Catholic school enrollments dropped quickly and precipitously after 1965, almost without warning. By 1968, the figure had dropped to 3.9 million and would continue to drop each year for the next twenty-five years. It was an ironic twist for Catholic educators who until the mid-1960s had been plagued with overcrowded classrooms and excess demand.[8]

The core group of Catholic parents and educators did not give up hope, of course. Tenacity had been a fundamental tradition of parochial education in 1770 and 1870, and it would be no different in 1970. And during the last half of the 1970s it was increasingly common for Catholic educators to again ask a question that had been debated for more than a century—could public money underwrite the future of parochial schools?

The champions of that particular campaign for public aid for parochial schools were an unlikely trio of politicians. Senator Daniel P. Moynihan, Democrat of New York, was joined by Senator Robert

Packwood, Republican of Oregon, in proposing legislation to allow Catholic parents a tuition tax credit to partially cover the expense of sending their children to parish schools. They were later joined in their campaign by Ronald Reagan, the conservative former governor of California, who included a tuition tax credit proposal in his 1980 presidential campaign platform.

These three men offered hope for many pastors and parents. If Moynihan and Packwood could convince their Senate colleagues to pass a bill, and Ronald Reagan could be elected president, perhaps a tuition credit would become a reality. Certainly this was on the minds of Catholic educators as they looked to a new decade.[9]

The early 1980s brought predictions for the future, and, not surprisingly, the fate of parochial education was a popular topic among Catholic educators. Catholic schools had suffered through fifteen years of decline. Indeed, the Catholic school population had plummeted by more than two million students between 1965 and 1980. Catholic educators tenaciously predicted that the 1980s would bring change. Yet these predictions of a brighter future were laced with doubt. The 1980s were a decade both of hope and uncertainty for Catholic education.

Throughout the 1980s, the mood of many Catholic educators shifted from hope to despair and back to hope again depending on the education news of the day. No one—even the most pessimistic commentators—expected the Catholic schools to continue to decline at the disastrous rate of the late 1960s and 1970s. Yet neither did the most optimistic commentators expect the 1980s to usher in years of growth like the 1950s and the early 1960s. In fact, Catholic educators throughout the decade focused on the uncertainty of the future.

And this uncertainty was reflected in the Catholic press. Many of the essays in Catholic newspapers and magazines tried to shore up the sagging spirits of parents and educators who were losing hope for parish schools. Throughout the decade, journalists called their readers to arms in essays entitled "Let's Support Catholic Schools at Any Price," "Can Catholic Schools Survive the Economic Crunch of the 1980s?," "Catholic Grade Schools: An Idea Whose Time Has Passed?," "Stop Killing Catholic Schools," and "Keeping Catholic Schools Open Is a Family Affair."[10]

Yet the most ardent supporters of parish schools—that essential core group—were not shaken in their faith. Year after year these advocates hammered away at the value of parish schools. "The real economies of Catholic education," noted Father Michael O'Neill, one of the most tenacious and vocal Catholic educators, "lies in such intangibles as vision, hopes, spirit, conviction, morale, program quality, staff satisfaction, personal relationships between school, staff, clients, public image, feelings of involvement in decision-making, openness and trust."[11] Other articles reinforced O'Neill's theme with case studies of schools across Catholic America.[12]

One source of optimism for Catholic school advocates was the election of Ronald Reagan as president in 1980. He alone of all the candidates of either party had endorsed the concept of tuition tax credits. Catholic school advocates had worked hard for Reagan's victory and expected him to keep his promise to support aid to private schools. Such aid would go a long way toward securing the future of parochial education.

After several false starts, Reagan finally delivered on his promise in the spring of 1982. In mid-April, the president appeared before the annual meeting of the National Catholic Educational Association. In clear, unequivocal language, Reagan promised to honor his campaign pledge. "Our bill will be aimed at the middle and lower income working families who now bear the double burden of taxes and tuition, while still paying local taxes to support public schools."[13] His promise was greeted by applause.

But the president's support was not enough to enact a law, and Congress had little interest in tuition tax credits. In fact, there were some Catholics who were downright cynical about Reagan's support. "I think it was a con job," commented one priest after the speech. "There is no way tuition tax credits can pass. He served up apple pie and ice cream and that's all."[14]

Even the most optimistic supporters of tuition tax credits knew it would be a battle. Throughout the summer, supporters saw their chances of a law go from slim to none. Even though a compromise bill did reach the floor of the Senate, it was dead on arrival. There would be no tuition tax credit law in 1982.[15]

Without any prospect of public aid, it was not clear how Catholic parish schools could survive in the next century. The decline in the number of parish schools and students had leveled off again in the mid-1980s and this ebb gave advocates the luxury to ask themselves more questions about the future of their schools.[16]

The future of Catholic education, most journalists concluded by the mid-1980s, would be determined by the determination of the Catholic people—bishops and pastors as well as parents. All of these groups came in for criticism from Catholic school advocates. "When you get down to it," concluded one beleaguered school principal, "it really becomes a question of priorities. What would you do if you didn't spend money on schools? Spend the money on yet another program? Buy new stained glass windows? What could you spend the money on that would prove more effective?"[17] These tough questions often were met with embarrassed silence, or worse, indifference.

The 1980s were years of uncertainty, but out of that uncertainty came a new identity. Once a haven of white immigrant children making the transition from Europe to America, the Catholic schools of the 1980s had become visible symbols of the commitment of some parents—both Catholic and non-Catholic—to the education of their children. To be sure, many Catholic parishes had closed their schools and other parishes were unwilling to open new schools. But just as important were the many parishes in the inner cities as well as in the affluent suburbs that made great sacrifices to sustain their schools. As Andrew Greeley and others had said in the Catholic press, the future of Catholic education rested on the foundation of parental commitment.[18]

The 1990s have been years of speculation on many aspects of American life and culture. Certainly the future of American Catholic parochial education has been discussed generally and specifically in the thousands of parochial schools across the nation. Not surprisingly, after twenty-five years of sustaining Catholic schools through sheer tenacity, Catholic educators are reluctant to predict a bright future for their schools.

But it is possible that Catholic educators are too pessimistic. What these prognosticators have left out of their cautious calculations is the substantial value of the long-standing Catholic educational traditions of tenacity, adaptability, and community.

The current appeal of these traditions is evident in the recent and ongoing call for public school reform, education vouchers, and charter schools. Essays in the *Wall Street Journal,* the *New York Times, Time* magazine, *Newsweek,* and other national publications stimulated public discussion and praise for parochial education in 1996.[19]

The two 1996 presidential candidates, state and local politicians, and scores of commentators also weighed in with their own views. Bill

Clinton argued for "charter schools"—public schools that would emulate Catholic schools in every way except catechesis. Bob Dole championed "education vouchers" to lighten the financial burden of parents who wanted to send their children to private or religious schools.[20]

Clinton's victory put an end to the voucher movement for the time being, but the charter school movement is still very much alive. It is interesting to note in passing that Clinton is the only president to have the "privilege" (his word) of attending a Catholic school!

Yet even with all the recent attention and publicity given to the Catholic traditions of adaptability and community, and a strong tradition of tenacity, Catholic schools will continue to struggle. The good news is that Catholic school enrollments have been increasing for the past several years. But the hard truth is that sustaining Catholic schools is arduous even in the best of times.

So why are these schools struggling, if they are doing such a good job? The answer is complex, intertangled with changing social values, changes in family structure, changes in the forms and content of public education, and the rising cost of private education relative to other living expenses. All of these factors contributed to the decline over the past thirty years and all of these factors will continue to affect parochial schools in the next century.

The major factor that continues to affect parish schools is the changing structure of the American family. Where once the typical American Catholic family consisted of two parents and a gaggle of kids, the American Catholic family of the 1990s is often a single parent with one or two children. Even in two-parent households, both parents work and are in need of day-care facilities and after-school programs. In short, Catholic families no longer have the time or energy to contribute to the operation and maintenance of a private parish school.

Related to the change in the structure of the typical Catholic family over the past thirty years is a change in American values. "We as a nation," notes William J. Byron, former president of the Catholic University of America, "are now more than ever possessed by our possessions. Wisdom leads the list of casualties in a conflict of values where greed, promoted by popular culture, is on the rise and sacrifice, proclaimed as a value by the Catholic tradition, is on the decline."[21]

Another factor is competition from public education. Many Catholic parents, particularly those in the suburbs, are attracted to public schools by the quality of the facilities, teachers, and courses. The principal concern of all parents—Catholic as well as non-Catholic—is the future careers and economic security of their children. Unlike their parents and grandparents, Catholic parents today do not value the spiritual development of their children as highly as their career development.

But the most powerful reason that Catholic parents do not support parish schools in the manner of their parents and grandparents is that there is no pressure to do so. "There is nothing like the presence of an external enemy," adds Father Byron, "to solidify a community in shared identity and mutual support. Catholics are more comfortable in the United States today. They are less rigid about their religious practice."[22] Their grandparents and parents saw parish schools as a form of protection and security for their children against a frequently hostile American society. Today, in an increasingly pluralistic, ecumenical world, discrimination against Catholics has become a distant memory.

When Catholic leaders first established parish schools—especially in the century between 1830 and 1930—their stated goal was to serve both their faith and their nation. "The fact is," noted David J. O'Brien more than thirty years ago, "that the hierarchy, clergy, and the laity, all wished to be both American and Catholic and their attempt to reconcile the two, to mediate between religious and social roles, lies at the heart of the American experience."[23] By all accounts and measures, parish schools did an extraordinary job of meeting those stated goals.

But if these goals have been met, is there a continuing need for parish schools? Public education is no longer a threat to Catholic children. Catholics as a group have blended into American society without the loss of their religious faith. Indeed, recent studies by the Educational Testing Service indicate that out-of-school religious education programs do an effective job—almost as effective as parish school programs—of passing on the faith.[24] It is not clear why Catholics should put an increasing percentage of their resources into institutions that have already fulfilled their stated goals.

Catholic educators respond that these schools should be supported precisely because the traditions of adaptability and community have been so effective in meeting those stated goals. Stated simply, these traditions have molded Catholic schools into a model alternative to public education. Where Catholic schools had once followed every innovation introduced in public education, the roles have been reversed. Catholic schools are now laboratories for the development of effective tools in reaching a broad cross section of children.

What can public education learn from parish schools? In a recent study entitled *Catholic Schools and the Common Good*, three social scientists outlined the successful hallmarks of Catholic education, hallmarks that could be adapted by public schools.[25] In fact, these are the very hallmarks that President Clinton has stated for his charter school movement.

Foremost among the qualities of parish-based education is decentralization—an extension of the tradition of community. To be sure, all parochial schools are nominally controlled by superintendents and diocesan boards of education. But for the most part, parish schools are administered at the local level. Funding for the schools comes from the community and teachers are hired by principals without outside interference. Parents have a greater involvement and effectiveness in the education process because they are working with a single institution in their neighborhood rather than a faceless bureaucracy downtown.

A second quality related to the first is the fact that parents, students, and faculty share a broad set of beliefs that give each school a moral purpose. Achieving this unanimity in a public institution may not be easy. But if our nation's motto means anything, then public institutions must do more to achieve "one out of many." Shared values are possible if parents, students, and faculty care about education.

This care is also reflected in a shared code of conduct that stresses "human dignity and the belief that human reason can discern ethical truth."[26] This code need not be religious, but neither can it be arbitrary. More important, it must stress a good greater than individual achievement or gratification. "It is difficult to envision," wrote the authors of *Catholic Schools and the Common Good*, "how unleashing self-interest becomes a compelling force toward human caring."[27]

Another hallmark of parochial schools worthy of emulation is size. The small size of most parish schools promotes interaction between students, parents, and staff. Because teachers serve in many different roles during the school day—disciplinarians, counselors, and friends as well as specialists in one or more academic disciplines—they become mentors and role models. The small size of most parish schools insures that parents and teachers know one another and their children well. In short, small size facilitates communication.

Finally, parish schools place a special emphasis on academic sub-jects—an extension of the tradition of adaptability. Small size and lim-ited resources necessarily require administrators to concentrate on ba-sics. The end result is a student body well grounded in the mathematical and literary skills so necessary for success at future educational levels. Large schools with cafeteria-style curricula may very well meet short-term demands for relevant instruction, but there is little evidence that courses in industrial management and family living are as valuable as literacy and mathematical skills in a constantly changing society.

But in spite of all that Catholic education has to offer as an alterna-tive and an example to public schools, there has not been a flood of re-sources to support these institutions. Society is generally grateful for the civic contributions of parochial education, but Americans are re-luctant to provide public monies—even in the form of vouchers—to support parish schools. The hard truth is that Catholics will have to pay for parish schools themselves.

Parish schools face an uncertain future in the next century because the cost of parish education is high—much higher than the spread sheets reveal. In spite of belt-tightening and other economies, few parishes can continue to raise the funds necessary to maintain their own schools. This is particularly true in the inner-city neighborhoods of America's largest cities. Poverty is an obstacle that has been almost insurmountable, even for the most dedicated Catholic educator.[28]

And yet there is no sense of resignation among Catholic educators, because the long-standing tradition of tenacity continues to flourish. It is clear that the future of Catholic parochial education will be deter-mined by the parents of the children who are educated in these schools. More than two centuries ago, the parents and pastor of St. Mary's parish in Philadelphia established the first parochial school in this country. And as long as there are parents and pastors interested in parochial education, these schools will survive.

And with this reflection comes a new vitality. Catholic schools seem more willing to experiment with new ideas and to respond to the di-verse and changing needs of today's Catholic students. In short, Catholic schools have become leaner, more cost-effective institutions than their public counterparts. Out of adversity has come a new identity.

These traditions—tenacity, adaptability, and community—form the foundation of the dramatic story of a social institution that ingeniously responded to almost constant change in American society without abandoning its two basic goals—the preservation of the religious faith of Catholic children and the preparation of these children for productive roles in American society.

It is a story that is worth telling and a story that Catholic parents, pastors, and educators should not overlook in the day-to-day effort to support Catholic education. Just as past generations survived and even thrived, so will future generations of American Catholic schools thrive in the next century. The traditions of our past keep our future in perspective.

Notes

1. This school is now known as St. Mary's Interparochial School and serves Philadelphia children from several inner-city parishes.

2. The most recent general survey of the history of Catholic education is Timothy Walch, *Parish School: American Catholic Parochial Education from Colonial Times to the Present* (New York, 1996).

3. Carl Kaestle, *The Evolution of an Urban School System: New York City, 1750–1850* (Cambridge, Mass., 1973), pp. 145–48.

4. Vincent P. Lannie, *Public Money and Parochial Education: Bishop Hughes and the New York School Controversy* (Cleveland, 1968), pp. 75–118.

5. Michael Feldberg, *Philadelphia Bible Riots: A Study of Ethnic Conflict* (Westport, Conn., 1975); Walch, *Parish School*, pp. 23–36.

6. Robert Cross, *The Emergence of Liberal Catholicism in America* (Cambridge, Mass., 1958), pp. 130–45, 162–81; Walch, *Parish School*, pp. 100–132.

7. Walch, *Parish School*, pp. 67–183.

8. Glen Gabert, *In Hoc Signo? A Brief History of American Catholic Parochial Schools* (Port Washington, N.Y., 1973), pp. 131–32; Patricia Byrne, "A Tumultuous Decade, 1960–1970," in Jay P. Dolan et al., *Transforming Parish Ministry* (New York, 1987), pp. 170–75.

9. *New York Times* (March 25, June 6, September 30, 1978; May 13, 1979; April 21, October 9, October 12, October 21, November 16, December 27, 1980).

10. William C. McCready, "Let's Support Catholic Schools at Any Price," *U.S. Catholic* 46 (November 1981): 12–17; Sister Mary Ann Walsh, "Can Catholic Schools Survive the Economic Crunch of the 1980s?" *Our Sunday Visitor* (December 13, 1981): 4, 16–17; Kris Tuberty, "Catholic Grade Schools: An Idea Whose Time Has Passed?" *U.S. Catholic* 47 (November 1982): 18–23; Dan Herr, "Stop Killing Catholic Schools," *U.S. Catholic* 49 (October 1984): 13–18; Julie Sly, "Keeping Catholic Schools Open Is a Family Affair," *Our Sunday Visitor* (April 21, 1985):3.

11. Quoted in Sister Mary Ann Walsh, "Planning for the Future," *Our Sunday Visitor* (December 13, 1981): 5.

12. William McGurn, "Our Catholic Schools;" Barry B. Bun, "Chicago: The Church Makes You Human"; Jane Frawley, "New York: Stressing Basics"; and Jim Orso, "St. Louis: Renewed Spirit"; all in the *National Catholic Register* (September 12, 1982). See also Vivian Dudro, "Hitting the Books," *National Catholic Register* (September 9, 1984), and Theodore M. Hesburgh, "Catholic Education in America," *America* (October 4, 1986):160−64.

13. Ronald Reagan, "Remarks to the National Catholic Educational Association, April 15, 1982," *Public Papers of the Presidents: Ronald W. Reagan, 1982*, 2 vols. (Washington, D.C., 1983), 1:465−69.

14. Quoted in "Tuition Tax Credits for Tuition?" *Newsweek* (April 26, 1982).

15. "Mr. Reagan and Tuition Tax Credits," *America* (May 1, 1982); "Educational Voucher Raises Questions," *Our Sunday Visitor* (May 8, 1982); Charles R. Babcock, "Reagan Sends Tuition Tax Credit Bill to Hill," *Washington Post* (June 23, 1982); "Tuition Tax Credits Are Formally Asked by Reagan," *Wall Street Journal* (June 23, 1982); Robert Pear, "Debate Begins on Tuition Tax Credits," *New York Times* (July 17, 1982); Charles R. Babcock, "Changes Sought in Tuition Credit Plan," *Washington Post* (August 10, 1982); Babcock, "Tuition Tax Credit Actions Blocked by Democrats," *Washington Post* (August 12, 1982); Lou Cannon, "Senate Group Seeks to Save President's Tuition Tax Credits," *Washington Post* (September 14, 1982).

16. Marjorie Hyer, "Catholic Schools' Rate of Decline Was Slowed," *Washington Post* (April 28, 1984), and Ann Mariano, "Transformation of Catholic Schools," *Washington Post Education Review* (April 21, 1985).

17. McGurn, "Our Catholic Schools," p. 8.

18. Andrew M. Greeley, "Catholic Schools: A Golden Twilight?" *America* (February 11, 1989): 106−8, 116−18.

19. Among others, see the following articles: Timothy Walch, "Catholic Schools Are Worth Saving," *Cedar Rapids Gazette* (February 1, 1996); Sol Stern, "Why the Catholic School Model is Taboo," *Wall Street Journal* (July 17, 1996); Andrew Greeley, "Why Catholic Schools Work So Well," *Washington Post* (July 28, 1996); Denis P. Doyle and Bruce S. Cooper, "Religious Schools Can Be a Solution," *Washington Post* (September 1, 1996); Margaret Carlson, "Hail, Mary and Regina," *Time* (September 23, 1996); Karen W. Arenson, "Parochial School Mystique," *New York Times* (September 22, 1996); and Kenneth L. Woodward, "Catechism Lessons," *Newsweek* (September 23, 1996).

20. Blaine Harden, "Dole Supports Public Funds for Private Schools," *Washington Post* (July 19, 1996); David S. Broder, "Awaiting A School Choice Showdown," *Washington Post* (July 24, 1996); Mary B. W. Tabor, "Ohio Upholds Public Funding of Private and Religious Schools," *New York Times* (August 1, 1996); Joe Klein, "Parochial Concerns," *Newsweek* (September 2, 1996); Rene Sanchez, "Cleveland Charts New Educational Course," *Washington Post* (September 10, 1996); Mona Charon, "Catholic Schools Could Succeed at Challenge," *Iowa City Press Citizen* (September 11, 1996); Charles J. Sykes, "Why Educators Fear School Vouchers," *San Diego Union-Tribune* (September 12, 1996); Jacques Steinberg, "New York Chancellor Won't Aid Parochial School Plan," *New York Times* (September 12, 1996); Mirta Ojito, "Private Program for Troubled Students

Echoes N.Y. Catholic School Plan," *New York Times* (September 12, 1996); and Richard Lacayo, "Parochial Politics," *Time* (September 12, 1996).

21. William J. Byron, "Catholic Education in America," *Vital Speeches of the Day* 61 (June 1, 1990):489.

22. Ibid.

23. David J. O'Brien, "American Catholicism and Diaspora," *Cross Currents* 16 (Summer 1966): 308–9. See also Marvin Lazerson, "Understanding American Catholic Educational History," *History of Education Quarterly* (Fall 1977):298–99.

24. Meg Sommerfeld, "Study Compares Religious Education of Parish Programs, Catholic Schools," *Education Week* (August 3, 1994); [Catholic News Service] "Educators Are Doing a Good Job," as published in *Davenport Catholic Messenger* (July 28, 1994) and other Catholic newspapers.

25. Anthony S. Bryk, Valerie E. Lee, and Peter B. Holland, *Catholic Schools and the Common Good* (Cambridge, Mass., 1993).

26. Peter Steinfels, "Why Catholic Schools Succeed: A Community of Shared Values," *New York Times* (April 17, 1994).

27. Quoted in Joseph P. McDonald, "The Greening of St. Madeline's," *New York Times Book Review* (September 5, 1993).

28. David Gonzalez, "Poverty Raises Stakes for Catholic School," *New York Times* (April 17, 1994); Marla K. Kale, "Inner-city Schools: What's in It for Catholics?" *U.S. Catholic* (April, 1992): 21–28; Peter J. Daly, "Who Needs Catholic Schools?" *Washington Post* (September 1, 1991).

10 Ethnic, Catholic, White

CHANGES IN THE IDENTITY OF
EUROPEAN AMERICAN CATHOLICS

Timothy Meagher

It has been a "significant and inspiring chapter in the
growth and fulfillment of American institutions," Daniel
Boorstin has said. It is the story of peasant immigrants,
clinging desperately to old-world loyalties and despised for
their religious faith, transformed into confident members
of the middle class, thoroughly American in culture and allegiances, and moving freely without check, or even notice,
in all levels of American society. It is testimony to America's ability to make "this new man" (and woman) out of
foreigners, and elevate impoverished, "huddled masses" to
prosperity. It is less a paradigm of American social change
than the embodiment of American myth. It is the story of
the millions of American Catholics who trace their roots to
Europe.[1]

And yet the history of European American Catholics has
not been quite that simple. The categories and transitions—
immigrant ethnic to American—are too neat and clean.
Ethnic identities among white Catholics stubbornly persisted after the immigrants, so stubbornly that some observers thought them primordial, bred in the bone. Nor
did Catholic ethnics move directly into an American mainstream. Indeed, for much of the twentieth century, many
European American Catholics—perhaps most by the
1950s—considered themselves first and foremost as neither ethnics nor simply as Americans, but as American

Catholics, a new people and a new identity that they had created for themselves.

Nor was the process of change a simple, inevitable, almost unconscious assimilation worked by the heroic striving of immigrants and their descendants and the beneficent blessings of American freedom and wealth. There is much to say for the broad play American liberties has given to individual achievement and expression for white Americans, and the dynamism of the American capitalist economy in providing opportunity for these achievements. But this emphasis on an inevitable, unconscious process of assimilation can be carried so far that it becomes ahistorical and abstract and ceases to have much explanatory power. As Kathleen Conzen and others have suggested, examination of how ethnic and religious groups change needs "to be restored to the province of history." Catholic ethnics did not assimilate through a timeless process into a timeless American culture. Neither the cultures they came from, nor the ones they created here in America, nor the American culture they encountered were timeless essences. They were all concrete and dynamic, changing and changing again, over time. Moreover, ethnic or Catholic religious identities did not persist or disappear only because Catholic ethnics did or did not maintain distinct cultures. European American Catholics defined and redefined their identities, mapped and remapped the boundaries of their groups as they negotiated relations with other groups, relations that were shaped and reshaped by the changing distribution of power in America. Catholic ethnic or religious identities were created, persisted, changed, or disappeared because relations among groups in America—particularly power relations—helped or did not help, create them or keep them alive.[2]

Understanding the evolution of group identities and boundaries among European American Catholics is critical to understanding the history of Catholic schools in America. The principal motive for establishing Catholic schools in the United States over much of the nation's history has been to preserve separate group identities and maintain group boundaries whether the group in question was defined as an ethnic entity—German, Polish, Irish for example—or a more broadly religious, American Catholic one. In the last few decades, that sense of a separate identity has faded and group boundaries have washed away as most European American Catholics appear to have melted into America's white majority. Because of that, Catholic education has entered a new and uncertain era.

Ethnic Identities

Most immigrants, historians have long asserted, come to America with very narrowly drawn concrete notions of group identity. Their "people" were not the people of nations like Italy and Germany (albeit new ones), or would-be nations like Ireland, Poland, or French Canada, but people of their village, or, at best, their county or province. Historians have assumed that immigrants push out the boundaries of their people to national borders after they came to America. The importance of regional loyalties has varied significantly from group to group, however. Italian migration was very dependent on extensive migration chains from old-country villages and thus led to heavy concentrations of Italians from the same villages or groups of villages in American cities. Homeland town or regional loyalties often remained very strong among Italian Americans throughout the immigrant generation.[3]

The reasons for this persistence of old-world town or village loyalties is not hard to understand. Immigrants, particularly the poorest and least skilled, were dependent on the networks of fellows from home to provide jobs and places to live. June Alexander has found that such networks among Slovaks not only helped bring new immigrants to America but guided and sheltered them as the newcomers sought employment in travels from town to town here in the United States. Immigrants, especially recent arrivals, were thus tied to their fellows from old-country villages or regions by links of interest.[4]

But communal rituals and symbols signified and reinforced these networks. Many of these rituals and symbols, most notably *festas* or saints' days were rooted in the folk Catholicism of their homelands. Some groups, the Italians most notably, were successful in transmitting these rituals to America and perpetuating them through annual festivals. For many American Catholic ethnics, then, religious identities and worship inhered in village or provincial identities and cultures from back home that had been preserved in the new world.[5]

Communal village or provincial loyalties were hard to maintain or at least maintain as the primary definition of identity, however. There were practical difficulties in maintaining the old local identities. Village or even provincial groups were usually too small in most American cities to fulfill many critical functions that their members needed. They provided only a very limited marriage market, for example. They also had too few members to support any but the smallest organizations or compete successfully in any but the smallest political jurisdictions against other groups. Moreover, others, outside the nationality, non-Germans or non-Italians or non-Irish, rarely distinguished among group members on the basis of region or village; they saw all Italians, Germans, or Irish as the same and saw them all as either enemies or friends in competition for resources. These perceptions of others thus also encouraged broader identities.[6]

Such loyalties, so specific, so concrete, were also hard to pass on to new generations who did not share experiences of the same villages or towns. Robert Orsi found that new generations of Italian Americans were willing to join in the celebration of Italian *festas,* but for them, Orsi suggests, participation affirmed loyalties to a general Italianness or to the American neighborhood and family, not to the old-world village. Because they were so specific and concrete, village or county loyalties had to be passed down through family or small associations; schools, passing on heritage through teachers recruited from many old-country backgrounds and using published texts, were poor means of transmitting the specific, concrete lore of the village back home.[7]

Understanding of oneself as part of a broader people did not just come out of necessity, however, or out of the perceptions of "others." Members of many immigrant groups brought some sense of a national identity with them. Ironically, but also understandably, such protonationalist sentiment seemed strongest among those people who had no nation, the Irish, the Poles, and the French Canadians. Moreover, in all three of these countries, nationalism built upon an already deeply entrenched and widely understood sense of difference between Catholic natives and non-Catholic conquerors: Irish and French Canadian versus English; and Pole versus German or Russian. In all three cases, importantly as we shall see, the differences were understood as much in religious terms as in national ones: Catholic Irish and French Canadians versus Protestant English; Catholic Poles versus Protestant Germans and Orthodox Russians. The equation of nationality and religion would prove very important for these groups in America, as, conversely, the lack of such an equation among groups such as the Italians, or many immigrants from Latin America, would also prove important.[8]

It is not clear how fully articulated nationalism was among peasants in the old world, but if they did not learn nationalism there, former peasants, now immigrants, would certainly learn it in America.
The Fenians, or Irish Republican Brotherhood, for example, were mas-
ters of propaganda, if failures at revolutionary conspiracy, and their
songs and tales rallied immigrants demoralized by the Famine and the
journey into cruel urban poverty in America and created a nationalist
language for Irish America that would last for generations. Even struggles and factional fights within ethnic nationalist movements, as Victor Greene points out, seemed to advance the nationalist cause rather
than hinder it. Greene argues that debates between leaders of the
Polish Roman Catholic Union and Polish National Alliance, bitterly
fought out in Polish American clubs and newspapers, helped teach
peasant immigrants the concept of a Polish nation and the goals of
Polish nationalists. Through plays, books, community parades and
rituals, holiday speeches, newspapers, and religious imagery suffused
with nationalism, the Poles and Irish, in Matthew Jacobson's phrase,
created a "diasporic imagination" that inspired immigrants with the
glories of their nation's (or would-be nation's) past and tied them to
its future.[9]

Yet these broader national identities also had many more practical
advantages as foci of identification than village or provincial loyalties.
National traditions, unlike village ones, could be passed on through formal education. Of those traditions none was more important than language. The spread of literacy and the codification of language were criti-
cally important to the emergence of nationalist movements in the
nineteenth century. Language became the most easily recognizable and
powerful marker of national identities for the new would-be nations.
For some groups like the French Canadians, language, religion, and nationality became inextricably mixed together in a strategy for ethnic
self-preservation called *survivance.* French Canadians were thus quick to
establish parochial schools in America to preserve all three. Poles, in-
tensely nationalistic too, also established parochial schools quickly. By
1921 an astounding two-thirds of Polish immigrant children in America
attended Polish parochial schools.[10]

On the other hand the Irish, vitally interested in nationalism, did not
look to schools to carry it on. Though perhaps as many as a quarter to
a third of Irish immigrants to America in the nineteenth century spoke

Irish and English, few Irish parishes sought to keep Irish alive as an everyday language through their schools. Indeed, Irish American schools not only taught in English but displayed little interest in anything more than superficial aspects of Irish culture. At the turn of the century, for example, the Ancient Order of Hibernians initiated a campaign to encourage public and parochial schools to place Irish history on their curriculums, but the effort had limited reach and little lasting effect. Irish American clergy were certainly self-conscious about their heritage and ethnicity, but they were even more eager to assert their claims as leaders of an American Catholic church over all other Catholic ethnics. Most Irish priests and bishops would not endanger those claims with overzealous promotion of Irish culture. In some parts of the country, then, most notably Boston and other parts of New England, the Irish seemed largely indifferent to parochial schools.[11]

Italians also seemed indifferent to parochial schools but for other reasons. Italian immigrants had little sense of being oppressed as Italians or Catholics; indeed, if anything, the Church and the new unified Italian state seemed to be the oppressors to the millions of southern Italian and Sicilian immigrants who came to America. The Italian government, dominated by northerners after reunification, imposed harsh taxes and army levies on the south and Sicily in the late nineteenth century and brutally repressed any resistance to those policies. The Italians, then, did not have the same inbred sense of the vital connections among religion, nationalism, and language as say the French Canadians and Poles and had little confidence in an institutional Church that seemed only to buttress the rule of local elites.[12]

Ethnic identities did not persist simply because of schooling, of course, or even because ethnics in America became enmeshed in the affairs of the homeland. In many cities the cores of old ethnic neighborhoods endured for two or three generations after the immigrants had passed away because of a paradoxical combination of high home-ownership rates and sluggish occupational mobility. Catholic ethnics of almost every nationality, as John McGreevey has noted recently, abandoned central cities much more slowly than white Protestants or Jews. Through their shops, clubs, churches, and other institutions, such persisting ethnic neighborhoods offered concrete and visible symbols of the ethnic group's survival and rallying points for its revitalization even for ethnics who did not live in the old districts.[13]

As much as anything else, however, political and economic competition helped keep ethnic identities alive. Groups struggled for recognition or more tangible benefits of power, jobs, and wealth in municipal and state politics, labor unions, and even the Church. Paradoxically, second- or third-generation ethnics were far better equipped to fight the battles of municipal, Church, or union politics than the immigrants and much more ambitious for the rewards that victories in those battles could offer. As Raymond Wolfinger pointed out long ago, ethnic groups or communities do not emerge as significant, independent players in political competition until the American-born generations—more upwardly mobile, more savvy about America, and more eager to get ahead than the immigrants—grow to maturity and replace their foreign-born fathers and mothers.[14]

This competition sharpened ethnic boundaries and enhanced ethnic solidarity. For Catholic ethnics like the Italians and Poles this competition was frustrating through most of the twentieth century as they struggled to break Irish strangleholds on politics, Church, and the unions. Some groups followed their own ethnic political interests even if it meant jettisoning old political partisan loyalties. In the 1950s one Irish American wag from Massachusetts claimed that the state had three parties: the Democrats, the Republicans, and the Italians. Ethnic interests, reinforced by repeated competition, encouraged groups to invent new ethnic traditions and rituals, such as St. Patrick's, Columbus, or Pulaski Day parades, even when many older customs inherited from homelands had already been washed away in the new environment.[15]

Ethnic identities, apparently fading in and out throughout the first half of the twentieth century, never really went away. The immigrant past was still close enough for millions of Catholic ethnics to remember even as late as the 1960s. Indeed, as late as that decade over half of the nation's Catholic adults were still immigrants or the children of immigrants. Institutionalization through schools and associations, residential stability, and the survival of core neighborhoods, and in particular, competition for status, power, and wealth helped keep these ethnic identities alive. When the right circumstances combined in the late 1960s, as we shall see, white European ethnicity revived and caught fire once again.[16]

Still, ethnic identities could be hard to maintain over the long run. Ethnic competition might keep identities alive, but acculturation slowly diluted ethnic cultures and made it difficult to perpetuate cultural values, customs, or traditions that distinguished groups from each other and gave members of each group a focus for their solidarity. Language was, perhaps, the most common, significant marker for most groups and despite the extensive networks of schools that groups like the French or Germans created, language was difficult to maintain in America. As Joshua Fishman pointed out long ago, language rarely survived second-generation ethnics as a cultural marker of group identity, much less as a viable means of everyday communication. When language and ethnic loyalties clashed with religious allegiances, Fishman suggests, most religious clerics felt bound more by loyalty to their institution than by the language of their ethnic group. By the 1930s and 1940s few European American Catholic ethnic communities established new national parishes, much less ethnic-language schools.[17]

AN AMERICAN CATHOLIC IDENTITY

Historians have often spoken of American Catholic history in a neat periodization where an immigrant church gives way to an American church. But such phases, as we noted earlier, are rarely neat. Ethnic identities, as we have seen, have persisted long beyond the immigrants (and among Latinos may endure into the forseeable future). Similarly Catholics have been trying to define an American Catholic religious identity since the arrival of Europeans and Catholics on the North American continent. In the wake of the American Revolution and long before the Catholic immigrant masses, John Carroll, the first American bishop, worked hard to hammer out such a definition.[18]

About a century later in the 1880s and 1890s, James Cardinal Gibbons of Baltimore and Archbishop John Ireland of St. Paul led a broad, ambitious effort to open up a now far larger Church to American culture. These Catholic Liberals encouraged Catholic ethnics to acculturate to American norms and customs and even to mingle with non-Catholics. The Liberals publicly endorsed parochial education but did not denounce public schools and tried hard to fashion some kind of compromise between public and parochial education. It is hard to determine, however, whether this Liberalism had any impact on the spread of parochial schools.[19]

Liberalism crashed in the 1890s, a victim of a crackdown by the Vatican and a revival of nativism in America, but efforts to define an American Church did not. Indeed, even after Leo XIII condemned a heresy called "Americanism," American Catholic leaders continued to proclaim the essential harmony of American and Catholic principles. In many respects, the patriotic rhetoric even of the most convinced twentieth-century Catholic conservatives like Francis Cardinal Spellman seemed eerily similar to the speeches of the nineteenth-century Liberals like John Ireland and Dennis J. O'Connell.[20]

The effort to reconcile, or, as it turned out, to fuse American and Catholic identities, thus did not end with the Liberals; indeed, it could not have ended with them. The emergence of new generations of the American-born ethnics insured that that effort would continue. In the 1880s, the American-born already outnumbered the immigrants in the Irish community and formed a substantial proportion of the German American population, but many of those American-born Irish and Germans were still young. By 1900, members of the second generation outnumbered immigrants among adults in both the Irish and German communities, and as both Irish and German immigration ebbed in the 1890s, those two communities would be increasingly dominated by the American born as the twentieth century unfolded. Most of the American born in both communities, as noted, were fiercely proud of their American birth and avid participants in an emerging new American urban popular culture. In 1909, for example, one novelist invented Mickey O'Hooligan as America's archetypal baseball fan.[21]

There was a second shift of consequence in the early twentieth century that encouraged Catholic efforts to forge an American Catholic identity: the growth of Catholic numbers and power. In 1870, as noted, the Catholic population of the United States was only about 9 percent; by 1906 it had risen to about 17 percent, a dramatic leap forward. In that time the nation's Catholic population had multiplied fourfold. Growth was even greater in the big metropolitan areas that had come to dominate the economic and cultural life of the nation. The migration of new groups, Italians, Poles, Lithuanians, Slovaks, and others was one important reason for this growth; the maturing of second generations of the older Catholic immigrants like the Irish and the Germans was another. By 1910, over 70 percent of the populations of New York, Chicago, Boston, Cleveland, Buffalo, Milwaukee, and Detroit were first- or second-generation ethnics. Not all of those ethnics, of course, were Catholics, but a substantial and growing proportion were. Catholics had thus become the largest and fastest-growing group in metropolitan America.[22]

These numbers concentrated in the nation's metropolises promised to give Catholics enormous power if all the various Catholic ethnic groups could be brought together. Catholic politicians, many of them second-generation ethnics themselves, understood this. From the 1880s through the 1920s, Catholics took over most of the big cities and then began to compete for control of many of the big industrial states throughout the northeast and midwest. Alfred E. Smith's "revolution" of 1928 seemed a perfect demonstration of the new potential of growing Catholic power. Although Smith lost, he carried the nation's largest cities for the Democrats for the first time in more than a generation, largely by mobilizing the Catholic vote for the Democratic party. By the early twentieth century, Catholics were no longer minorities needing to prove themselves worthy to powerful Protestant majorities in most northeastern and midwest cities; by then, when unified, they were a majority in those cities and ready to reap the benefits of their power.[23]

Catholics, then, had enormous potential power. But they could wield such power only if they could be brought together as a group bound by a loyalty that transcended their diverse ethnic allegiances. That loyalty was not a given. American-born Catholics might be tempted to abandon a Church that could impede their dreams for upward mobility. More important, ethnic differences and rivalries threatened to fracture Catholic solidarity, and losers in the intrachurch ethnic competition might become alienated and leave the Catholic fold. Yet there were trends within and without the Church that encouraged Catholic unity and thus nourished the formation of an American Catholic identity.

From without, the persistence of anti-Catholic discrimination and prejudice contributed to Catholic unity. Anti-Catholic crusades swept the nation twice in the turn-of-the-century period: the American Protective Association in the 1890s; and the Ku Klux Klan in the 1920s. In Oregon, the Klan-controlled state government attempted do away with parochial education, turned back only by the United States Supreme Court. Protestant-Catholic tension and rivalry persisted throughout the "tribal twenties" culminating in the 1928 presidential election between Alfred E. Smith and Herbert Hoover. That election was a referendum on religion for many American voters, a referendum that the Catholic Smith lost.[24]

As important as the great nativist movements was the persistence of a systemic anti-Catholic prejudice that excluded Catholics from most elite economic and social positions. Over the course of the late nineteenth and early twentieth centuries, the Protestant economic and social elite transformed their privilege into a well-organized "Protestant establishment" through a network of newly founded or recently revived preparatory schools and academies, men's eating clubs, country and tennis clubs, and annual social events. This network attempted to perpetuate the rule of the WASP elite by strengthening its boundaries and reinforcing its internal solidarity. This establishment's openness to Catholics varied by region but the overall effect was to enhance a Catholic sense of exclusion.[25]

While pressure on the boundaries of the Catholic community from without persisted or even increased in the late nineteenth and early twentieth centuries, a trend within the Church to tighten discipline and centralize authority and power gained momentum at the same time. In 1899, as noted, the Vatican had cracked down on the alleged heresy of Americanism through the encyclical *Testem Benevolentiae.* This encyclical was widely perceived as an attack on Catholic Liberals and followed a series of statements by the Vatican reasserting its support of parochial schools and condemning Catholic membership in non-Catholic secret societies. Pope Pius X's condemnation of Modernism in 1907 discouraged Catholic experimentation with new ideas and seemed to further seal American Catholics in a cultural and social religious ghetto. In addition to these pronouncements, Rome tightened control of appointments to the American hierarchy. Roman connections, always helpful, now became paramount for ambitious clerics seeking to move up in the American Church. William Cardinal O'Connell of Boston and Francis Cardinal Spellman of New York were both excellent examples of this trend, for both were adept and sedulous players of Roman politics and owed their prominence to their Vatican connections.[26]

Trends to centralization were occurring within America as well. The National Catholic Welfare Conference (NCWC), a lobbying group and national spokesman for the Church, the National Catholic Educational Association (NCEA), and the National Conference of Catholic Charities (NCCC) all emerged in the early twentieth century. Along with the

NCEA and the NCCC , the NCWC permitted Catholics across the country to address issues in concert and gave a tangible national focus to an American Catholic identity.[27]

The trend to centralization and administrative tightening on the diocesan level, however, probably had the most immediate and powerful effect on the lives of most Catholics. Dioceses in the nineteenth century had often been run like feudal kingdoms. Bishops with only the tiniest central offices (even in the largest dioceses no more than one or two secretaries) had to cajole, bluff, and maneuver their "feudal barons," entrenched pastors and heads of religious orders. In the twentieth century, several bishops, but most notably Cardinal Mundelein in Chicago, broke the independent power of the pastors and centralized control of more and more functions like schools and charities in new, growing chancery bureaucracies. The American church, therefore, became far more centralized and well disciplined in the twentieth century than it had been in the nineteenth.[28]

All these trends, maturing American-born generations, greater potential power in a larger but more diverse population, anti-Catholic pressure from without, and increasing discipline and centralization of authority within, encouraged the formation of a new and powerful religious identity among American Catholics. This identity was patriotically American, militantly Catholic and panethnic or supraethnic, attempting to weld together a large, but ethnically diverse Catholic population into a single community.[29]

American patriotism was a critical hallmark of the new identity, and lay and clerical church leaders alike encouraged Catholic devotion to the United States. Assertions of patriotism were common among American bishops. During World War I the bishops, even German American bishops, were virtually unanimous in their support of war mobilization. American bishops in later years were steadfast backers of American anticommunism during the Cold War. Yet fervent patriotism was also common among the Catholic laity. No Catholic lay organization trumpeted American patriotism more effectively or vigorously than the Knights of Columbus. Through its work among soldiers on the homefront in World War I, its publications, rituals, and holiday celebrations, the Knights ceaselessly promoted the loyalties reflected in its Fourth Degree ceremonial: "Proud in the olden days was the boast 'I am a Roman Catholic'; prouder yet today is the boast 'I am an American citizen'; but the proudest boast of all times is ours to make 'I am an American Catholic citizen.'" The Knights were not only the principal promoters of the American Catholic identity, but their growth from 42,000 members to 782,000 between 1899 and 1922 was proof that this fusion of Catholicism and Americanism was becoming increasingly popular among American Catholics in the early twentieth century.[30]

Catholic schools, of course, played an important role in encouraging Catholic identification with the United States. English-language schools, as Timothy Walch has pointed out, had been doing so since the late nineteenth century. Such efforts received a significant boost in 1938 with the creation of the Commission on American Citizenship at Catholic University. The commission, was dedicated to creating "an enlightened conscientious American citizenship" among Catholic schoolchildren. The Commission published the *Young Catholic Messenger,* a children's magazine, *Treasure Chest* comic books, and the *Faith and Freedom* series of school readers. These publications were broadly popular. At one point in the early 1940s the *Faith and Freedom* readers were used in nearly three-quarters of the nation's parochial schools. One of the *Faith and Freedom* readers, *These Are Our People,* reminded young Catholic schoolchildren that "God, Our Father, made a plan for us in our country . . . the people who fought to make our country great knew God's plan. . . . We the children of America must help to carry on God's plan for our great country." These publications did more than just promote good citizenship and patriotism, however. They also helped invent a new past for millions of Catholic ethnic children, an American Catholic past, that was filled with Catholic heroes who had played critical roles in American history. *These Are Our People* and *These Are Our Freedoms,* another reader in the series, introduced students to the "contributions of Catholic Americans to our basic freedoms" through stories about people like Father Isaac Jogues, missionary to the Iroquois; Father White of the Maryland colony; Father Gallitzin, frontier pastor in Pennsylvania; Father Marquette, explorer of the Mississippi; and John Barry and Tadeusz Kosciuszko, Revolutionary War heroes. Some such heroes, of course, were celebrated by individual ethnic groups—Barry by the Irish and Kosciuszko by the Poles—but taken together and presented together as Catholics and Americans they became the honored history or tradition of a new group, the American Catholics.[31]

Liberals in the late nineteenth century had coupled their emphasis on Americanization with efforts to integrate Catholics into American society, but in the twentieth century American Catholics were militant Catholics as well as patriotic Americans. Stung by the revival of anti-Catholic prejudice, chastened by renewed Vatican conservatism, and increasingly confident because of their growing power, twentieth-century American Catholics sought no rapprochement with Protestants but instead turned to creating a Catholic world, a Catholic ghetto, as institutionally complete as they could make it. Throughout the twentieth century, but especially after the return of prosperity in the 1940s and 1950s, Catholic dioceses across the country built furiously. Schools were essential to the Catholic ghetto; indeed, they were its foundation stones. Dioceses like Chicago, which had been at the forefront of school construction in the nineteenth century kept pace in the twentieth century. In 1890 Chicago had 100 schools; by 1940 it had 388. In other dioceses such as Boston or Portland, Oregon, where school construction had lagged in the nineteenth century, the pace accelerated. Boston had only 50 parochial schools in 1890, but 149 by 1940. Portland had but 9 in 1890, but 53 in 1940. As important, Catholics also began to build their own high schools in this era. As Leslie Tentler points out, Catholic high schools played a critical role in sealing the ghetto. Tentler notes that religious intermarriage stopped rising and began to level off in Detroit after the archdiocese's construction of Catholic high schools there in the middle decades of the twentieth century.[32]

This vast Catholic ghetto needed a Catholic culture to hold its various parts together. It had to be a Catholic culture that appeared, at least, to be above any one group, one that would appeal to Catholics of all ethnic backgrounds. Americanization was part of that effort to pull Catholic ethnics together, but Catholic leaders trying to forge such unity also needed to create a distinctly Catholic culture that all Catholic ethnics could participate in and yet would distinguish them from other Americans. They borrowed much of that culture from Rome. One aspect of it was a cult of the popes. In the often fractious world of ethnically diverse American Catholicism, the pope stood above ethnic particularisms as the living embodiment of Catholic unity. Ultramontanism had roots in the middle nineteenth century among American Catholics, but, as Patricia Byrne notes, the "personal cult of the popes" reached its apogee during the reign of Pius XII in the 1940s and 1950s. Beyond the cult of the popes, the American Church, often prompted by Rome, promoted devotions that cut across ethnic lines: some were new like St. Therese of Lisieux, the "Little Flower," or Our Lady of Fatima; others old, like St. Joseph; still others were devotions to saints like St. Anthony of Padua, who emerged from a single ethnic group to gain a broad panethnic following. Mass devotional demonstrations and spectacular ritual celebrations, like the Eucharistic Congress in Chicago in 1926, became common in the early and mid-twentieth century, and both embodied and reinforced panethnic unity and power.[33]

By the 1920s and 1930s, there were also more mundane and prosaic, but nonetheless powerful, symbols in American popular culture that served as important icons of American Catholic identity. The 1930s, for example, were the golden age of Catholic college football. Notre Dame became the nation's premier team, but Catholic University, Holy Cross, Fordham, Georgetown, and St. Mary's of California all achieved prominence and went to bowl games. Pat O'Brien played not only Knute Rockne of Notre Dame but Frank Cavanagh, the "Iron Major," coach of Fordham and Holy Cross, in popular films of the era.[34]

American Catholics shared more than common rituals or symbols, sacred or profane; they shared a common philosophical perspective and values. A revival of Thomist philosophy began among American Catholics in the late nineteenth century but after 1920 became the foundation stone of Catholic philosophy in America. Revived Thomism reinforced the Church's resistance to modernist trends in thought and art, and encouraged Catholics' confident conviction in moral certainties and fixed standards of aesthetic value. Catholics thus remained committed to the old ways, to the values and standards of American "innocence," in William Halsey's terms (borrowed from Henry May), when others had begun to discard those moral certainties as stale pieties.[35]

It was not just the force of the Thomist revival nor even the encouragement or admonitions of Rome that made such cultural conservatism so attractive to American Catholics, however. Such moral certainties and strict rules were helpful to Catholics still trying to raise themselves out of the sometimes chaotic urban slums. After studying Catholicism among the Irish on the West Side of New York in the early twentieth century, Hugh McLeod concluded: "it seems fair to interpret the militant respectability of these Catholics as a means of protecting their families from aspects of local life that were unpleasantly prominent. Their Catholicism looks less like the famous opium than a stimulus to the sanctification of values that offered a basis for pride in a situation of suffering and humiliation and some defense against its effects." Second-generation men and women, in particular, may have found this Catholic moral rigor a useful, if also painful, aid to their efforts to postpone marriages in order to achieve a modicum of prosperity and respectability. There was a price for Catholic moral and cultural conservatism, as novelists from James Farrell to Mario Puzo have depicted: the price was a starched, even bleak moral puritanism driving out some of the earthy joy of a peasant, immigrant world. Yet eager to escape the poverty of their parents' lives, many American-born ethnics appeared ready to accept that price.[36]

Mixing American and Catholic culture, the new American Catholic identity thus had a broad appeal, especially among American-born ethnics. Advocates of the new identity, however, always risked the consequences of insisting too firmly on the assimilation of immigrants or ethnics into this new American Catholicism. Ethnic identities never really went away, and bishops, priests, or lay leaders who ignored ethnic loyalties could provoke nasty rebellions or even wholesale defections by ethnic minorities. Revolts against Irish or American-born German bishops were common among French Canadians, Poles, Italians, and others in the late nineteenth and early twentieth centuries. By the 1920s, most such rebellions had subsided (although the Sentinelle controversy in Woonsocket traumatized French Canadians throughout New England in the mid-1920s), and by the next decade even the creation of new national parishes and ethnic parochial schools seemed to slow or stop in most dioceses.[37]

With ethnic identities apparently in decline but religious allegiance still intense, the American Catholic religious identity reached its high point in the 1950s. Anti-Catholic feeling subsided in the 1930s, remained dormant through the war, but reemerged in the late 1940s and 1950s. Traditional Protestant evangelicals from the right, and liberal intellectuals from the left, assailed the Church with just enough force to provoke Catholic solidarity and intensify Catholic boundary maintenance. Meanwhile, Catholic upward progress during the war and after it greatly enhanced the Church's resources of money and talent. The result was a Catholic building boom of epic proportions in the fifties—a blizzard of Catholic yellow brick—and record numbers of nuns, priests, and Catholic school students. It was the ghetto church triumphant.[38]

WHITE AMERICANS

In the 1960s the great Catholic ghetto began to crack and crumble. Church attendance began to fall; schools and parishes closed: and priests and sisters began to leave the church. Old religious boundaries dissolved or, at least, had so little meaning that they scarcely impeded socializing or even intermarriage. Ethnic and even religious identities for whites, once fierce loyalties, became matters of choice abandoned with a shrug.

With hindsight it sometimes seems a wonder that such changes had not happened earlier, but it is important not to see these changes as inevitable. Even as late as the late 1950s and early 1960s several informed observers confidently predicted religion's persistence as a defining identity in America. "Religion and race seem to define the major groups into which American society is evolving," said Moynihan and Glazer in 1963; "in our major cities," they continued, "four major groups emerge: Catholics, Jews, white Protestants, and Negroes, each making up the city in different proportions . . . religion and race define the next stage in the evolution of the American people." Gerhard Lenski agreed in 1961. He found "a drift toward compartmentalization" along religious lines, "increased religious group communalism," the principal trends defining the future of Detroit's society.[39]

So how did the virtual disappearance of religious boundaries happen in the twentieth century? The easy answer is that Catholics assimilated; they became Americans. Educating and refining themselves to take advantage of American bounty, they moved up the economic ladder and out to ethnically mixed suburbs. As Catholics "proved" themselves through economic success and acculturation they became more acceptable and less threatening to non-Catholics and faded into an American mainstream.

Catholics certainly did move up the economic ladder. By the 1960s they had pulled even with or ahead of Protestants in occupational status nationally. Some Catholic ethnics, particularly descendants of the "old immigrant" Germans and Irish, moved even farther up the ladder and more quickly. Catholics were somewhat slower to suburbanize than members of other religious groups, but by the late 1950s and early 1960s white Catholics were moving out to the suburbs in enormous numbers. The Chicago archdiocese built 72 new suburban parishes and 25 in peripheral areas of the city in the 1940s, 1950s, and early 1960s. The simple answer, then, is that Catholics simply "made it."[40]

But that answer is too simple, and suggests an inevitability that is ahistorical. It ignores too many of the very contingent events that occurred between the 1920s and the 1960s that were critical to the changes among American Catholics. In the 1920s, Catholics were largely working-class, politically powerful but in a party seemingly condemned to permanent minority status, and on the wrong side of a culture war. Within four years the country would plunge into depression. The largely WASP elite that ruled the nation's business was thoroughly—if temporarily—discredited. Beginning with the New Deal, but really reaching fruition with World War II and its aftermath, there would be a fundamental shift in power and resources in the United States, and Catholics would be among the chief beneficiaries of this shift.

The first important change was that Catholics became an integral part of the ruling political coalition and reaped the benefits of that coalition's victories. They reaped it in access—they were listened to at the highest levels. Cardinals Mundelein and Spellman, Bishop Sheil of Chicago, and Father John J. Burke of NCWC all had an ease of access to the White House that no Catholic clerics had ever had. They reaped it in political patronage and power: more federal judges, federal agency heads, or cabinet undersecretaries. Most important, they reaped it as leaders of stronger city and state Democratic parties from Boston to Chicago.[41]

Yet it was not just the achievement of political power, but its use, that was important. There were, of course, the temporary measures for Depression relief, but more important were the long-term policies of the New Deal and Fair Deal that bolstered the bargaining power of union labor, provided low-interest loans for suburbanization, underwrote the education of millions of American veterans, and during World War II significantly redistributed the profits of a burgeoning economy to the middle and working classes. These policies were not aimed at Catholics. If they had been they would never have won widespread legislative support. Instead they took place behind what was largely a class coalition that cut across religious and even racial lines and was fashioned in public imagery as the "people." With Catholics, still largely lower-middle and working-class people, as integral members, that coalition, nonetheless, revolutionized the nature of power and wealth in America in ways that helped Catholics.[42]

Catholics could boast not only growing political power but cultural power as well. They were heavily represented in the burgeoning popular culture and commercial athletic industries of the mid-twentieth century. Catholics, particularly Irish Catholics were prominent among popular journalists and newspaper columnists of the 1940s and 1950s. Citing Jack O'Brian, Ed Sullivan, Jimmy and Dorothy Kilgallen, Bob Considine, Red Smith, and Jimmy Cannon, James Fisher argues that Catholics "by the 1950s . . . had achieved sufficient cultural authority to reshape not only their own image but to craft . . . a vision of gritty urban sophistication which influenced an entire culture."[43]

The number of Catholic cultural consumers and their strategic location in major metropolitan areas coupled with the increasingly centralized authority in the Church, gave Catholics significant power over the movie industry in the middle decades of the twentieth century as well. Exploiting the financial vulnerability of the big movie studios after the 1929 stock market crash, Catholic authorities won substantial influence over Hollywood films. This helped Catholics block films they found morally distasteful, but also encourage films, from war movies like "The Fighting Sullivans" to celebrations of Catholic priests like "Going My Way" and "Boys Town," that put the Church and Catholics in a better light.[44]

The new, positive image of Catholics portrayed on Hollywood's screens was not simply a reflection of Catholic influence in Hollywood but part of a change in the national ethos that began to make "cultural pluralism the very essence of American democracy." The New Deal fought its fights on economic grounds in behalf of "the people" or working men and women against the plutocrats or Wall Street financiers. Liberals in that decade, Gary Gerstle notes, studiously avoided issues of race, culture, and religion lest they sidetrack or disrupt pursuit of their economic goals. Rural WASPs or even New England Yankees, not African or even Italian or Irish Americans, were self-consciously elected to represent the New Deal "folk" in images generated in the popular culture. The rise of Nazism and the nation's confrontation with it in World War II forced Americans to consider race and culture anew. In reaction to Nazi racism American war propaganda began to deliberately highlight a cultural diversity in America as both an attribute of American democracy and a source of its strength: hence "The Fighting Sullivans," and many more films with the inevitable foxhole filled with a potpourri of American ethnic and regional types. Liberal intellectuals also began to trumpet the virtues of American cultural tolerance in response to vicious Nazi racism. The new ethos coupled with the migration of millions of African Americans to northern and southern cities and the beginnings of a black climb up the American economic ladder would inspire and sustain a rebirth of the black civil rights movement. Yet it would also help encourage acceptance of once alien and despised white ethnics like the Catholic Irish, Italians, and Poles.[45]

After the war, trends in racial politics further eased the full integration of Catholics into white America. As African Americans moved into northern cities in increasing numbers in the 1940s and 1950s, became players in the political arena, and began to assert their claims to jobs and housing, old distinctions and conflicts among European Americans—even old religious distinctions and conflicts—began to fade away. The racial gap between blacks and whites had always existed in America, but now it became such a fiercely contested political and social fissure in northern American cities that it seemed to render most old ethnic or religious differences among whites irrelevant.[46]

Despite the long-term changes undermining old religious boundaries in America over the middle of the twentieth century, the ghetto Church, militant American Catholicism, was still waxing strong through the 1950s. It was not until the climactic changes of the 1960s, that the ghetto Church began to crumble. When the collapse came, however, it was catastrophic. The proportion of Catholics attending church regularly fell from nearly three-quarters to one-half between 1963 and 1974; the proportion seeking confession regularly dropped from 37 to 17 percent; over 10,000 men left the priesthood from 1966 to 1978; the number of nuns fell by over 30 percent from 1966 to 1980; and the number of seminarians by over 70 percent from 1964 to 1984. Catholic school attendance, which had peaked in 1964, now plummeted. Between 1964 and 1984, 40 percent of the nation's Catholic high schools and 27 percent of its Catholic elementary schools closed.[47]

This revolution in Catholic life was a long time in the making, but there were specific events in the 1960s that finally brought it to fruition.

Most Catholics today look back to the Second Vatican Council as the principal cause of the ghetto Church's collapse. The council's endorsement of ecumenism and the opening of the Church to the modern world certainly helped sap the old militancy and undermine the separatist raison d'être for the ghetto Church and its institutions. Catholics could no longer build institutions just to maintain the boundary that separated them from Protestants. But there were other reasons why the 1960s were a watershed for Catholics and, indeed, all Americans. John F. Kennedy's election in 1960 and elevation to martyrdom after his subsequent assassination in 1963 ended forever fears of Catholics as president and helped undermine discrimination against Catholics in general. The civil rights movement also helped eliminate such discrimination by smashing official ideologies of prejudice. A new consensus on civil rights emerged in the country: if discrimination against blacks was no longer legitimate, discrimination against Catholics seemed a silly anachronism. Finally, controversies over the Vietnam War helped undermine the old militant American Catholic fusion of patriotism and religious devotion in the crusade against communism.[48]

In the aftermath of the collapse of militant American Catholicism, many Catholics retreated from that broad religious identity back into narrower ethnic identities. In what has been called the "ethnic revival" of the 1960s and 1970s many Catholic Americans rediscovered Irish, Italian, Polish, or other old-country roots. Such loyalties, however, could never be as meaningful as they had been for parents or grandparents. Not only had cultures eroded, but there was no social or political basis for such loyalties. European American Catholic ethnics were not discriminated against because they were Irish or Italian or Polish or any other specific European ancestry. Some turned to those ancestral roots in order to mobilize against growing African-American power, but such particularisms had to eventually dissolve into whiteness, for it was the black-white boundary that was the important one.[49]

The rapid decline of militant American Catholicism and—after a brief flurry—ethnic loyalties has suggested the possibility that European American Catholics might quickly disappear into a larger white American world. That seems unlikely now. Church attendance rates have stopped falling among American Catholics. Parochial school enrollments have also leveled off (though parochial education's share of the school-age population has not). Other measures also point to the persistence of Catholic distinctiveness. Catholic and Protestant patterns of voting for the presidency had been converging in the 1970s and 1980s, for example, but have stopped in the last few elections.[50]

Yet it is important to recognize that European American Catholics entered a new era in the 1960s and left a past that can never be recovered even if most of them wanted to recover it. The configuration of power relations and social conditions that nourished ethnic identities and later militant American Catholicism in the nineteenth and twentieth centuries has disappeared and will not return. Unlike earlier eras, white Catholics today seem to have no clearly defined political or economic interest that separates them from other European Americans. Catholics, for example, are not discriminated against or barred from positions even at the highest levels of the economy. Issues of public morality, specifically issues of sexual morality, also no longer seem to define Catholics—at least the laity—as different. Now securely middle class and thus no longer as worried about respectability, less ghettoized and less responsive to authority, and perhaps influenced by the Democratic party's civil rights tradition, Catholics seem to differ very little from Protestants on gay rights and many other issues of sexual morality. Indeed, of the eleven states with gay rights laws, three, Massachusetts, Connecticut, and Rhode Island, have the largest proportionate Catholic populations in the country, and five others, New Jersey, Wisconsin, New Hampshire, Vermont, and Minnesota, are among the top ten states with the largest proportion of Catholic populations in the country.[51]

Catholic strategies for parochial education thus must be formulated to fit the conditions of a new era, and not be burdened by efforts to live up to a past that is long gone and cannot be revived. That past is not irrelevant. It may, in fact, provide useful models for today's educators. European American Catholics were one of the first peoples in the history of the world to successfully move, almost en masse, from a premodern, agricultural peasantry to a modern, industrial bourgeoisie. That transformation meant negotiation of the drastic ruptures and harsh stresses and strains of newly industrializing economies by a people who began the process with few relevant skills and obsolete understandings of how to make it in the world. It was an impressive achievement and Catholic schools played a critical role in it. Perhaps Catholic educators can parlay some of the lessons of that experience into helping new groups trying to make similar transitions. But if the past offers some models and more inspiration, the numbers of schools or students in that older era should not stand as a benchmark of success or failure for today's educators. The old European American Catholic rationales for parochial schools were rooted in separatist desires to defend the boundaries of ethnic or religious identities. Yet Catholic and ethnic identities among European Americans in the past were sustained as much by external pressure and practical necessity as internal will or cultural habit; they cannot be revived by Vatican fiat or self-conscious efforts to reconstruct a cultural uniformity that no longer seems necessary to most American Catholics. European American Catholics have not built schools to perpetuate national identities for more than a generation, and few of them today would build schools simply to shore up the walls of a Catholic ghetto that has long since crumbled. Any new strategy for Catholic education of European Americans must be fashioned in a realistic understanding of this new era in their history.

Notes

1. R. Laurence Moore, *Religious Outsiders and the Making of Americans* (New York: Oxford University Press, 1986), p. 49.

2. Kathleen Neils Conzen, David A. Gerber, Ewa Morawska, George E. Pozzetta, and Rudolph J. Vecoli, "The Invention of Ethnicity: A Perspective from the U.S.A," *Journal of American Ethnic History* (Fall 1992), pp. 4–5. Because the process of change in identities is contingent and dependent on specific and concrete circumstances, it is important to note that it had many regional variations. The history of Catholicism and thus white Catholic identities was surely not the same in the Southwest or even the South or the Pacific Northwest as in the Northeast or Midwest. It was not even the same in Boston as in New York or Chicago. Which Catholic ethnic groups settled in a region, when they arrived there, in what numbers, what other groups were there; the ethnic composition, permeability, and stability of local elites; and the dynamism of the local economy, were key variables affecting local Catholic experiences. What follows is an analysis based largely, but not exclusively on white Catholic experience in the Catholic heartland of the Northeast and Midwest where most Catholics have lived, but it is important to keep in mind these important regional differences. Thomas T. McAvoy, *The Great Crisis in American Catholic History* (Chicago: Henry Regnery, 1957), pp. 19–28; John Higham, "Another Look at Nativism," *Catholic Historical Review* 44, no. 2, (1958), pp. 155–58.

3. Donna Gabbacia, *From Italy to Elizabeth Street* (Albany: SUNY Press, 1983), and Gabbacia, *Militants and Migrants: Rural Sicilians Become American Workers* (New

Brunswick: Rutgers University Press, 1988); Josef Barton, *Peasants and Strangers: Italians, Roumanians and Slovaks in an American City, 1890–1950* (Cambridge: Harvard University Press, 1975); John T. Ridge, "Irish County Societies in New York, 1880–1914," in Ronald Bayor and Timothy Meagher eds., *The New York Irish* (Baltimore: Johns Hopkins University Press, 1996), pp. 275–300.

4. Charles Tilly, "Transplanted Networks," in Virginia Yans McLaughlin, *Immigration Reconsidered: History, Sociology and Politics* (New York: Oxford University Press, 1990), pp. 79–95; June Granitir Alexander, "Moving Into and Out of Pittsburgh: Ongoing Chain Migration," in Rudolph Vecoli and Suzanne Sinke, *A Century of European Migrations, 1830–1930* (Urbana: University of Illinois Press, 1991), pp. 200–220, and 134–57.

5. Robert Orsi, *The Madonna of 115th Stret: Faith and Community in Italian Harlem, 1880–1950* (New Haven: Yale University Press, 1985); Rudolph Vecoli, "Contadini in Chicago: A Critique of *The Uprooted*," *Journal of American History* 51 (December 1964), pp. 404–17.

6. John Walker Briggs, *An Italian Passage: Immigrants to Three American Cities, 1890–1930* (New Haven: Yale University Press, 1978); Conzen, "The Invention of Ethnicity," pp. 12–13.

7. Orsi, *The Madonna of 115th Street*, pp. 168–71.

8. John J. Bukowcyk, *And My Children Did Not Know Me: A History of the Polish Americans* (Bloomington: Indiana University Press, 1987), pp. 1–15; Matthew Frye Jacobson, *Special Sorrows: The Diasporic Imagination of Irish, Polish and Jewish Immigrants in the United States* (Cambridge: Harvard University Press, 1995).

9. Kerby Miller, *Emigrants and Exiles: Ireland and the Irish Exodus to North America* (New York: Oxford University Press, 1985), pp. 436–41; Roy Foster, *Modern Ireland, 1600–1972* (New York: Penguin, 1988), pp. 345–99; Jacobson, *Special Sorrows;* Victor Greene, *For God and Country: The Rise of Polish and Lithuanian Ethnic Consciousness in America* (Madison: State Historical Society of Wisconsin, 1975).

10. Benedict Anderson, *Imagined Communities;* Bukowcyk, *And My Children Did Not Know Me*, p. 72.

11. Ellen Skerrett, "The Catholic Dimension," in Lawrence McCaffrey, ed., *The Irish in Chicago* (Urbana: University of Illinois Press, 1987), pp. 42–47; Miller, *Emigrants and Exiles*, pp. 531–35; John O'Dea, *History of the Ancient Order of Hibernians and Ladies' Auxiliary* (New York: A.O.H., 1923), vol. 3, pp. 1434–44; James W. Sanders, "Catholics and the School Question in Boston: The Cardinal O'Connell Years," in James M. O'Toole and Robert E. Sullivan, *Catholic Boston: Studies in Religion and Community, 1870–1970* (Boston, Archdiocese of Boston, 1985), pp. 71–121; *Hoffman's Catholic Directory, 1890*, Summary Tables.

12. Gabaccia, *Militants and Migrants;* William DeMarco, *Ethnics and Enclaves: Boston's Italian North End* (Ann Arbor: UMI Research Press, 1981).

13. John McGreevy, *Parish Boundaries: The Catholic Encounter with Race in the Twentieth-Century Urban North* (Chicago: University of Chicago Press, 1995), pp. 18, 132; John Bodnar, *Lives of Their Own: Blacks, Italians and Poles in Pittsburgh, 1900–1960* (Urbana: University of Illinois Press, 1982), pp. 113–261.

14. Raymond Wolfinger, ed., *Readings in American Political Behavior* (Englewood Cliffs: Prentice-Hall, 1970).

15. Bukowcyk, *And My Children,* pp. 70–71, pp. 82–83, p. 87; Conzen, "Invention of Ethnicity," pp. 18–21; Murray Levin, *The Compleat Politician: Political Strategy in Massachusetts* (Indianapolis: Bobbs-Merrill, 1962), p. 213; Kathleen Neils Conzen, "Ethnicity as Festive Culture: Nineteenth Century German America on Parade," In Werner Sollors, ed., *The Invention of Ethnicity* (New York: Oxford University Press, 1989), pp. 44–76; For St. Patrick's Day parades, see John Bodnar, *Remaking America: Public Memory, Commemoration and Patriotism in the Twentieth Century* (Princeton: Princeton University Press, 1992), pp. 65–70.

16. Andrew Greeley, William C. McCready, and Kathleen McCourt, *Catholic Schools in a Declining Church* (Kansas City, MO: Sheed and Ward, 1976), p. 40.

17. Joshua Fishman and Vladimir Nahirny, *Language Loyalty in the United States: The Maintenance and Perpetuation of Non English Mother Tongues by American Religious and Ethnic Groups* (The Hague: Mouton, 1966).

18. Jay Dolan, "The Search for an American Catholicism," *Catholic Historical Review* 82, no. 2 (April 1996), pp. 163–86. On the early Americanism of Carroll, see Jay Dolan, *The American Catholic Experience: A History From Colonial Times to the Present* (New York: Doubleday, 1985; rpt. Notre Dame: University of Notre Dame Press, 1992), pp. 101–26.

19. Dolan, "The Search for an American Catholicism," pp. 175–80. The standard works on the Americanism controversy and the rise of Liberalism are Robert D. Cross, *The Emergence of Liberal Catholicism in America* (Cambridge: Harvard University Press, 1958), and McAvoy *The Great Crisis in American Catholic History.* See a special issue of the *U.S. Catholic Historian:* "The Americanist Controversy: Recent Historical and Theological Perspectives," *U.S. Catholic Historian* 11, no. 3 (Summer 1993); Paul Robichaud, "The Resident Church: Middle Class Catholics and the Shaping of American Catholic Identity, 1889–1899," Ph.D. dissertation, UCLA, 1989); John Tracy Ellis, *The Life of James Cardinal Gibbons* (Westminster, Md.: Christian Classics, 1987), p. 450; Marvin R. O'Connell, *John Ireland and the American Catholic Church* (Minneapolis: Minnesota Historical Society Press, 1988), p. 341. In 1890, the Boston archdiocese had 50 schools to 158 churches; the Springfield, Massachusetts, diocese, 23 schools to 107 churches; the Providence diocese 27 schools to 67 churches; the Denver diocese, 18 schools to 49 churches; the Los Angeles diocese, 7 schools to 38 churches; the San Francisco archdiocese, 29 schools to 93 churches; the Portland, Oregon, diocese, 9 schools to 50 churches; the Omaha diocese, 33 schools to 126 churches: *Hoffman's Catholic Directory, 1890,* Summary Tables.

20. John Cooney, *The American Pope* (New York: Times Books, 1984), pp. 137–40, pp. 211–45; Dorothy Dohen, *Nationalism and American Catholicism* (New York: Sheed and Ward, 1967); Edward R. Kantowicz, *Corporation Sole: Cardinal Mundelein and Chicago Catholicism* (Notre Dame: University of Notre Dame Press, 1983) pp. 24–26, pp. 115–16.

21. In 1900 there were 1.49 million second-generation German American males in the work force over age 14 compared to 1.27 million German American immigrants over age 14; there were 1.09 million second-generation Irish males in the work force over age 14 and .71 million Irish immigrant men: *Reports of the Immigration Commision,* vol. 28, *Occupations of the First and Second Generation Immigrants in the U.S,* pp. 474–75, 486; Roy Rosenzweig, *Eight Hours for What We Will: Workers and Leisure in an Industrial City, 1870–1920* (New York: Cambridge University Press, 1983); James R. Barrett, "Americanization

from the Bottom Up: Immigration and the Working Class in the United States, 1880–1930," *Journal of American History* 79, no. 3 (December 1992), pp. 996–1020; Mickey O'Hooligan in Allen Guttman, *Sports Spectators* (New York: Columbia University Press, 1986), pp. 111–15.

22. Roger Finke and Rodney Starke, *The Churching of America, 1776–1990* (New Brunswick: Rutgers University Press, 1992), p. 114; Howard Chudacoff, *The Evolution of American Urban Society* (Englewood Cliffs: Prentice-Hall, 1975), p. 91.

23. John Allswang, *A House for All Peoples* (Lexington: University of Kentucky Press, 1971); Gerald Gamm, *The Making of New Deal Democrats: Voting Behavior and Realignment in Boston, 1920–1940* (Chicago: University of Chicago Press, 1989); Steven P. Erie, *Rainbow's End: Irish Americans and the Dilemmas of Urban Machine Politics* (Berkeley: University of California Press, 1988), pp. 67–106; Christopher McNickle, *To Be Mayor of New York: Ethnic Politics in the City* (New York: Columbia University Press, 1993), pp. 1–73.

24. Kathleen M. Blee, *Women and the Klan: Racism and Gender in the 1920s* (Berkeley: University of California Press, 1991), pp. 86–94; Kenneth Jackson, *Ku Klux Klan in the City: 1915–1930* (New York: Oxford University Press, 1967); Allan Lichtman, *Prejudice and the Old Politics: The Presidential Election of 1928* (Chapel Hill: University of North Carolina Press, 1979).

25. Digby Baltzell, *The Protestant Establishment: Aristocracy and Caste in America* (New York: Vintage, 1966); Frederick Jaher, *The Rich, the Well Born and Powerful: Elites and Upper Classes in History* (Urbana: University of Illinois Press, 1973), on New York, 156–57, 169–70, 189–93, 203–5, 231–33, 245–64 and 275–81; on Boston, 15–125, on Chicago, 453–554, and on Los Angeles, 581–659.

26. Cooney, *The American Pope*, pp. 3–80; James M. O'Toole, *Militant and Triumphant: William Henry O'Connell, 1859–1944* (Notre Dame: University of Notre Dame Press, 1992), pp. 1–78; Gerald P. Fogarty, *The Vatican and the American Hierarchy from 1870 to 1965* (Wilmington: Michael Glazier, 1985).

27. Elizabeth McKeown, *War and Welfare: American Catholics and World War I* (New York: Garland, 1988), p. 74; Douglas J. Slawson, *The Foundation of the First Decade of the National Catholic Welfare Council* (Washington, D.C.: Catholic University of America Press, 1992); Gleason, *Contending With Modernity*, pp. 43–95; Dolan, *American Catholic Experience*, pp. 340–41.

28. Cooney, *The American Pope*, pp. 83–110, 169–208; Kantowicz, *Corporation Sole*, pp. 33–63; Leslie Woodcock Tentler, *Seasons of Grace: A History of the Catholic Archdiocese of Detroit* (Detroit: Wayne State University Press, 1990), pp. 297–360.

29. Charles Shanabruch, *Chicago's Catholics: The Evolution of an American Identity* (Notre Dame: Univeristy of Notre Dame Press, 1981); Paula Kane, *Separatism and Subculture: Boston Catholicism, 1900–1920* (Chapel Hill: University of North Carolina Press, 1994).

30. Skerret, "Catholic Dimension," pp. 46–51; Timothy Meagher, "Irish American Catholic: Irish American Identity in Worcester, Masachusetts, 1880 to 1920," in Meagher, ed., *From Paddy to Studs: Irish American Communities in the Turn of the Century Era, 1880 to 1920* (Westport: Greenwood, 1986), pp. 75–92; Christopher J. Kauffman, *Faith and Fraternalism: The History of the Knights of Columbus* (N.Y.: Simon & Schuster, 1992), pp. 133, 139, 316.

31. Timothy Walch, *Parish School: American Catholic Parochial Education from Colonial Times to the Present* (New York: Crossroads, 1996), pp. 71–75; *The Commission on American Citizenship* (Washington, D.C.: Catholic University of America, n.d.), pamphlet, Catholic University Archives; Sister M. Annunciata, O.P., "The Commission on American Citizenship," *Catholic University Bulletin* (October 1964), p. 7; Sister Thomas Aquinas, O.P. and Mary Synon, *These Are Our People* (Boston: Ginn, 1943); Sister M. Charlotte and Mary Synon, *These Are Our Freedoms* (Boston: Ginn, 1944), pp. 74–75, 133, 213, 218.

32. Tentler, *Seasons of Grace,* pp. 306–10, 348–60; Steven M. Avella, *The Confident Church: Catholic Leadership and Life in Chicago, 1940–1965* (Notre Dame: University of Notre Dame Press, 1992), pp. 77–81; Cooney, *The American Pope,* pp. 169–76; *Official Catholic Directory* (New York: P. J. Kenedy and Sons, 1940), general summary tables; *Hoffman's Catholic Directory, 1890,* summary tables.

33. Timothy Kelly, "Suburbanization and the Decline of Catholic Public Ritual in Pittsburgh," *Journal of Social History* (Winter 1994), pp. 311–26; Kantowicz, *Corporation Sole,* pp. 165–72; Patricia Byrne, C.S.J., "American Ultramontanism," *Theological Studies* 56 (1995), pp. 301–26; Paula Kane, *Separatism and Subculture;* Tentler, *Seasons of Grace,* pp. 408–14.

34. Leslie Halliwell, *Halliwell's Film Guide* (New York: Harper Collins, 1991), p. 565. Boston College, Catholic University, Fordham, and St. Mary's of California all went to bowl games in the late 1930s and early 1940s: Editors of *Sports Illustrated, Sports Illustrated 1997 Almanac* (Boston: Little, Brown, 1997), pp. 199–201.

35. William M. Halsey, *The Survival of American Innocence* (Notre Dame: University of Notre Dame Press, 1980), pp. 61–83, 139–68; Philip Gleason, *Contending With Modernity,* pp. 105–66.

36. Hugh McLeod, "Catholicism and the New York Irish," in Jim Obelkevich, Lyndal Roper, and Ralph Samuel, eds., *Disciplines of Faith: Studies in Religion, Politics and Patriarchy* (New York: Routledge & Kegan Paul, 1987), p. 350; Nancy S. Landale and Stewart E. Tolnay, "Generation, Ethnicity and Marriage: Historical Patterns in the Northern United States," *Demography* 30, no. 1 (February 1993), pp. 103–22; Mario Puzo, *Fortunate Pilgrim* (Greenwich: Fawcett Books, 1964); James T. Farrell, *Studs Lonigan: A Trilogy* (New York: Modern Library, 1938).

37. Gerard J. Brault, *The French Canadian Heritage in New England* (Hanover: University Press of New England, 1986), pp. 70–73, 86–89; Shanabruch, *Chicago's Catholics,* pp. 78–104; James M. O'Toole, *Militant and Triumphant,* pp. 143–72.

38. Robert Wuthnow, *The Restructuring of American Religion: Society and Faith Since World War II* (Princeton: Princeton University Press, 1988), pp. 72–76; Gerhard Lenski, *The Religious Factor: A Sociologist's Inquiry* (Garden City: Anchor Books, 1963), pp. 298–303.

39. Nathan Glazer and Daniel Patrick Moynihan, *Beyond the Melting Pot: The Negroes, Puerto Ricans, Jews, Italians and Irish of New York City* (Cambridge: M.I.T. Press, 1970; first published 1963), p. 314; Gerhard Lenski, *The Religious Factor,* p. 362.

40. Steven Avella, *This Confident Church,* pp. 78–79; McGreevy, *Parish Boundaries,* pp. 82–84; Greeley, *Catholic Schools,* pp. 42–75; Richard Alba, *Ethnic Identity: The Transformation of White America* (New Haven: Yale University Press, 1990).

41. George Q. Flynn, *American Catholics and the Roosevelt Presidency, 1932–1936* (Lexington: University of Kentucky Press, 1968), pp. 36–60; Kristi Andersen, *The Creation of a Democratic Majority, 1928–1936* (Chicago: University of Chicago Press, 1979); Cooney, *The American Pope*, pp. 211–62; Kantowicz, *Corporation Sole*, pp. 217–36: Lyle Dorset, *Franklin D. Roosevelt and the City Bosses* (Port Washington, N.Y.: Kennikat Press, 1977); Thomas Gobel, "Becoming American: Ethnic Workers and the Rise of the CIO," *Labor History* 29 no. 2 (Spring 1988), pp. 173–98.

42. Gary Gerstle, "The Protean Character of American Liberalism," *American Historical Review* 99, no. 4 (October 1994), pp. 1068–69; George Lipsitz, "The Possessive Investment in Whiteness: Racialized Social Democracy and the 'White' Problem in American Studies," *American Quarterly* 47, no. 3 (September 1995), pp. 369–427. Shammas claims, "However one counts, by household or by individual units, the last half of the twentieth century shows a noticeable improvement in the share [of wealth] captured from the top quintile by the remaining 80%": Carole Shammas, "New Look at Long-Term Trends in Wealth Inequality in the United States," *American Historical Review* 98, no. 2 (April 1993), pp. 412–31, p. 428; Jeffrey G. Williamson and Peter H. Lindert, *American Inequality: A Macroeconomic History* (New York: Academic Press, 1980), pp. 82–94, 245–51; Greeley, *Catholic Schools*, pp. 42–75; Suzanne Model, "The Ethnic Niche and the Structure of Opportunity: Immigrants and Minorities in New York City," in Michael Katz, ed., *The Underclass Debate: Views From History* (Princeton: Princeton University Press, 1992), pp. 172–74.

43. James T. Fisher, "Alternative Sources of Catholic Intellectual Vitality," *U.S. Catholic Historian* 13, no. 1 (Winter 1995), p. 87.

44. Gregory Black, *Hollywood Censored: Morality Codes, Catholics and the Movies* (New York: Cambridge University Press, 1994), pp. 37–71; Ian C. Jarvie, "Stars and Ethnicity: Hollywood and the United States, 1932–1951," in Lester Friedman, ed., *Unspeakable Images: Ethnicity and the American Cinema* (Urbana: University of Illinois Press, 1991), pp. 82–111; Les and Barbara Keyser, *Hollywood and the Catholic Church: The Image of Roman Catholicism in American Movies*, (Chicago: Loyola University Press, 1984), pp. 41–194.

45. Gary Gerstle, "The Working Class Goes to War," *Mid America* 75, no. 3 (October 1993), pp. 315–16; Gerstle, "Protean Character of American Liberalism," pp. 1070–73.

46. Gary Gerstle, "The Working Class Goes to War," pp. 315–16; Arnold R. Hirsch, "Massive Resistance in the Urban North: Trumbull Park, Chicago, 1953–1966," pp. 522–50, Thomas J. Sugrue, "Crabgrass-Roots Politics: Race, Rights and the Reaction against Liberalism in the Urban North, 1940–1964," pp. 551–78; and Gary Gerstle, "Race and the Myth of the Liberal Consensus," pp. 579–86—all in *The Journal of American History* 82, no. 2 (September 1995); McGreevy, *Parish Boundaries*, pp. 79–207; Eileen M. McMahon *What Parish Are You From? A Chicago Irish Community and Race Relations* (Lexington: University of Kentucky Press, 1995).

47. Dolan, *American Catholic Experience*, pp. 433–34.

48. Dolan, *The American Catholic Experience*, pp. 421–54; David J. O'Brien, *The Renewal of American Catholicism* (New York: Oxford University Press, 1972); Tentler, *Seasons of Grace*, pp. 519–27; Steven Avella, *The Confident Church;* Eileen McMahon, *What Parish Are You From?* pp. 116–89; Barry A. Kasmin and Seymour P. Lachman *One Nation*

Under God: Religion in Contemporary American Society (New York: Harmony Books, 1993), pp. 255–56; Lawrence H. Fuchs, *John F. Kennedy and American Catholicism* (New York: Meredith Press, 1967); Greeley, *Catholic Schools*, pp. 103–54. Greeley claims the biggest impact on changing Church attendance came from the encyclical *Humanae Vitae*, not the council. Robert Wuthnow, *The Restructuring of American Religion: Society and Faith Since World War II* (Princeton, New Jersey: Princeton University Press, 1988) pp. 132–214.

49. Jonathan Rieder, *Canarsie: The Jews and Italians of Brooklyn Against Liberalism* (Cambridge: Harvard University Press, 1985), pp. 57–167; Richard Krickus, *Pursuing the American Dream: White Ethnics and the New Populism* (Bloomington: Indiana University Press, 1976); Conzen et al., "The Invention of Ethnicity," pp. 26–30.

50. George Gallup, Jr., and Jim Castelli, *The American Catholic People: Their Beliefs, Practices, and Values* (Garden City: Doubleday, 1987), pp. 27–28, 64–74, 126–37. The Catholic and Protestant presidential votes converged to within thirteen percentage points in 1980 but widened to a seventeen-point difference in the last election: *New York Times*, November 10, 1996.

51. Kosmin and Lachman, *One Nation Under God*, pp. 88–89; Rieder, *Canarsie*, p. 69.

11 Not Just Religious Formation

THE ACADEMIC CHARACTER
OF CATHOLIC SCHOOLS

Jerome Porath

*Thus it follows that the work of the school is irreplaceable
and the investment of human and material resources
in the school becomes a prophetic choice. On the threshold
of the third millennium . . . [the Catholic school]
is still of vital importance.*

These closing words from the Sacred Congregation for Catholic Education's brief statement *The Catholic School on the Threshold of the Third Millennium* may shock some Catholic leaders.[1] The schools are important, but are they, in fact, "irreplaceable"? Is the investment of human and material resources really a "prophetic choice"? Are they still of "vital importance"?

The answers may well be "no," "no," and "no," as long as Catholic educators attempt to justify the existence of the Catholic school solely in terms of the school's religious dimension. Under pressure since Vatican II, Catholic school leaders have sought cover under the umbrella of the catechetical ministry of the Church. The origins of Catholic schools in the United States and the convenience of using the word "education" both for schools and catechetical formation gave plausibility to the religious-dimension (or catechetical ministry) approach. However, defining the special character of Catholic schools in this way neither justifies the claims of the Sacred Congregation for Catholic

Education nor adequately explains the true distinctive nature of the schools.

The Catholic school is one of the primary ways in which the Catholic Church is engaged in the world. The bishops at the Second Vatican Council issued a statement on the Church's involvement in such "secular" activities: The Pastoral Constitution on the Church in the Modern World. In this rich document lies a set of elements that distinguishes the Catholic school.[2] Along with the school's religious dimension, these elements constitute its Catholic character.

The present chapter will examine the implications of The Church in the Modern World for Catholic schools. First it will be useful to understand the problem encountered by seeing the "Catholicity" of the schools solely from a religious-formation perspective. Several earlier chapters of this book help illustrate the problem.

After that review comes an explanation of how the Church sees itself engaged in the secular world through the lens of The Church in the Modern World. This document becomes the guide to identify the characteristics of the school (as school) that are distinctively "Catholic." Other official Church writings will then be offered to explicate how the institution of the school fulfills this "irreplaceable," "prophetic," and "vital" function within the Catholic Church.

The "Religious Formation" Approach

In his chapter in this book, "The Past Before Us," Timothy Walch succinctly recounts the paradox of the recent history of the schools. On the one hand the schools are praised for their academic successes; on the other they are struggling to meet rising costs. Walch attributes the problems to changing social values, changes in family structure, changes in public education, and the rising cost of private education. In particular he asserts that parents no longer value Catholic schools as they once did because "there is no pressure to do so."[3] While Walch finds valuable lessons for public schools, he certainly brings no evidence for a claim that "the investment of human and material resources in the school becomes a prophetic choice." Neither the Church nor parents appear ready for the needed level of commitment.

The history of Catholic schools in the United States is clearly a story of a community that protects its own. No one more clearly depicts both the ethnic and religious overtones to that protectionism than Timothy Meagher. His chapter, "Ethnic, Catholic, White," traces the differences among ethnic groups and changes in the schools over time. Meagher's analysis supports the thesis that, without a defensive posture, the forces to hold the schools together may be gone.

> Ethnic and religious identities had thus dissolved and with them the rationales that had sustained separate Catholic schools in America for over a century. . . . Before the 1960s no such agonized searches for purposes were necessary; it was assumed Catholic schools served a useful purpose simply because they were Catholic in a hostile secular or Protestant world. After the 1960s, even for the best schools, identity and purpose could no longer be assumed.[4]

As Meagher correctly points out, the debates over Catholic school identity began in earnest only after the threat of the Protestant public school was gone.

The post–Vatican II era also saw the mass exodus of members from religious orders. Schools without sisters, brothers, and priests seemed to many to have lost their religious character. Even a quick reading of the contributions to this book by Jacobs and Mueller supports that feeling. Members of religious orders were a significant part of the history of Catholic schools. Richard Jacobs gives clear examples of the dedication and sacrifices of the religious; he further offers suggestions that today's lay teachers can emulate some of their characteristics and practices to strengthen the religious character of the schools.

In his chapter on the sponsorship of schools, Frederick Mueller shows the relationship between the charism of a religious order and the spiritual identity of the school. He analyzes the various approaches to "sponsorship" as a means for a religious order to extend its influence without supplying the personnel to staff the institution. The influence of the religious order is offered to support the religious identity of the school.[5]

While Catholic schools were losing enrollment and religious through the 1960s to the late 1980s and continuing through the 1990s to struggle financially, they could always claim to be the best at religious education. After all, the American bishops said they were: "Of the educational programs available to the Catholic community, Catholic schools afford the fullest and best opportunity to realize the threefold purpose of Christian education among children and young people."[6] In this book John Convey reports the high esteem that Catholic schools continue to enjoy among the hierarchy and, to a slightly lesser extent, among the clergy. However, priests, in significant numbers, worry about the cost and would consider replacing the schools with religious education programs.[7]

Nonetheless, in 1994 Catholic school leaders were outraged when they read reports of George Elford's research on the effectiveness of schools and religious education programs.[8] Some of Elford's findings are briefly summarized in his contribution to this book. With a new test of religious beliefs and values, Elford had the tools for sound quantitative analysis of religious education outcomes. The good news for Catholic schools that he reports in this book is that most Catholic schools do a better job than most parish programs. The bad news is the shocking finding that some parish programs are getting better results than some schools. The "gospel" of the "best means available" is being severely challenged.

A result of all of these challenges has been the "seemingly endless" discussion on the Catholic character (or "identity" or "culture"). Catholic schools are not worth keeping if they are not Catholic. So what does being "Catholic" mean? For most people today the answer has something to do with religion. That answer is understandable given their history; the Catholic schools in the United States grew as a form of religious instruction.[9]

The contributions to this book on Catholic character by Carr, Dooley, Galetto, and Schuttloffel have their significance in this context of religious instruction and formation. What is either a curious omission by the editors of this book on Catholic character or the result of prevailing sentiment about nature of Catholic schools (or both) is the absence of any discussion to this point about the academic function of schools.

Is what is "Catholic" about the schools their religious formation and the "school part" just the vehicle for this faith formation? Is there anything "Catholic" about the rest of the curriculum and programming in Catholic schools?

In an address to diocesan leaders of Catholic education on Catholic "culture," The Most Reverend Daniel Pilarcyzk, archbishop of Cincinnati, seemed to say "No!" to the latter question. He offered a framework for analyzing this issue of the Catholic "character" (or "culture" or "identity") of Catholic schools. Pilarcyzk proposed that the Catholic character of an institution is found in its continuing the work of Christ as Prophet, Priest, and King. More specifically he identified the activity of sanctification through the sacraments (Priest) as central, with sanctification supported by instruction in Church doctrine (Prophet) and carried out in affiliation with the established Church structure (King).[10] Pilarcyzk illustrated his idea by examining the institutions of the family and Catholic health care, as well as the Catholic school. He labeled the institutions as the "context."[11]

The Importance of Being a School

The critical question is whether "being a school" means anything important for the school's "being Catholic." The question may be put: if all the Church wants is religious formation, why does it even bother to operate schools? If the answer is only found in the historical conditions that led to the widespread organization of schools in the United States, then maybe the time for Catholic schools is over. If the answer is that Catholic schools are most often the better means of religious education, then maybe it is time to improve catechetical programs. If Catholic schools are no more than a "vehicle" or "context" for religious education, there is no wonder about the fuss over Catholic character for the last thirty years.

The fact of the matter is that schools are much more than a "vehicle" or "context." If the accidents of history had not occurred, then the Church would still want to operate schools. Even if every parish religious education program achieved better results (as measured by Dr. Elford's test or any other instrument of religious beliefs and values) than every Catholic school, Catholic schools would still be irreplaceable. A framework for understanding both the why and what of Catholic schools can be found in The Church in the Modern World.

The Church in the Modern World presents the Church as both situated in the world and engaged with that world. This is the secular world, the material universe apart from the human institution of the Church. The fundamental rationale for the Church's engagement with the world is to help persons become more human.[12] The human person is seen in

Catholic theology as made in God's image and as the center or pinnacle of creation. Helping each person achieve the maximum perfection of humanity that is possible is helping each person achieve his or her destiny. This is no dichotomy between helping a person become holy and helping a person become human.

With this understanding, The Church in the Modern World presents three ways that the Church can help:

1. The Church's beliefs can give meaning to human existence.
2. The Church's formation of individual members will provide for the world persons who will make for a better world.
3. The Church can take action on behalf of the betterment of persons (where conditions call for the Church to do so).[13]

This third way is the basis for the organization of an institutional presence within society, e.g., schools, hospitals, social services.

The establishment of an institutional presence within the political, economic, or social order is a function of the Church's religious mission.

> Christ, to be sure, gave His Church no proper mission in the political, economic, or social order. The purpose which He set before her is a religious one. But out of this religious mission itself comes a function, a light, and an energy which can serve to structure and consolidate the human community according to divine law. As a matter of fact, when circumstances of time and place create the need, she can and indeed should initiate activities on behalf of men. This is particularly true of activities designed for the needy, such as works of mercy and similar undertakings.[14]

While The Church in the Modern World affirms the religious mission of the Church, it also asserts that the Church's work in the secular world supports that mission.

The Catholic Church understands that its organization of institutions serves simultaneously to enhance human dignity and build the kingdom of God on earth. However, as noted in the preceding passage, institutions are not created to serve a political, economic, or social purpose. They are created to support the dignity of human beings and thereby are a means of fulfilling the Church's religious mission, which is the salvation of all persons. Further the Church organizes such institutions only when the "circumstances of time and place create the need."

According to The Church in the Modern World human dignity is supported in four different ways, by the (1) development of the whole person—integral formation; (2) unification of persons into the human community; (3) liberation of persons from all forms of oppression; and (4) progress of culture or the completion of creation.

While the notion of the development of the whole person is often used in educational literature, the concept advanced by The Church in the Modern World must be understood in the context of a particular philosophy. Two philosophical positions are being used. One is that human beings are endowed with an intellect and a free will. The other is that all truth is related in an organic whole and the human intellect is capable of coming close to knowing it. True wisdom, ultimately known only to God, but able to be closely approximated by the human intellect, is the unification of all knowledge.

The human person is made in God's image, is made to know and love God and to become master of all creation.[15] The human person's first likeness to God is found in the intellect. The word "intellect" has obvious cognitive connotations, but in the underlying philosophy being used it refers to all aspects of conscious sentient life. "Intellect" includes therefore the affective aspects of consciousness (feeling, attitudes, aspirations, and so forth).

Because of intellect, human beings are above the rest of creation; The Church in the Modern World highlights this fact:

> Man judges rightly that by his intellect he surpasses the material universe, for he shares in the light of the divine mind. By relentlessly employing his talents through the ages, he has indeed made progress in the practical sciences, technology, and the liberal arts.[16]

By developing this intellect, human beings perfect themselves, become more God-like; and at the same time, in God's plan for creation, they control the rest of the material universe.

As the human intellect studies the world, it discovers more penetrating truths, theories or explanations that are not confined to observable data. The deeper reality leads to humanizing wisdom that in turns leads one to an openness to truth knowable only through faith.[17] As the "human spirit grows increasingly free from its bondage to creatures," it is "more easily drawn to the worship and contemplation of the Creator."[18]

The person in God's image is also capable of true freedom, but liberty is not license; it is the pursuit of the good.

> Hence man's dignity demands that he act according to knowing and free choice. Such choice is personally motivated and prompted from within. It does not result from blind internal impulse or from mere external pressure. Man achieves such dignity when, emancipating himself from all captivity to passion, he pursues his goal in a spontaneous choice of what is good, and procures for himself, through effective and skillful action, apt means to that end.[19]

By their nature, humans are oriented towards the truth and the good, and so they mirror's God's image. However, human beings also move away from both. This dynamic tension recognized in human beings is part of the human condition. Sociologists and anthropologists can report this finding as readily as philosophers and theologians. The theological explanation is "original sin." Even though human beings are made in God's image, they are free to choose to be like God (their full human potential) or not. The Church's interest is in assisting human beings to become God-like or fully human through the development of the intellect and the formation of conscience to direct the will.

The second way in which human dignity is supported is through the unification of the human community. Human beings are meant to be in community. "For by his innermost nature man is a social being, and unless he relates himself to others he can neither live nor develop his potential."[20] Though human beings are social beings by nature, people frequently put up barriers between each other. Barriers create the tensions within the human community that are obvious to any observer. In Catholic theology the barriers to community are the direct result of human being's "fallen nature" or sinfulness.

The communitarian nature of human beings is also recognized in the way in which civilization progresses. People are dependent on one another. No one knows everything. Each generation builds on the successes and failures of the preceding generation.

Only when a person is free from oppression can he or she attain full potential both materially and spiritually. The third way in which the Church can affirm human dignity is by speaking and acting for social justice.

Therefore, there must be made available to all men everything necessary for leading a life truly human, such as food, clothing, and shelter; the right to choose a state of life freely and to found a family, the right to education, to employment, to a good reputation, to respect, to appropriate information, to activity in accord with the upright norm of one's own conscience, to protection of privacy and rightful freedom even in matters religious.[21]

These are basic human rights that apply to all persons. To work towards their achievement is to work for human dignity.

The recognition that all persons share in the same human rights does not imply that all people are exactly the same. There are rightful differences among people, but in regard to their basic dignity all are the same. This equality is the foundation for social justice, for the distribution of goods among people—not so that everyone has an identical amount, but so that each one's basic dignity is respected and his or her freedom is supported.[22]

Making a better world for all people is the fourth way in which human dignity is affirmed and promoted. Making a better world is, from a theological perspective, the completion of creation, and it is a task entrusted to all persons. Productive human activity within the world is how the world's creation is completed.

Throughout the course of the centuries, men have labored to better the circumstances of their lives through a monumental amount of individual and collective effort. To believers, this point is settled: considered in itself, this human activity accords with God's will. For man, created to God's image, received a mandate to subject to himself the earth and all it contains, and to govern the world with justice and holiness; a mandate to relate himself and the totality of things to Him Who was to be acknowledged as the Lord and Creator of all. Thus, by the subjection of all things to man, the name of God would be wonderful in all the earth.[23]

While it is true that the Church's mission is to bring all people into unity with God so that they might enjoy eternal life, that mission is not in opposition to the advancement of the material world. "Hence it is clear that men are not deterred by the Christian message from building up the world, or impelled to neglect the welfare of their fellows, but that they are rather more stringently bound to do these very things."[24]

The Implications for the Catholic School

The Catholic school derives its place in the Church's ministry precisely as an institution organized to enhance human dignity. Enhancing human dignity both justifies its existence and gives the school its distinctive character.[25] Not only does the Catholic school support and further human dignity, the school is uniquely suited to do so in all four of the ways described in The Church in the Modern World. How this statement is true will be shown through a presentation of the goals of Catholic schools as described in several key documents on Catholic schools written by the Sacred Congregation for Catholic Education.

Before the goals are examined, the purpose of all schools can be clarified. The proper role of a school in society is to transmit culture to the next generation. The Sacred Congregation presents this definition in *The Catholic School:*

> A close examination of the various definitions of school, and of new educational trends at every level, leads one to formulate the concept of school as a place of integral formation by means of a systematic and critical assimilation of culture. A school is, therefore, a privileged place in which, through a living encounter with a cultural inheritance, integral education occurs.[26]

In school students learn from the experience of others, from their successes and failures. Through their teachers and books and other means, they meet the world as people of other times and places know it. In school the wealth of knowledge is passed along.

The word "culture" needs an explanation. Here is the definition as found in The Church in the Modern World:

> The word "culture" in its general sense indicates everything whereby man develops and perfects his many bodily and spiritual qualities; he strives by his knowledge and his labor, to bring the world itself under his control. He renders social life more human both in the family and the civic community, through improvement of customs

and institutions. Throughout the course of time he expresses, communicates and conserves in his works, great spiritual experiences and desires, that they might be of advantage to the progress of many, even of the whole human family.[27]

There are other definitions of culture that are more common. These generally refer to customs or practices of a community or organization. Such meanings of culture would include typical art forms and styles of communicating. Obviously, culture in this more commonly used sense is important to schools also. However, when used in the Church documents relied on here, culture frequently has the much broader meaning.

The Sacred Congregation makes a point in defining the school to say that schools are involved with the "critical" communication and assimilation of culture. Here the word "critical" is used in the sense of "applying a set of criteria." Schools cannot possibly give students the totality of knowledge and skill accumulated by the human race. There must be choices; and every choice is made according to some criterion. Having a set of criteria leads directly into the first way in which human beings are supported, namely an integral education.

The four goals for Catholic schools as "schools" are formulated in the following areas.

A. Integral Education

As described in the previous section, integral education may be considered in three ways: the education of the whole person, the unification of knowledge, and the inclusion of all forms of knowing. The first of these is the most commonly understood in educational circles. Most schools generally offer a well-rounded education providing experiences in the language arts, mathematics, the natural and physical sciences, the fine arts, and the health sciences and physical education.

However, all of the information gleaned from human experience is so many bits of separate data unless it can be organized into some kind of a pattern. The human intellect is capable of progressively higher-order abstractions from the data of experience. These are penetrations into a form of knowledge that is a derivative of experience. It may be called in the sciences "theoretical" knowledge, and in the sciences it is said to be "explanatory" of the data. Providing students information, and even natural and social science theories, is commonplace in schools. What is not so common in all schools, but a distinct characteristic of the Catholic school, is the higher-order unification of the knowledge and skills, along with the values, into something that might be called a "worldview."

The second meaning of integral education described in The Church in the Modern World is having a "worldview." The presentation of all human learning and experience as a unified whole is given in *The Catholic School* as a central purpose of the school:

> She [the Church] establishes her own schools because she considers them as a privileged means of promoting the formation of the whole man, since the school is a center in which a specific concept of the world, of man, and of history is developed and conveyed.[28]

It can be implied from this statement that the Catholic Church has a "specific concept of the world, of man, and of history." While the source of this worldview is religious belief (faith), the worldview is not about religious tenets but about the world itself. Space does not allow for a description of the elements of such a worldview as it might apply to learning in a Catholic school. However, in case anyone might think that the presentation of a worldview is something purely philosophical, a look at a primary-grade approach to one aspect might be helpful.

The complex notion of life after death is not fully understandable by an eight-year-old (or for that matter even fully understandable by an eighty-year-old). In the Catholic conception of life (worldview) there is included the idea of immortality. For an eight-year-old death is not a completely foreign experience. Pets die, grandparents die, and sometimes even parents or siblings die. Teachers use such opportunities to talk about the importance of relationships and the meaning of death. Precisely because of the strength of a relationship and corresponding feeling of loss, a connection can be made that all life does not come to an end because of death. Wanting a deceased grandparent to still be alive, a small child is comforted by a very simple idea of a life after death, like "Grandpa is now with God in heaven." Suddenly life is not so harsh; hope is a reality. The Christian's view of life begins to take shape.

In the public schools neutrality is supposed to be the rule. Not only are religious teachings expressly prohibited, but to the extent possible the schools are expected to be value-neutral. But neutrality is problematic because it is virtually impossible to teach without taking some position on basic human beliefs and values. Even the selection of course material itself involves the application of some criterion that is based on some value system.

The approach of Catholic schools is in marked distinction to that of contemporary public schools. The distinction is not that Catholic schools have a religious education program, or that they are able to incorporate or make reference to religious beliefs and values while teaching academic subjects. The real difference is that Catholic schools use the beliefs and values of the Catholic religion as determining factors of a worldview and communicate that basic and unifying view of life and knowledge to their students. This unifying vision is restated by the Sacred Congregation in its most recent document:

> There is a tendency to forget that education always presupposes and involves a definite concept of man and life. To claim neutrality for schools signifies in practice, more times than not, banning all reference to religion from the cultural and educational field, whereas a correct pedagogical approach ought to be open to the more decisive sphere of ultimate objectives, attending not only to "how", but also to "why", overcoming any misunderstanding as regards the claim to neutrality in education, restoring to the educational process the unity which saves it from dispersion amid the meandering of knowledge and acquired facts, and focuses on the human person in his or her integral, transcendent, historical identity.[29]

The third way of integral education is the inclusion of all forms of knowing, specifically the inclusion of faith. Now accepting the truth of information based on the word of another (a classic definition of faith) is commonplace in all schools. Most knowledge is accepted as truth because some authority has attested to its accuracy. No person has enough time to test personally or experience everything. What is not acceptable in so-called secular and ideologically neutral schools is "religious faith"; that is, the acceptance of something as true because God has revealed it. It is important to note that what is different between accepting something as true on faith in some scientific authority and by faith in some religious authority is not the type of knowledge. Rather, the difference is in the form of justification.[30] Catholic schools are different from the secular schools because they accept divine revelation as a justification for belief.

> [The school's] task is fundamentally a synthesis of faith and culture, and a synthesis of faith and life: the first is reached integrating all the different aspects of human knowledge through the subjects taught in the light of the Gospels; the second in the growth of the virtues characteristic of a Christian.[31]
>
> The endeavor to interweave reason and faith, which has become the heart of individual subjects, makes for unity, articulation and coordination, bringing forth within what is learnt in school a Christian vision of the world, of life, of culture and of history. In the Catholic school's educational project there is no separation between time for learning and time for formation, between acquiring notions and growing in wisdom.[32]

What the Sacred Congregation on Catholic Education is saying in these two important documents issued twenty years apart is something significantly more than that Catholic schools offer religious formation. In an earlier chapter, Schuttloffel examined Catholic elementary school curricula. Her finding on what made a curriculum "Catholic" was that it received its coherence from the Catholic Church's mission of "faith formation within its students."[33] That is not precisely correct in light of the statements previously quoted. It is possible to have "a Christian vision of the world, of life, of culture and of history" without being a Christian. The "vision" is a unification of human understanding which is dependent on information accepted on religious faith; the "vision" itself is not a set of religious truths.

None of this is to deny that Catholic schools have a role to play in faith formation. Indeed, that is the point of saying that integral formation is completed by faith. Catholic schools provide an integral education in all three ways: educating all aspects of the human person, offering a unified view of the world, and providing faith formation. Integral education is more than the acquisition of intellectual values, it is learning a lifestyle, according to *The Catholic School*.

When seen in this light, a school is not only a place where one is given a choice of intellectual values, but also a place where one is presented an array of values, which are actively lived.[34]

B. Formation of the Human Community

A second purpose for the Catholic school can be found in its support for the social nature of human beings. Recognizing that all persons are made to live in community with others and understanding the tensions of interpersonal relationships that are common among people, the schools strive toward building an experience of the benefits and opportunities of working harmoniously with others. The schools fulfill this goal in two ways: by demonstrating the interdependence of human beings in the development of knowledge and by offering positive interpersonal experiences.

The first means is readily understandable simply from the definition of a school. The communication of knowledge and skills is the sharing of human experience. The recognition that what is learned is both for oneself and for the good of others ought to be readily understood from the activity of schooling itself.

> Education is not given for the purpose of gaining power but as an aid towards a fuller understanding of, and communion with man, events and things. Knowledge is not to be considered as a means of material prosperity and success, but as a call to serve and to be responsible for others.[35]

Unfortunately, education can also be pursued for personal gain. Schools need to point consciously to the benefits of education beyond oneself.

All schools also have the opportunity of building on the clear need for positive interpersonal relationships. *The Catholic School on the Threshold of the Third Millennium* states:

> During childhood and adolescence a student needs to experience personal relations with outstanding educators, and what is taught has greater influence on the student's formation when placed in a context of personal involvement, genuine reciprocity, coherence of attitudes, life-styles and day to day behaviour. While respecting

individual roles, the community dimension should be fostered, since it is one of the most enriching developments for the contemporary school.[36]

These relationships are both within the community of the school and beyond in other communities. In the first instance teachers can show students that special care and attention that both fosters growth in self-concept and satisfies a need for being wanted and accepted. This experience of community is an extension of the family. Unfortunately, in contemporary society not all families provide this for their children.

In the second instance schools can make connections for young people among persons of different races, cultures, economic conditions, and so forth. Learning not only that the human community is composed of diverse peoples but also that being human makes all people the same is an essential means of promoting the human community. Many schools through programs of multicultural education or understanding of diversity go far to reach this end. Catholic schools are distinctive because such programs are not simply "course offerings" or "extracurricular experiences" but rather essential elements of the schools' programming.

C. Liberation from All Forms of Oppression

Essential to the character of Catholic schools is a commitment to social justice. As noted earlier, social justice is the distribution of the goods of this world so that all persons can live with dignity. According to *The Catholic School*, the schools promote this purpose in two ways:

> Since it is motivated by the Christian ideal, the Catholic school is particularly sensitive to the call from every part of the world for a more just society, and it tries to make its own contribution towards it. It does not stop at courageous teaching of the demands of justice even in the face of local opposition, but tries to put these demands into practice in its own community in the daily life of the school.[37]

Involved in the education of individuals, the Catholic school first has the opportunity to teach social justice. Justice is part of the worldview that is fashioned through the curriculum. Additional projects, such as those called "Christian service programs," also are means to this instruction of students. If anything marks them, students who complete Catholic schooling ought to be characterized by a passion for social justice.

Just as important as individual formation is the institutional activity of the school in establishing a more just society. Concern for the poor and others in need of an education is a special part of the character of Catholic schools and why they are so valuable to the Church.

> Spurred on by the aim of offering to all, and especially to the poor and marginalized, the opportunity of an education, of training for a job, of human and Christian formation, it can and must find in the context of the old and new forms of poverty that original synthesis of ardour and fervent dedication which is a manifestation of Christ's love for the poor, the humble, the masses seeking for truth.[38]

In the history of Catholic schools in the United States the urban flight of the Catholic community during the 1950s and 1960s is well known, as is the resulting dramatic increase in African-American and non-Catholic students in the schools that continued to operate. For some, the large number of non-Catholics was a reason for closing these schools; for others, the needs of the poor were more than adequate to justify their continuation.[39]

However, the service to the urban poor must not be seen only as a fortuitous historical accident. Just as the Catholic Church operates schools in developing countries, irrespective of the religious affiliations of the students, the Church's work with the poor is of concern to the Church in the United States. Especially today when Catholic education is seen as very effective in lower-income communities,[40] the Church has the perfect opportunity to use the institution of the school to promote human dignity.

D. Completing the Work of Creation

When man develops the earth by the work of his hands or with the aid of technology, in order that it might bear fruit and become a dwelling worthy of the whole human family and when he consciously takes part in the life of social groups, he carries out the design of God manifested at the beginning of time, that he should subdue the earth, perfect creation and develop himself. At the same time he obeys the commandment of Christ that he place himself at the service of his brethren.[41]

Preparing human beings for the world of work is often stated as the goal of schooling. This goal is valid for Catholic schools but distinctive in that the productivity of work is for the progress of the human community. Work is not for personal gain; work is for everyone's gain. Fashioning such an attitude or value is important for Catholic schools.

Equally important is the understanding that the Catholic schools are not merely custodians of antiquities. Catholic schools transmit the knowledge of past generations but do so to create the knowledge and skills for succeeding generations. This suggests that Catholic schools ought to be recognized by their forward-looking focus. Education in basic skills with a core curriculum is the recognized mark of Catholic schools. Yet, if that focus is at the expense of failing to prepare persons to be productive in contemporary skills, then the Catholic schools have not recognized a key element of their distinctive character.

> Moreover, in spite of numerous obstacles, the Catholic school has continued to share responsibility for the social and cultural development of the different communities and peoples to which it belongs, participating in their joys and hopes, their sufferings and difficulties, their efforts to achieve genuine human and communitarian progress.[42]

This task of preparing students for their place in the world is affirmed in *The Catholic School on the Threshold of the Third Millennium*.

"Genuine human and communitarian progress" is at the center of the Catholic school's academic nature. Seeking to be the very best academically is not a distraction from the school's purpose. Rather, not to be the very best in its academic programs is to deny the Catholic school's essential character and role in the progress of culture.

> Thus the Catholic school should be able to offer young people the means to acquire the knowledge they need in order to find a place in a society which is strongly characterized by technical and scientific skill.[43]

The Catholic character of the Catholic school is clearly more than its role in faith formation. Catholic schools are institutions organized by the Church to support and promote human dignity. They do so by offering an integral education, fostering the development of the human community, working for liberation from all forms of oppression and promoting the progress of culture.

These characteristics place monumental demands on the curriculum, the faculty, the financing, and the organization of Catholic schools. Clearly more work is needed to further develop the implications of these ideas for Catholic schools. The Pastoral Constitution on the Church in the Modern World remains a valuable resource for reflection by Catholic educators because of its clear focus on how the Catholic Church engages with the world.

What has been written here could leave one with the feeling that the religious dimension of the Catholic school is unimportant, because it is not addressed. Clearly Catholic schools as they have been historically organized in the United States have held this religious dimension at their center. There is no reason why this should not be the case. On the other hand Catholic schools without formal religious education programs have been organized in other parts of the world.[44] It may even be possible to make a case for such schools in the present-day United States.[45]

"Irreplaceable," "prophetic choice," and of "vital importance"— these were the words of the Sacred Congregation for Catholic Education that opened this chapter. As important as the work of faith formation is, faith formation alone does not justify the resources invested in Catholic schools, nor does it adequately describe its true character. Only when one fully grasps the importance of "being a school," only when one understands how "being a school" can promote human dignity, can he or she truly value the character of Catholic schools on this threshold of the third millennium.

NOTES

1. Sacred Congregation for Catholic Education, *The Catholic School on the Threshold of the Third Millennium* (1997), no. 21.

2. Rev. J. Byran Hehir suggested the use of this document from the Second Vatican Council in an application to Catholic colleges and universities in light of the Vatican document *Ex corde ecclesia.* Although Hehir does not fully elaborate on The Church in the Modern World's themes in relation to education, his discussion of the balance that The Church in the Modern World gives to the Dogmatic Constitution on the Church parallels in part the argument to see the schools as *both* instruments of religious formation *and* means for engagement with the world. J. Bryan Hehir, "Observations and Conversation," Occasional Papers on Catholic Higher Education, I (1955), 34–43.

3. Walch, draft, p. 14.

4. Meagher, draft, pp. 31–32.

5. "Thus, sponsorship was not simply a question of governance but inextricably tied into religious motivation and values as well." Mueller, draft, p. 7.

6. The National Conference of Catholic Bishops, *To Teach As Jesus Did* (Washington, D.C.: United States Catholic Conference), no. 101, p. 28.

7. Convey, draft, p. 8.

8. George Elford, "Towards Shaping the Agenda: A Study of Catholic Religious Education/Catechesis" (Washington, D.C.: Educational Testing Service, 1994).

9. Cf. Meagher, draft.

10. It is no accident that Pilarcyzk's presentation of Catholic culture closely parallels the Second Vatican Council's description of the Church in the Dogmatic Constitution on the Church.

11. Daniel Pilarcyzk, "Catholic Culture—What Does It Mean to Be a Catholic?" Address to the chief administrators of Catholic education, NCEA, Orlando, Fla. (1998).

12. Second Vatican Council, Pastoral Constitution on the Church in the Modern World, nos. 11–12.

13. Ibid., no. 40–43.

14. Ibid., no. 42.

15. Ibid., no. 12

16. Ibid., no. 15.

17. Ibid.

18. Ibid., no. 57.

19. Ibid., no. 17.

20. Ibid., no. 12.

21. Ibid., no. 25.

22. Ibid., no. 29.

23. Ibid., no. 34.

24. Ibid.

25. To be more precise, the justification for the existence of the school also requires a judgment that the circumstances of time and place demonstrate a need for the Church to organize schools. These circumstances might be practical ones, such as no other means of schooling are suitable or available; or perhaps more theoretical, such as the nature of a pluralistic society calls for the organization of schools with different systems of beliefs and values. (On the latter point, cf. Sacred Congregation for Catholic Education, *The Catholic School* [1977], no. 12). Space does not allow anything more than the presumption that current circumstances do demonstrate a need. A general statement

to that effect can be found in the Introduction to the Declaration on Christian Education (Second Vatican Council).

26. Sacred Congregation for Catholic Education (1977), no. 26.

27. Second Vatican Council, Pastoral Constitution on the Church in the Modern World, no. 53.

28. Sacred Congregation for Catholic Education (1977), no. 8.

29. Ibid. (1997), no. 10.

30. Further discussion on this point would require a discussion of theories of knowledge and that is well beyond the scope of this chapter.

31. Sacred Congregation for Catholic Education (1977), no. 37.

32. Ibid. (1997), no. 14.

33. Schuttloffel, draft, p. 11.

34. Sacred Congregation for Catholic Education (1977), no. 32.

35. Ibid., no. 56.

36. Ibid. (1997), no. 18.

37. Ibid. (1997), no. 58.

38. Ibid. (1997), no. 15.

39. Timothy Walch, *The Parish School: American Catholic Parochial Education from Colonial Times to the Present* (New York: Crossroad, 1996), pp. 183–84.

40. Ibid., pp. 202–5.

41. Second Vatican Council, Pastoral Constitution on the Church in the Modern World, no. 57.

42. Sacred Congregation for Catholic Education (1997), no. 5

43. Ibid., no. 8.

44. Cf. Sacred Congregation for Catholic Education, *The Religious Dimension of the Catholic School* (1988), no. 108.

45. A justification might be found in the failure of public education to meet the needs of the poor and the availability of public funding if religious education is absent. Catholic Charities has consistently done much good for society with a similar justification.

Contributors and Editors

Kathleen Carr, C.S.J., a Sister of St. Joseph of Boston, earned a Ph.D. in educational administration at Catholic University of America in Washington, D.C. Her particular interest is in leadership development of Catholic school principals. She has been involved in the ministry of Catholic education for more than thirty years as teacher, principal, Regional Director of Elementary Education, and currently, Director of Marketing and Public Relations for schools in the Archdiocese of Boston.

John J. Convey is Provost and the St. Elizabeth Ann Seton Professor of Education at Catholic University of America. He received a Ph.D. in research and evaluation from Florida State University in 1974, a M.Sc. in mathematics from Ohio State University in 1968, and a B.A. in mathematics from La Salle College in 1962. During the 1986–87 academic year he was a Senior Research Fellow in the Office of Research at the United States Department of Education. Dr. Convey is the author of *Catholic Schools Make a Difference: Twenty-Five Years of Research*, published by the National Catholic Educational Association in 1992. He served on the Education Committee for the United States Catholic Bishops from 1992 to 1994 and was the 1991 recipient of the C. Albert Koob Award, given by the National Catholic Educational Association for outstanding national service to Catholic schools.

CATHERINE DOOLEY, O.P., Ph.D., is an associate professor in the Department of Religion and Religious Education at Catholic University of America. She has published widely in catechetical and liturgical journals and has written a number of texts and resource materials for catechesis and religious education. She is the co-editor of *The Echo Within: Emerging Issues in Religious Education* (Thomas More, 1997) and author of *Listen and Tell: A Commentary on the Introduction to the Lectionary for Masses with Children* (Pastoral Press, 1993).

GEORGE ELFORD has combined experience in the administration of Catholic education with extensive work for the Educational Testing Service (ETS) and ACT. He has created several programs that provide catechetical assessment services; more recently he has begun work on using the Internet for both survey and assessment services to Catholic schools and parishes.

PAUL W. GALETTO, O.S.A., Ph.D., is currently President of St. Augustine College Preparatory School in Richland, New Jersey. He has taught both at Catholic University of America and Villanova University. He is an occasional speaker on educational concerns for the National Catholic Educational Association and on the local circuit. His book, *Building the Foundations of Faith* (1996), was based upon a national survey he conducted of over 2,200 teachers of religion in Catholic elementary schools and describes their religious knowledge, belief, and practices.

RICHARD M. JACOBS, O.S.A., is an associate professor at Villanova University. He earned his Ph.D. at the University of Tulsa. Jacobs studies U.S. Catholic education, in particular, its historical, philosophical, and theological underpinnings. In 1994 he delivered the 12th annual Seton-Neumann lecture, and from 1995 to 1997 he served as member of the United States Catholic Conference Committee on Education.

JEFFREY A. MCLELLAN is a Research Associate of the Life Cycle Institute at Catholic University of America. His areas of research include Catholic education, school and church-based community service programs for youth, and adolescent social development. He is a developmental psychologist by training and editor of *The Role of Peer Groups in Adolescent Social Identity: Exploring the Importance of Stability and Change* (1999).

TIMOTHY MEAGHER is Director of the Irish Studies Program and Adjunct professor of history at Catholic University of America. He has written extensively on American ethnic and religious history. He is editor of *From Paddy to Studs: Irish American Communities in the Turn of the Century Era, 1880 to 1920* and, with Ronald Bayor, *The New York Irish*. His study of the emergence of new generation and changes in Irish American identity in Worcester, Massachusetts, between 1880 and 1928, is forthcoming (University of Notre Dame Press).

FREDERICK C. MUELLER, F.S.C., Ed.D., a member of the De La Salle Christian Brothers, is currently Headmaster/Principal of La Salle Center, a K-12 school located in Oakdale, Long Island, New York. He has served as a teacher and administrator at the elementary and high school levels. In addition, he was the director of the Secondary Teacher Education Program at Salve Regina University. He holds a doctorate in educational administration from Boston College; his doctoral dissertation studied sponsorship issues in LaSallian schools in the United States.

JEROME R. PORATH has been Superintendent of Schools for the Archdiocese of Los Angeles since 1991. He previously held the same post for the Archdiocese of Washington, D.C., and Diocese of Albany, New York. Dr. Porath did his college studies in St. Louis and received his Ph.D. in education from St. Louis University. He is an active member of the National Catholic Educational Association and is a past board member and past president of its department of Chief Administrators of Catholic Education. He has taught graduate courses in education at Catholic University of America, Loyola Marymount University, and the University of San Francisco.

MERYLANN J. SCHUTTLOFFEL is Assistant Professor of Educational Administration and Policy Studies at Catholic University of America. She received her Ph.D. from the University of Tulsa in educational administration and research. Her research interests include reflective practice in teaching and educational leadership, innovation and school change, and the transformation of educational beliefs and practice.

TIMOTHY WALCH is Director of the Herbert Hoover Presidential Library and associate editor of the *U.S. Catholic Historian*. He is the author or editor of fifteen books, including *Parish School: American Catholic Parochial Education from Colonial Times to the Present* (New York: Crossroad/Herder, 1996).

JAMES YOUNISS is Professor of Psychology and former director of the Life Cycle Institute at Catholic University of America. His most recent research is focused on the developmental consequences of community service on youth. His recent books include *Community Service and Social Responsibility in Youth*, with M. Yates (University of Chicago Press), and *Catholic Schools at the Crossroads: Survival and Transformation*, co-edited with J. Convey (Teachers College Press).

Index

Munley, A., 39–40, 44, 45, 53; *Threads for the Loom*, 41

National Catechetical Directory, 164, 166
National Catholic Educational Association (NCEA), 15, 62, 149, 181, 200; Secondary School Department 1987 symposium on the high school teacher, 40–41
National Catholic Welfare Conference (NCWC), 200–201
National Conference of Catholic Charities, 200–201, 239n45
national identity, European, sentiments among different immigrant populations, 193–94
nativist movements, in late nineteenth and early twentieth centuries, 199–200
Nazism, influence on American cultural diversity, 208–9
networks, regional, as collaboration models of sponsorship, 58
New Deal era, legislation and attitudes toward Catholics, 207, 208
New Orleans, LA, archdiocesan curricula guides, 115
non-Catholics, as students in Catholic schools, 7, 26, 235
non-Catholic teachers, as elementary school catechists, 132, 136 table
Notre Dame Journal of Education, The (periodical), 96

O'Brien, David J., 184
O'Brien, J. Stephen, survey of bishops and priests on Catholic schools, 15–36
O'Brien, Pat, 204
occupational mobility, among Catholic immigrants, 195

O'Connell, Dennis J., 198
O'Connell, Cardinal William, 200
Office of the Catechism, role in text materials, 167–68
O'Neill, Rev. Michael, 181
On Our Way (series, Sister Maria de la Cruz), 157, 158
oppression, liberation from, social justice as promoted by Catholic schools, 234–35
Oregon, Ku Klux Klan's attempt to close parochial schools, 199
Orsi, Robert, 193
O'Shaugnessy, Sister Mary Michael, O.P., 158
O'Shea, Mother Francesca, 82, 85
out-of-school religious education programs, compared to parish school programs, 184
ownership, institutional, question of under sponsorship agreements, 42

Packwood, Robert, 179–80
parents: financial futures of children as major concern, 184; influence on local schools' curriculum, 108; involvement in school governance and bishop/clergy opinions, 22–23, 25, 34–35 *tables;* role in schools' mission, 55, 170, 183; Vatican II's document on, as central figures in education, 159
parishes: Catholic schools as strengthening unity within, 20–21, 24, 30–31 *tables;* effect of Catholic migration from urban centers to suburbs, 2–3; influence on local schools' curriculum, 108; support of schools by, views of bishops and priests on, 21–22, 32–33 *tables;* views on whether they should remain synonymous with schools, 86